Crossover

The New Model for Youth Basketball Development

Third Edition

By Brian McCormick

Cross Over: The New Model of Youth Basketball Development / Brian McCormick

ISBN 978-0-557-02588-6

1. Sports – Basketball. 2. Coaching. 3. Physical Education and Training – Basketball. I. McCormick, Brian, 1976 -

Copyright 2008 © Brian McCormick

All rights reserved. No part of this book may be reproduced in any manner without the express written consent of the publisher. All inquiries should be addressed to:

Brian McCormick

highfivehoopschool@yahoo.com

Published by Lulu.com

Printed and bound in the United States of America

Cover design: John Hayashi / Inkblot Creative Asylum / inkblot.ca@gmail.com

Thank you to my editors: Thomas McCormick III and Brianna Finch

Photographer: Brianna Finch

Thank you to my advisors: Rick Allison, Adrian Flynn, C.J. Lee, Vincent Minjares, Jeff Olivio, Sandy Sandago and Derek Vargas.

Other Books published by Brian McCormick:

180 Shooter

Blitz Basketball

Brian McCormick's Hard2Guard Player Development Newsletter, Volume I

Championship Basketball Plays

Hard2Guard: Skill Development for Perimeter Players

Developing Basketball Intelligence

E-books available at www.180shooter.com

Paperbacks available at www.lulu.com/brianmccormick

Table of Contents

Chapter 1: Philosophy of Long Term Athlete Development — 5

Chapter 2: Athletic Skills — 23

Chapter 3: Tactical Skills — 55

Chapter 4: Technical Skills — 89

Chapter 4B: Technical Skill Progressions — 109

- Ball Handling
- Finishing
- Passing
- Post Play
- Shooting

Chapter 5: Psychological Skills — 143

Chapter 6: Practice Planning — 157

Chapter 7: Coaching Effectiveness — 167

Chapter 8: Learning — 179

Appendix I: Injury Prevention — 189

Appendix II: Dynamic Warm-up — 197

References — 201

Chapter 1:
Philosophy of Long Term Athlete Development

<u>Cross Over: The New Model of Youth Basketball Development</u> outlines a step-by-step skill acquisition and competitive model based on physical, psychological and physiological development stages. The Cross Over model uses a Long Term Athlete Development philosophy to accomplish two primary goals:

1. Create a better environment for all youth basketball players.
2. Develop global players more prepared for elite basketball competition.

The Cross Over Movement, a grassroots effort started after the publication of the First Edition, aims to accomplish these goals through two primary means:

1. Educating coaches, parents and organizations about Long Term Athlete Development (LTAD) and the different development stages that each individual progresses through during childhood.
2. Providing a template for coaches to follow to ensure each player develops and has the opportunity to maximize his potential.

The Cross Over Movement web site focuses on educating parents, coaches and organizations about the development model and different issues relating to youth basketball development. <u>Cross Over</u>, the book, provides the coaching template.

To create a template, or develop a system, we must envision the end-result and work backward. The end-result for this model is to:

1. Create programs that meet players' needs at each distinct stage of their development and ensure that players' motivations, not the adult's, guide the team and league environment.
2. Develop elite players with advanced athletic, tactical, technical and psychological skills.

Most people see these as opposing goals. However, through the LTAD model, coaches, parents and organizations can meet the needs of all players at each stage of development and develop better all-around players.

Talent Development as a Process

The best business franchises use a system or process which achieves consistent results. When you eat at McDonald's or go to Starbuck's, you know what to expect. These companies have a process which guides the production of their product and a philosophy which guides their business practices.

<u>Cross Over: The New Model of Youth Basketball Development</u> is a system based on the LTAD philosophy. A book, however, cannot guarantee results. A philosophy to guide youth basketball organizations guarantees a similar atmosphere, just as Starbuck's philosophy guarantees a similar experience every time you go to Starbuck's, whether in Los Angeles or Beijing. Every employee plays his or her part; the philosophy does not guarantee against a barista providing poor service if she had a bad morning or a longer line than usual, but the philosophy empowers individuals to make decisions based on the company's guiding principles. The philosophy illustrates the goal to

its employees and offers a system to achieve its goal. Employees adhere to the system and meet the goal – providing an experience to its customers rather than simply serving coffee – or the employee quits or gets fired.

A basketball development program does not ensure that every coach will be good or know everything about basketball, but it offers a framework. If organizations monitor parents and coaches and emphasize the philosophy throughout its programs and correspondences, the philosophy slowly changes the approach to youth basketball and develops the process to develop better players in a better environment. In an organization adopting and promoting the Cross Over Model, coaches learn about the model and its purpose, and they coach to meet this goal – using appropriate strategies at the appropriate age and with the appropriate motivations to maximize the players' experience and develop more global basketball players.

When a coach is unsure of what to do, the philosophy guides him. When faced with a practice for nine-year-olds, what should a coach emphasize? The philosophy does not dictate every drill or limit a coach's creativity or individuality, but creates a mindset throughout the youth basketball system which concentrates on creating the right atmosphere for players based on their developmental levels. The philosophy empowers individual decision-making.

Cross Over introduces the philosophy of Long Term Athlete Development. The mission is to create a more balanced approach to youth basketball which emphasizes age-appropriate skill acquisition and meets the developmental needs of youth basketball players. This approach creates a better youth basketball environment and nurtures the players' development. The overall system must have a goal which directs every coach, parent and player. We demand players write down their goals, make them specific and measurable and give them a timeline in order to keep players focused on the effort required to turn their goals into reality. To create an overarching philosophy to guide coaches, parents and players, we need to establish such a goal.

Cross Over's goal is to advocate for the philosophy of Long Term Athlete Development, outline a step-by-step and skill-by-skill guide to implement the philosophy, emphasize a Growth Mindset and learning orientation and educate coaches through supplemental information to enhance coaching effectiveness.

Why Long Term Athlete Development?

Within this system, the goal is a player-centered environment which maximizes the experience of all players. However, the end-goal developmentally is to prepare players athletically, tactically, technically and psychologically to excel at the college or professional level: players who move quickly and efficiently and possess strength, agility and explosiveness; players who read and react to their opponent using the appropriate tactical skills, whether a cut, screen or other move; players who shoot with good mechanics, handle the ball adeptly, utilize the Hard2Guard position, finish with either hand and possess flawless footwork in the post or on the perimeter; and players who possess a Growth Mindset, learning orientation, coachability, self-confidence, self-awareness, internal motivation and a good work ethic.

While no philosophy can ensure every player develops equally, as an individual determines his own success, the LTAD philosophy creates the best environment for development, giving coaches, parents and players the best opportunity to develop the desired end-product.

Athlete-centered, Coach-driven, Performance-based

The USA Track and Field Coaching Education program uses the motto "Athlete-centered, Coach-driven and Performance-based." It emphasizes this approach throughout its curriculum, training coaches to approach their team and their athletes with this mindset. Winning is not a part of the motto, though performance is. Winning is controlled externally; winning often depends on the opponent. A team with greater talent typically beats a team with inferior talent. However, a loss does not equal a poor performance. In the development system, we want to emphasize performance as opposed to outcome because we control performance internally. In Track and Field, if a long jumper jumps a career best, but loses to another competitor, should he be proud of his performance and personal best or disappointed with the ultimate result? Within the Cross Over Model, his performance signals his growth and development as a long jumper, which is the ultimate goal.

Winning	Performance
External	Internal
Result	Effort
Scoreboard Outcome	Personal Improvement
Compare to Others	Contrast with Self
Mistakes not OK	Mistakes mean learning

At any developmental stage and in any given season, the primary objective is the athlete's physical, social and psychological development. When we consider the purpose of youth sports and our time and financial investments, its true purpose is more than wins, trophies, personal accolades, scholarships or professional careers. We support youth sports because we believe it has a powerful and positive impact on a child's life and development. Creating an athlete-centered coaching philosophy emphasizes this development. An LTAD program supports and creates an athlete-centered environment by focusing the curriculum on age-appropriate skills, activities and motivations rather than attempting to accelerate the development process.

The coach drives the development process through the environment he creates, his instruction, his communication and his emphasis. When a coach emphasizes wins and losses with nine-year-olds, he strays from an athlete-centered environment because nine-year-olds want to learn new skills and play with friends. However, a varsity coach who ignores competition and pretends that winning does not matter also moves from an athlete-centered environment because 17 and 18-year-olds play to win. A coach must be mindful of his athletes' needs and motivations and acknowledge the different developmental stages rather than treating all youth basketball players the same.

The Philosophy of Long Term Athlete Development

Long Team Athlete Development (LTAD) is a model created by Dr. Istvan Balyi to guide the athletic development process from pre-puberty through retirement. The LTAD approach emphasizes age-appropriate skill acquisition to maximize the athlete's potential: "it takes 8-to-12 years of training for a talented player/athlete to reach elite levels. This is called the 10-year or 10,000-hour rule," (Balyi and Hamilton; Ericsson).

Parents and coaches rush the development process and use adult training protocols with young players to get a head start. "Parents and coaches in many sports still approach training with an attitude best characterized as 'Peaking by Friday,' where short-term approach is taken to training and performance with an over-emphasis on immediate results," (Balyi and Hamilton). The *Peak by Friday* mentality stifles development because "overemphasizing competition in the early phases of training will always cause shortcomings in athletic abilities later in an athlete's career," (Balyi and Hamilton). If players never achieve a base level of athleticism, their athletic career will end prematurely.

The opposite of the *Peak by Friday* mentality is not an abdication of competitive play or the desire to win. Instead, the LTAD model creates a balanced approach: players play to win, but train to improve. Teach basic skills like lateral movement, ball handling and shooting mechanics with some practice time devoted to game preparation. Encourage the team to compete, play hard and play to win, but emphasize the performance over the result. Emphasize *how* the team plays rather than the outcome. *Peak by Friday* coaches concentrate on the win, not on performance. "The reason why so many athletes plateau during the later stages of their careers is primarily because of an overemphasis on competition instead of training during the important period in their athletic development. The "Learn to Train" and "Training to Train" stages are the most important phases of athletic preparation. During these stages, we make or break an athlete," (Balyi and Hamilton). A performance orientation approach enhances skill acquisition compared to an outcome orientation.

Children progress through different stages as they develop; the LTAD model reconciles athletic development with natural development. "From early childhood to maturation, people go through several stages of development, which include pre-puberty, puberty, post-puberty and maturation. For each development stage there is a corresponding phase of athletic training" (Bompa). Sport scientists use these principles to take a proactive approach to athlete development. These models guide athletes, coaches and league organizers so each athlete receives the best opportunity to reach his peak performance, which should be everyone's end-goal.

The LTAD creates a gradual progression whereby coaches teach the game in stages, rather than all at once, coordinating instruction and programs with the athletes' motivations at different ages and development phases. With pressure to win, youth coaches have little time to teach the basics and prepare for games; so, *Peak by Friday* coaches prepare for the game to the detriment of their players' development. Instead, for younger players, actual basketball skills should comprise very little of the practice time, as players must learn to move without a ball before dribbling: one adds and subtracts before doing long division, and athletes need to move well before dribbling and playing defense.

Young students learn a foreign language easier than adults because the child's mind is "ripe" for learning. Sensitive periods of athletic development also exist; teaching young athletes these skills at the appropriate ages enhances their development.

Girls	Item	Boys
9-10	Balance	10-11
8-13	Movement Adequacy	8-13
6-7 & 10-11	Kinesthetic Differentiation	6-7 & 10-11
8-10	Reaction to Acoustical & Visual Signals	8-10
7-9	Rhythmic Motion	9-10
12-14	Spatial Orientation	12-14
6-8	Synchronization of Movement	6-8

(Grasso)

In New Zealand, all athletes between 9 and 14-years-old, regardless of sport, participate in the same training as part of the Long Term Athletic Development System of New Zealand. The following outlines the basic curriculum:

Day One: Aquatics (stroke technique, conditioning)

Day Two: Ball Skills (hand-eye, foot-eye and dexterity development)

Day Three: Gymnastics (spatial awareness, systematic strength, dynamic balance, torso strength)

Day Four: Strength Training (skill acquisition, system strength, torso strength)

(Grasso, Vol. 80)

Imagine a youth basketball coach spending an entire practice on gymnastics, rather than ball skills. But, are spatial awareness, systematic strength, dynamic balance and torso strength important to basketball? Is there transfer between the fundamental motor skills learned in one activity and another activity? These skills are imperative for basketball success, yet a revolt would ensue if a coach used gymnastics to train basketball players. Parents prefer their son or daughter learn another half-dozen out of bounds plays than practice something with no obvious correlation to basketball.

The *Peak by Friday* mentality approaches youth sports as a series of one-year careers, while an LTAD approach plans for a 10-year career. In the series of one-year careers, the one season matters and coaches play to win without thought to the players' future. In Little League, this approach results in young pitchers throwing too many innings and injuring their arms. In basketball, it means running set plays to get the best player open shots and running a gambling press which takes advantage of the opponents' weaknesses. While effective in accomplishing short-term goals, players may or may not improve. If players fail to improve, the season may end their basketball career as they dislike the experience and quit or they get cut the following season. Studies show that 70% of kids quit sports by the age of 13, and very few kids give losing too many games as a reason. With an LTAD approach, players play to win, but coaches ensure players develop and improve through the course of the season to extend their playing careers.

Sport scientists understand there is a better way to train athletes, and the LTAD is a model for this enhanced, balanced training. The LTAD rationalizes athletic development and emphasizes the needs of the athlete, not the coach, parents or administrators. By following the LTAD model, recreational athletes learn more skills and have more fun, while elite athletes develop a greater base of skills to enhance their play as they reach the Performance Stage. Athletes do not develop overnight or by accident. The LTAD provides a model to guide athletes from pre-puberty through adult basketball in a sensible, efficient manner.

The End-Goal: The Global Basketball Player

To develop a global basketball player, we must define the terms. What is a global basketball player?

> "We want to develop 'global players'. This means every player develops every skill. We encourage this through 15-16 years old. After this it is recommended to train players in all skills, but in competition we know coaches will begin to specialize. We are trying to discourage coaches from constantly selecting the early maturing athlete," says Mike MacKay, Canada's Manager of Coach Education and Development.

In middle school, my team featured a dominating post player. He led us to P.A.L. Championships in 6th and 8th grade and dominated at camps. However, he never played varsity high school basketball. He dominated in middle school because he hit puberty early. In 6th grade, he was

...scle definition. In 8th grade, he was 5'10, which is as tall as he grew. As a ... in 8th grade, he dominated. However, by the time we reached varsity high ... guards were over six-feet. As a junior varsity player, he excelled against bigger ... of his desire, athleticism and post footwork. He was no longer a dominating ... second or third best player on a team that won its last 24 games. Unfortunately, ...erimeter skills to transition to the varsity level.

... not unique. Coaches often sacrifice a player's future for immediate success. I ... played the post in middle school because she was the tallest girl. However, she was only ... her freshman year of high school, her coach told her never to dribble. Her entire role was to be tall, stand near the basket and make lay-ups if the ball found a way into her hands. She never grew beyond 5'10, which is a small post player at the varsity high school level even for girls. How is a player supposed to improve if her coach prohibits her from trying skills that she needs to acquire to continue playing? At the varsity level, the same coach now criticizes the player because she lacks a diverse skill-set.

A global approach to player development means training all skills for all players, regardless of size. This means not pigeon-holing a player into a position at a young age. It means using a system which enables all players to use their global skills, rather than sticking the tall girl under the basket. It also means training all skills, not just preparing players for games. To develop into a great player, the player first needs to be a great athlete. Basketball is an athletic game which requires great lateral movement, agility, quickness, strength, power, explosiveness, hand-eye coordination, visual acuity, flexibility, balance, body control and more. Therefore, to develop a global player, these skills must be a part of the overall development plan.

Society narrowly defines athleticism. We see a player who runs fast and jumps high and label him "athletic." However, if he cannot stop his forward momentum or if he lacks hand-eye coordination, is he really athletic? In today's game, Steve Nash is the most misunderstood player. We marvel at his success despite his perceived lack of athleticism. However, Nash is a phenomenal athlete. If he wanted, he likely could have played professional soccer, like his father and brother. Besides his ability to perform in two sports, he excels in many athletic areas which go unnoticed.

Steve Nash may not soar through the sky, but he is athletic: he possesses great hand-eye coordination, lateral quickness, reaction time, agility, conditioning, dexterity, balance, core strength and more. While not a dunker, he can do some athletic feats that most basketball players will not try; for instance, he stands on a stability ball and catches medicine balls. While the relevance to basketball success is small, it illustrates supreme body awareness, core strength and balance, three athletic skills important to basketball success.

An elite player must be a great athlete, which requires more than the ability to dunk. Jumping is an important skill, but it does not define athleticism. A basketball player needs a multitude of athletic skills, including:

- Hand-eye Coordination
- Balance
- Body Control
- Agility
- Reaction Time
- Flexibility
- Power
- Quickness (linear and lateral)
- Strength
- Anaerobic Conditioning
- Aerobic Conditioning
- Visual Acuity
- Dexterity
- Core Strength
- Explosiveness

Second, an elite basketball player requires refined mental and psychological skills like:

- Competitiveness
- Concentration
- Confidence
- Stick-to-itiveness
- Motivation
- Decision-making
- Open-mindedness
- Mental Toughness
- Growth Mindset
- Learning Orientation

We use these words frequently, but few people understand their true meaning or how to develop these traits in a young player. We throw around words like mental toughness when a player makes a free throw late in the game. However, if we believe it is such an important skill, do we practice mental toughness? And, if we did, what would we do to train the skill?

Similarly, coaches often yell at players to tell them to concentrate. However, the coach's yelling actually interferes with their concentration. The yelling distracts the player from the task as he shifts his concentration to the coach's instructions. We wonder why young players struggle at the free throw line, but their parents yell instructions and their coach yells instructions and the player suffers paralysis from analysis because the parents and coaches want the player to concentrate, but misunderstand concentration.

Sports psychology plays a major role in talent development and sports success, yet few coaches and players understand the process. To maximize talent, we need a better understanding of these and other concepts.

Third, an elite player requires technical skill development:

- Shooting
- Finishing
- Passing
- Ball Handling
- Footwork
- Hard2Guard Moves
- Post Moves
- Individual Defense

Finally, an elite player needs game awareness or tactical skill development:

- Using a screen
- Movement in relation to dribble penetration
- Court Spacing
- Pick-and-Roll
- Dribble Hand-offs
- Flex Screens
- Defensive Rotations
- Zone Spacing
- Handling a Trap

With this end in mind, how can we best develop such a player?

The Five LTAD Stages

The *Cross Over Development Model* features five stages: (1) Foundation; (2) Fundamentals; (3) Training; (4) Competition; and (5) Performance. This book covers stages one through four, which encompass youth development; the fifth stage covers adult basketball, competitive (college or professional) or recreational.

In past generations, teams developed in the winter and players developed in the summer; multilateral skills developed naturally through playing multiple sports and engaging in an active childhood. Early specialization, overuse injuries and year-round club basketball did not exist; consequently, a plan for year-round development or an organization to oversee basketball development was unnecessary.

However, youth sport is now a billion-dollar industry supporting personal trainers, private workout facilities, year-round teams and exposure events. Athletes play one sport and train competitively before they are potty-trained. These changes demand more planning and organization to nurture the talents of recreational and elite players.

Some national sport federations organize long term athlete development to maximize its athletes' potential. The Spanish Federation's Youth Basketball Program utilizes Player Development Centers for players from 14 to 18-years-old. The Spanish system starts with summer camps for 10 to 14-year-olds where coaches teach and evaluate potential prospects that they follow through the year. Select individuals join the Player Development Centers where "the goal is to help basketball players between 14 and 18 years of age train in the most efficient way so basketball is compatible with their studies and personal development" (Sergio).

The Centers emphasize "long-term training." In a results-driven system, young athletes train like mini-professionals, not children, and "adult training programs are superimposed on young athletes. This is detrimental because it means that coaching is conducted without regard for the principles of childhood development" (Balyi). A child is not a small adult; a child experiences different stages of physical and psychological development which cannot be rushed or ignored.

The *Cross Over Development Model* uses these developmental periods to maximize training for each athlete and provide a general guideline for youth coaches. Different styles, approaches and emphases are appropriate in each stage, though a general philosophy of long term development through fun, learning and development remains constant.

The **Foundation Stage** (ages 7-10) builds the athlete's base through games, play and basic instruction to ensure proper motor skill development. The introduction of a wide array of basketball and athletic skills through fun, active training sessions is more important than winning games. Players must develop their basic general movement skills during this stage or their basketball fundamentals will peak prematurely. 3v3 games rather than 5v5 provide the best competitive learning environment for these young players. Players shift from a recreational (fun) emphasis to a developmental (learning) emphasis as they join organized teams during this age group.

The **Fundamental Stage** (ages 11-14) emphasizes basketball fundamentals, using the general athletic skills developed through the Foundation Stage to build sport-specific skills. While some players continue to play for fun, most players in organized leagues are developmental athletes and learning continues to take precedence over winning. Progress to full 5v5 games and leagues, but maintain a focus on developing individual and team skills.

The **Training Stage** (ages 15-16) is a transitional stage as developmental athletes transition into competitive athletes through higher training intensity and volume. However, do not rush the process; being a competitive athlete at an earlier age does not make a player better; in fact, rushing the developmental process almost always results in a player peaking early. Develop strength and fitness during this stage and expand tactical awareness through exposure to more tactical skills and greater decision-making responsibility.

The **Competition Stage** (ages 17-20) is comprised of competitive athletes and increases the intensity from the Training Stage. Players specialize in one sport and train year-round to improve performance in order to compete and become an elite athlete. While most never reach an elite level, many compete at this level and strive to reach the Performance Stage (college and/or professional basketball). Players specialize their skills and positions, fill their role on the team and build the competitive fire.

Within each stage, players train Athletic, Tactical and Technical skills. Other skills and attributes contribute to success; however psychological and mental skills contribute and complement these skills. Athletic, Tactical and Technical skills develop interdependently, as each skill requires and complements the others.

During Stages 1 and 2, athletes learn and train a wide variety of skills. Stage 3 transitions athletes from the learning stages to the competitive stages through increased emphasis on training and intensity. In Stage 4, training specificity, testing and performance training increase. Basketball is a simple game; the following four-stage progression gradually builds upon simple concepts, teaching players how to play the game and progressing from simple to more complex and general to specific. Use this model to guide basketball development over a period of years, not a matter of days.

Stage 1: The Foundation Stage

The Foundation Stage is the initial stage when a young child is introduced to the game, often informally, and eventually joins a team. This stage emphasizes:

- Fun
- Exploration
- Freedom
- Love of the Sport

Develop and introduce skills through game play, rather than instruction and drills. The coach organizes the activity and takes on a role like a cheerleader: supportive, active, encouraging, positive and involved. This is not the stage for strategists or even great fundamental teaching. This stage is for coaches to have fun and ensure the players enjoy practice and playing the game.

During this stage, coaches and parents work to:

- Develop a work ethic
- Ensure some measure of success to encourage children to keep playing the sport
- Encourage responsibility for one's actions
- Develop a love of the sport
- Make each player feel important

My friend coaches his seven-year-old son's youth basketball team in East Los Angeles. As with many youth leagues, the players sign up and then the league has an evaluation day where the kids play and the coaches pick their teams. My friend picked his team. The next day, a new team signed up. A coach from a previous season hand-picked the top players, had them skip the evaluation day and formed an all-star team.

This coach used an adult sensibility. Adults value winning. Adults believe that stacking a team displays their cunning and coaching skills. He played to the parents' values of winning and protecting their own kids rather than to their sense of fair play and true competition.

Kids never would have stacked the teams. Kids are uninterested in creating competitive advantages. When kids play without adult interference, they choose even teams, usually using equally talented captains.

While adults value competition and winning, kids value fun. However, fun is different for kids of different ages. A research study found that eight-year-olds believe "being able to do the skill" is fun (Harris and Ewing). Nine-year-olds like "learning and improving skills," and 10-year-olds like "playing with friends." If an eight-year-old believes that fun is "being able to do the skill," shouldn't we spend more time and energy teaching players to do the skill and less time concentrating on stacking teams and winning games? Shouldn't parents focus their comments on skill development and the player's effort rather than the results?

Recreational athletes dominate Stage 1. Fun and activity motivate this group, not winning trophies or making all-star teams. Learning new skills motivates the others. While coaches and parents argue that their athletes prefer competitive athletics, these attitudes reflect the environment the parents and coaches create, as children want to please authority figures, especially parents or coaches. "What seems to be missing in North American youth sport is the whole concept of activity without immediate purpose," (Grasso).

When I coached an under-9 AAU team, we traveled to AAU Nationals. The players enjoyed spending the night in each other's room and watching *Remember the Titans* as much as playing the games. They sang "Everywhere we go" every day and showed off their ball handling tricks to a team from Minnesota. They competed and loved the game while playing, but, when it ended, they wanted to go swimming. Winning and losing hardly affected their attitudes, as they had fun either way.

In countries like Italy and Lithuania, kids start playing basketball when they are five or six-years-old, but they do not play on teams. They join a basketball club, but they do not play games against other clubs. Instead, they learn skills and play fun games with the other kids in their club. When they are nine or 10-years-old, the clubs form teams and play games. However, for several years, the focus is not competition, but developing skills and having fun playing the game.

Stage 1 is the foundation, the base of a child's athletic career. The foundation for athletic enjoyment begins with a positive environment where parents and coaches encourage athletes to have fun and develop their skills without performance pressure. Similarly, the future professional develops the athletic tools which blossom into the skills and attributes of a professional athlete. While most view the foundations for the future pro and the recreational athlete differently, each develops through the same dedication to fun and learning at this age.

Competition – and learning to be competitive – is an important skill, regardless of athletic dreams and goals. However, coaches and parents must accept the athlete's motivation and not superimpose adult attitudes or expectations. While some adapt, adjust and excel when a coach emphasizes winning, many young athletes lose interest and quit sports: 70% of kids quit youth sports by age 13 (Thompson).

Beyond the athlete's motivation, Stage 1 sets the foundation for athletic development. During this stage, athletes develop running, jumping, stopping, landing, squatting and other basic and essential movement patterns. If these patterns develop incorrectly, the athlete eventually must re-learn the skill or see his sport-specific development peak as others improve. While children learn these skills naturally, they may not learn them correctly. Proper development gives athletes an advantage as they move toward more competitive athletics. Entering children into competitive athletics at a young age increases initial sport-specific development. However, long term, these athletes peak early, while the athletes with a broader and better athletic foundation blossom. Developing these skills does not require a technician's knowledge of each motor skill. Instead, coaches cue players to certain things to enhance their natural development. For instance, many players learn to run without using an arm swing. By cuing the players to swing their arms from "shoulder to your back pocket" and "drive the opposite arm and opposite leg," coaches direct the players learning while not interfering with their natural development.

Rather than concentrate on game preparation and 5v5 Tournaments, use small-sided games to teach basic rules and strategy. Play is more important than instruction or drills; however, players lack the strength, spatial awareness and cognitive skills to play 5v5 games, so one player typically dominates the action. Small-sided games allow more players to play, building interest and motivation. Small-sided scrimmages and informal leagues keep players active, reduce the performance pressure and offer more opportunities to improve ball skills.

I once worked a summer camp and worked with the 10-year-olds. The group hated softball, but whiffle ball in the handball court was their favorite game. Softball was hard. Most could not hit a pitched ball and few could field or throw, so games were a disaster. But, whiffle ball made the game easier *and* more challenging – when nobody on the field can hit, throw or field, where is the challenge? In whiffle ball, nearly every play involved every player. We played 4v4 or 5v5, so the kids got more at-bats and more chances to field and throw the ball. Playing small-sided games or changing the rules – like from softball to whiffle ball – involves more young athletes while teaching the skills needed to play the real sport.

Whether the goal is to develop an appreciation and interest in sports for health or social reasons or to prepare a young athlete for elite sport participation, Stage 1's mission is the same: create a positive environment with an emphasis on fun, learning and activity. "The object is to remove the idea that play must become work if children are to improve, so challenges replace technique practices, and drills make way for carefully structured games," (Launder). This is a preparation stage, the first step toward a life of sports activities, not a season-long quest for a championship.

Stage 2: The Fundamental Stage

The Fundamental Stage builds on the athletic and general basketball skills and emphasizes fundamental skill execution. Developmental players dominate Stage 2: learning, discovering and improving motivates players. Fun is important, but accomplishing a task, mastering a tough drill or making shots excites players.

The Fundamental Stage dominates youth basketball. Unfortunately, coaches and parents often ignore this stage in their rush to competitive basketball. This phase emphasizes:

- Learning
- Technique
- Mastery of Skills
- Social Development: Part of a team

Players are hungry to learn new skills and try new things. The best coaches explain and demonstrate the basic fundamental skills and use their creativity to enhance the players' learning through new drills or teaching methods. The more a coach understands the skills he teaches and the basic progression or process to master the skills, the better his coaching.

The Fundamental Stage lasts longer than the Foundation Stage, as learning and mastering the basic fundamentals takes time. Rushing the process to reach the next stage often stifles development, rather than enhancing it, as athletes need time to concentrate on skill development.

Coaches should have a gradual system of progressions for the development and mastery of the necessary technical skills. While teams compete and play games, games should not interfere with the learning process, but provide additional motivation and an opportunity to measure one's improvement.

In this stage, contrast, rather than compare improvement. Contrasting is a term developed by Jerome Green of the Hoop Masters AAU program in Los Angeles to describe the process of contrasting one's development over a period of time, rather than comparing one player to his peer group. Because players grow, mature and develop at such a different rate, comparisons are problematic. On a 12-and-under team, one player may already have finished his major growth spurt, while others may not have reached puberty. Comparing these players is unfair, as the players with the older biological age (physical maturity) should have higher expectations. At this age, the goal is not to be better than other players or teammates, but to improve over a period of time. Contrasting is more individual and personal and compares one player's progress over a period of time, maybe one season, rather than comparing one player to another.

By this stage, most players play in organized leagues. Children are aware of winning and losing. For most, the final score is not their primary motivator; adults increase its importance. Players want to play and feel important; winning beats losing, but winning is not everything. One study found that 11-year-olds consider fun to be "competing with others of about the same ability," while 12-year-olds consider fun to be "competing against a challenging opponent," (Harris and Ewing). Competition is healthy, but the "will to win must come from within the child. Parents, activity leaders and trainers must create conditions, through organizing matches and giving training sessions, in keeping with the perceived world of the child," (Michels).

Developmental athletes use competition to measure improvement. When players stop improving, the game loses its fun. "In many countries, the development of the young players is inhibited. The players do not reach their full potential because they are too early on sacrificed for the result. Their development is stagnated for the principle 'the result takes precedent over how it is achieved," (Michels).

In an article titled "Winning vs. Player Development," German lecturer and coach Horst Wein outlines the objectives "To win" and "To promote development." The development objectives offer a good list for Stage 2 coaches. By giving freedom to players, encouraging creativity, focusing on individual and team skills and giving everyone a chance, all players stay motivated, have fun and improve. Through the improvement and fun, players work harder, practice on their own and continue playing.

Objective: To Win	Objective: To promote development
There is little room for younger, less skilled or underdeveloped players. The game is undemocratic.	Everyone has the same right to play, regardless of physique and ability. The game is democratic.
Tactics are overemphasized, starting around the age of eight.	Matches highlight players' skills and allow them to gain tactical experience gradually
The point of training is to win the match and championship. Players have to obey the coach, who gives orders from the sideline.	The coach's aim is to improve the performance of each individual player and of the team as a whole. Players rely on their own perception and judgment to decide what their next move will be, rather than the coach deciding for them.
The game plan has been thought out by the coach. There is no time or room for flair.	Individuals are allowed to introduce their flair, skill and imagination.
Young people are prematurely exposed to adult competition instead of age-appropriate competition, which would make for more efficient learning.	In the interest of learning the complex game more efficiently, competition is adapted to players' physical and intellectual abilities at each stage of their growth. Fun and self-esteem are guaranteed.
Physical skill and working out are overemphasized because these factors get results most quickly.	Through exposure to a variety of competitions each season, players gain coordination and the ability to play under different conditions.
In the interest of winning, training relies primarily on traditional methods of teaching.	In the interest of understanding the game and making fewer mistakes, training emphasizes the discovery of skills and capacities in simplified games.

During this stage, athletes work to master the required technical skills and physical attributes. As these skills near mastery, motivations shift, as players look for more ways to use their skills and physical tools. Competition is more meaningful and biological age balances with chronological age, so the discrepancy between the early and late bloomers lessens. At this point, players progress to the Training Stage.

Stage 3: The Training Stage

Stage 3 is a transition period between the preceding fun and learning and forthcoming competition. The fun is the increased challenge, the formal school or club-based competitions and the pride of making a team. Learning requires training the previously learned skills at a higher intensity and tempo, while adding new skills and concepts. For instance, the challenge is no longer to learn proper shooting mechanics, but to make game shots from game spots at game speed. This transition occurs for all the basic fundamental skills as training, tweaking and refining previously learned skills replaces strictly learning new skills.

The Training Stage emphasizes:
- Increased training intensity
- Off-Season Training
- Off-court Workouts (Strength, plyometrics, etc.)
- Greater specificity of training
- More emphasis on the team game and individual roles

Many athletes and coaches ignore this transition from the learning stages to the competitive stages. Games lose their learning and development components as winning takes over. When a coach tells a freshman never to dribble, how is she supposed to improve? "The reason why so many athletes plateau during the later stage of their careers is primarily because of an over-emphasis on competition instead of training during this period in their athletic development," (Balyi and Hamilton, 2003). While teams compete to win, players need room to grow, develop and learn from mistakes without fear of failure.

This stage is the "window of accelerated adaptation to aerobic and strength training," (Balyi and Hamilton, 2003). Incorporate resistance training. While players have a large window of growth for basketball skills, adding strength, quickness and power can elevate a player even more. A gradual program which incorporates flexibility, stability, strength and power enhances on-court player development, develops players into better athletes and enables players to perform at a higher level. Aerobic conditioning is of lesser concern; through playing, players develop good fitness levels without much additional running. If conditioning is necessary or desired, use interval training. Mile runs (or longer) use different energy systems and muscle fibers. Basketball is primarily an anaerobic sport requiring fast-twitch muscle fiber for quick, explosive actions; steady-state running trains the aerobic system and slow-twitch muscle fiber.

This stage is essential to a player's growth and development, yet many ignore the preparatory stages completely. Teams prepare to win; they do not prepare to improve. There is a significant difference, though commonly misunderstood, and this difference impedes players' development. During the second and third stage, we "make or break an athlete...Athletes who miss this phase of training will not reach their full potential," (Balyi and Hamilton).

Regardless of system, well-coached teams exhibit several characteristics and traits:
1. Play hard
2. Play unselfishly
3. Make good decisions

4. Shoot high percentage shots
5. Share the basketball
6. Protect the basketball
7. Defend relentlessly
8. Hustle
9. Exhibit mental toughness
10. Compete

Emphasize these attributes to focus players on their performance, not just the result. At this age, teams are often unbalanced, so winning the game is sometimes virtually guaranteed and other times nearly impossible. Rather than focus on won-loss record, motivate players to focus on their performance as a means to success. Emphasize and reward these traits and attributes during practice drills, scrimmages and games. Coaches accentuate the negatives, commenting on mistakes. Rather than focus on the mistakes, comment on the positives. Reward the positives rather than punishing the negatives. When a player uses the screen properly but misses the shot, notice the proper use of the screen, not the missed shot. Players know when they make a mistake. They do not always know why they made the mistake, so there is room for teaching. However, spend more time commenting on positives than correcting negatives. Build players confidence and allow players to learn from their own mistakes.

Winning depends on talent and luck as much as effort, skill or execution. The bigger, faster more talented team wins most games. Therefore, "control the controllables," and focus internally on your team's performance rather than externally on the outcome. The game and the season are a process, not a result.

Stage 4: The Competition Stage

The Competition Stage is high school varsity basketball or u-18 and u-20 club basketball; for many players, this is the pinnacle of their competitive career; for the elite, Stage 4 is another step toward the ultimate goal, which is the Performance Stage: college and/or professional basketball. In the Competition Stage, one does not play basketball, but he identifies himself as a basketball player. Players specialize in one sport and commit more time and effort toward achieving their goals.

During this stage, players integrate their physical tools and technical skills into game performance. Players compete to make teams, to win games and championships and to earn the opportunity to play at the next level. The Competition Stage emphasizes:

- Integration of skills
- Individuality
- Understanding of the game
- Acceptance of roles
- Performance Goals

Training sessions are competitive; teaching continues, but more coaching occurs, as strategy increases. Every day includes basic fundamentals, but the in-season emphasis is game preparation and success, not mastering fundamentals, which occurs during the previous stages and the off-season. Fundamental skill practice occurs within the team's framework and is specific to a player's position and role and the team's system, as opposed to previous stages where skill development is general and less role, system and position-specific.

At this level, games matter; individuals subjugate their game for the good of the team and players specialize skills and positions. For most athletes, building the competitive fire translates directly towards the competitive season; however, for elite athletes, building the competitive fire adds motivation to succeed at the highest levels.

Coaches continue to enhance players' skills and maximize their talent through their system of play to develop a successful program. Coaches are not only teachers, but motivators, strategists, organizers, managers, decision-makers, mentors and more. A coach's role transitions from that of a teacher to that of a coach. Teaching remains important, but other roles take on great importance. In an old ESPN.com article, analyst Jay Bilas differentiated coaching and teaching like this:

> Generally, "coaching" consists of team preparation, the devising of game plans and schemes to defeat opponents. When you are coaching, you are dealing with strategies, different offenses and defenses, and putting in plays to take advantage of the skills, strengths and weaknesses of your players. The measure of a coach is the quality of the development of his system, and has been distilled into winning.
>
> "Teaching" consists of instruction and training of individuals in the fundamental skills of the game, and in teaching players how to play, instead of how to run plays. The measure of a teacher is not in winning, but in the fundamental soundness and skill level of the players taught. A player with excellent fundamentals and skills can play successfully in any system.

Team drills revolve around the team's system; some teams play fast and others play slow; some shoot outside shots, some pass until they get a lay-up; some defend full court, some drop into a zone. Practice decisions depend on the team's style, as a zone team trains differently than a pressing team. Players need time to master the team's system and to learn each other's tendencies, strengths and weaknesses.

The progression through the stages is an individual process and the duration of each stage differs from individual to individual. A coach's role is to understand the players' motivations and provide the environment necessary to promote enjoyment and success, while developing the requisite skill level to progress to the next stage and the next competitive level. It is not a race; the most successful players take the time to develop the physical and technical skills fully and possess the work ethic and psychological tools to maximize their talents.

Chapter 2:
Athletic Skills

Basketball is an athlete's game. The biggest, strongest, fastest kids dominate youth basketball, while the NBA features the world's best athletes, players with 40-inch vertical jumps, 5% body fat and a 300-pound bench press. Nobody succeeds without technical and tactical skills, but coaches choose the more athletic player when picking teams, recruiting players or drafting prospects.

Athleticism is a skill, like technical and tactical skills. Genetics play a part in determining one's size, body type and muscle type, but one can train athleticism through good instruction and proper training. Unfortunately, many coaches, teams and leagues ignore athletic development during the formative stages.

The term "athleticism" is often misunderstood. When we speak about athleticism, we generally mean players who look fast and jump high. We picture players like Atlanta's Josh Smith or Orlando's Dwight Howard. When they play, we see their athleticism. We see Howard's boulder-like shoulders and Smith's gravity-defying dunks. They make running and jumping look effortless.

Athleticism is the ability to execute a series of movements at optimum speed with precision, style, and grace (Gambetta). Howard and Smith define athleticism. However, Steve Nash does as well. Few people believe Nash possesses "NBA athleticism," though play after play, he executes a series of movements with speed, precision, style and grace. When Nash flies down court dribbling the basketball, changing directions and evading defenders and fires a pass which hits a teammate in stride for a lay-up, he illustrates athleticism which few players at any level can match.

Distinguishing between athletic, tactical and technical skills is difficult. Does Steve Nash draw a charge because of his great lateral quickness, great reaction time or great anticipation through tactical and strategic understanding? Yes. He understands the game and his opponent (tactical awareness), which allows him to anticipate the play, improving his reaction time (athletic skill) which makes his lateral movement quicker (athletic skill). During a game, these skills work together for successful performance.

While athletic, tactical and technical skills develop interdependently, athletic skills form the foundation. Without developed athletic skills, a player's tactical and technical skills disappear. When Nash flies down court dribbling, changing directions and evading defenders, he combines a multitude of general athletic skills into sport-specific performance. He uses locomotor skills (running) and manipulative skills (dribbling the ball). He reacts to a stimulus (the defender), exhibits core and upper body strength (the pass), agility (changing directions) and more. Before Nash executes this skill flawlessly at full speed during a game against similarly skilled and athletic players, he spent years developing these individual skills. When we watch Nash make this play look easy, we underestimate the athletic skill involved with performing these skills and we undervalue the instruction and training necessary for a young player to perform such a play.

Without athletic skill development, a player may develop the control with the basketball and the ability to fire the pass and he may understand when and where to pass the ball, but he will lack the ability to change directions, evade defenders and combine the skills flawlessly and gracefully. Many kids today develop superior technical skills (dribbling the basketball) and some even possess a high basketball I.Q., but they learn predominantly through drills and lack the shiftiness and evading skills necessary to use these technical and tactical skills in a game. Possessing great ball handling skill is useless if the player cannot use his skill to beat a defender.

It is easy to see who runs the fastest from baseline to baseline, who dunks with authority or who has bulging biceps. However, athleticism runs much deeper than straight-ahead speed, vertical jumping and biceps (unless you are a 100m sprinter). Speed kills, but only if the player can use the speed within the basketball rules. If a player is fast, but he cannot stop, is his speed useful? How many times does a fast player sprint ahead for a break-away lay-up but miss because he cannot control his body on his last step or he lacks the coordination to manipulate the ball at full speed? Everyone assumes a missed lay-up is a technical deficiency, and the player needs more practice. However, often an inability to control one's body causes the miss, not the actual lay-up execution. If the player can make a lay-up at half-speed, but not at full-speed, is the problem the shot or the speed?

Unfortunately, coaches and parents see the player race ahead of his peers and believe he is athletic. He is fast and speed is easy to see. To fix his problem, they address the way he shoots the ball because they believe the problem is his technical ability. They fail to address the athletic deficiency because he runs fast and fast equals athletic. The narrow definition of athleticism hinders the player's athletic development.

People describe Nash as unathletic because he does not dunk. Standing next to Josh Smith, nobody would pick Nash as the better athlete. However, if basketball is an athletic game featuring some of the world's best athletes, how is Nash able to compete?

Nash is, in fact, incredibly athletic when we broaden our definition of athleticism to include more than speed and jumping ability. His hand-eye coordination is as good as it gets in the NBA; his reaction time is unbelievable; his lateral movement is excellent; his ability to switch from a broad or soft-centered focus to a narrow, fine-centered focus is the best in the NBA; his body awareness is exceptional; his dexterity with both hands is tops in the NBA; his first step quickness is far above average for the NBA; his core strength is unparalleled in the NBA and likely the only reason he is able to play with his chronic back problems. In all these categories, he is in the top 1% of NBA players, but because he does not "look" athletic (sculpted muscles) or do obviously athletic things (dunk), we label him unathletic.

If one lacks great athletic skills, he can compensate to a certain degree with tremendous technical and tactical skills. Because Nash shoots a high percentage and uses his left and right hand equally well, we assume he succeeds through his technical ability and a great understanding of the game (tactical skill). However, his athletic ability enhances his technical ability. Could Nash sprint down court, stop on a dime, elevate and shoot if he lacked athleticism? We see the shot's technical execution, but the athletic ability to decelerate quickly is the more difficult skill. On the court, we do not notice Nash's athleticism because it blends with his basketball skills. How do you separate his hand-eye coordination from his ball handling and passing ability? How do you judge his reaction time without his tactical understanding?

Athleticism is more than what we see with the naked eye, and basketball involves more than running in a straight line and jumping high. Core strength, deceleration, balance, dynamic flexibility, hand-eye coordination, ability to shift from fine to soft focus and more contribute to successful skill execution and performance. These skills enhance or detract from a player's sport-skill execution.

With a base of athleticism, sport-specific training is more purposeful. Basic laws govern the acquisition of motor skills and abilities.

> "Any Athletic skill is actually a motor skill, which can be defined as an act or task that has a goal to achieve and requires voluntary body or limb movement to be properly performed. Many times – and wrongly so – the terms skills and ability are used interchangeably. Motor abilities (static and dynamic balance, visual acuity, response

time, speed of limb movement, eye hand/foot coordination, etc.) can be viewed as the foundational components of motor skill development, but are not skills by definition," (Mannie).

To develop sport skills, one must have basic motor abilities. There is a learning progression with motor skill development, just as with learning math. In mathematics, one learns the values of numbers, first learning to put the language – the spoken number four – together with a picture of four objects. Once one learns the value of the symbols used to represent things and language, the student learns addition and subtraction and works to the multiplication tables, division, etc. There is a rational order, and one cannot skip addition and subtraction and go straight to long division.

Similarly, in motor skill development, there is an order of skill acquisition. "The basic motor skills-*non-locomotor* (stationary, like bending and stretching), *locomotor* (traveling, like walking or hopping) and *manipulative* (object control, like bouncing and catching a ball) – have been called the ABC's of movement," (Pica). A person masters non-locomotor skills, most importantly balance, before moving to locomotor skills and finally manipulative skills.

These motor skills combine non-locomotor, locomotor and manipulative skills and allow a person to move to specific sport skills. "Fundamental motor skills such as hopping, jumping, skipping, kicking, throwing, catching and striking are prerequisites to the learning of sport specific skills such as those of basketball, football, gymnastics, tennis, badminton, etc. Sport-specific skills are comprised of fundamental skills and variations of them. It is very difficult to obtain proficiency in sport skills unless the prerequisite fundamental skills are present," (Smith).

When young children do not fully develop these basic fundamental skills, it hampers their sport-skill performance. Many high school players cannot skip; they can make a motion that approximates skipping, but they lack the coordination to skip. Other young people have difficulty catching balls because they cannot track the ball; their motor abilities – namely hand/eye coordination and visual acuity – are poorly developed. Rather than developing a faculty for skipping through hop scotch in the school yard, or learning to chase and track a ball playing stickball, children are exposed to motion and skills only in classes and practices where a coach, teacher or parent tells them what to do, rather than learning on their own. Language can only approximate the skill; it is not the skill itself and if the child is not given the time to translate the language and learn the skill, it may not develop fully at a young or appropriate age.

As we learn different movements, we progress through different stages or movement patterns, each with its own emphasis and performance cues.

> "Movement patterns is the term given to ten basic types of movements [sending, receiving, accompanying, evading, locomotions, landings, statics, swings, rotations, springs] the body engages in when participating in physical activity…these movement patterns are broken down into 'performance cues' at the beginner, intermediate and advanced levels…The beginner's performance cues are all related to body and space…the intermediate's focus is still on 'space' but more on 'force'…this means that the focus is on the application of power in order to move the body (starting and stopping) or applying power to a game object (badminton smash versus drop shot)…the [advanced] student's focus is somewhat on force but more on relationships…the adjustment made among body, space and force to change or further refine skill performance and strategies," (Saskatchewan Education).

A coach's awareness of his players' level focuses his attention on the proper cues. When teaching a player to dribble, the beginner focuses on his body position and the ball's distance from the body. Imagine a young basketball player dribbling for the first time: often they slap at the ball and the ball controls the player rather than the player controlling the ball. If the coach concentrates on intermediate or advanced cues, like the force of the dribble or the player's dribbling in relation to a defender, before focusing on the player's ball control and maintaining the proper distance between the ball and body, he undermines his coaching effectiveness. His points may be valid, but the player is not prepared to use the instruction because he must overcome the initial challenges first. If the coach understands the different levels and evaluates his players' levels correctly, his effectiveness increases as he offers instruction the player can use.

Stage 1: The Foundation Stage
Training Goals: Speed, coordination, execution of proper movement patterns, fundamentals of movements, and exposure to multiple skills.
Emphasis: Fun and games to develop skills and athleticism.

Coaches have a dual purpose: provide a positive, fun environment and prepare athletes for future participation. Stage 1 is pivotal for athletic development. During the first stage a coach should:
1. Expose athletes to a multitude of general skills.
2. Devote more time to athletic skills training than tactical or technical training to prepare players for long term development and success.
3. Utilize scientific principles in training.
4. Use fun games for skill development.

Exposure to General Skills

Introduce general movement skills and patterns, as these movements form the foundation of all athletic actions. Athletes move from general to specific skills and simple to complex movements. At this age, encourage players to play multiple sports. "If the children later decide to leave the competitive stream, the skills they have acquired during the [Foundation] phase will still benefit them when they engage in recreational activities, which will enhance their quality of life and health," (Balyi and Hamilton). The same skills enhance competitive opportunities. Before athletes exhibit the grace, balance and agility of an NBA superstar, they master the basic movement skills and train the five bio motor qualities (Speed, Strength, Flexibility, Endurance and Coordination). The movement skills are:

- Locomotor skills: running, skipping, jumping, bounding, etc.
- Non-locomotor skills: twisting, turning, balancing, etc.
- Manipulative skills: throwing, kicking, catching, trapping, and striking.

Some skills are beyond basketball, like kicking, striking and trapping. However, train the other skills. First, teach the movement without regard to speed. Next, increase the speed while maintaining movement precision; do not sacrifice quality for speed. Next, change the movements or execute them under different conditions. Finally, implement the sports-specific skill with the movement skill.

To teach jumping, start with single jumps in place. Once players demonstrate proper jumping and landing mechanics, move to multiple jumps, which increases the speed. Next, do broad jumps, jumping forward on each jump rather than straight up in the air or run into a jump, like a jump stop. Finally, combine the skill into a sport-specific skill, like jumping to shoot or dribbling into a jump stop. To a coach's perspective, dribbling into a jump stop is an easy skill as it is second-nature for coaches with playing experience. However, for a novice player, especially one who may lack coordination, dribbling into a jump stop combines several skills and attempting to teach all the skills at once impedes the learning process. In this stage, teach the skills individually and progress to the full sport-specific skill.

Running Mechanics

While children learn to run like they learn to crawl and walk – through watching their environment, mimicking others and trial and error – not all children develop proper running mechanics. While fun is the primary goal, use fun games to teach skills like running and stopping.

Running involves four phases:

- Propulsion Phase: push against the ground with power to drive the body quickly forward.
- Drive Phase: the opposite leg drives forward with the thigh horizontal. The opposite arm also drives along the body with the hand at shoulder height (arms are bent to 90-degrees). It is essential to keep the ankle dorsiflexed (locked up) to the landing phase.
- Landing Phase: the foot strikes the ground and quickly comes underneath the body
- Recovery Phase: the heel of the propelling leg quickly drives toward the butt while the opposite arm quickly moves forward.

Use the PAL System to evaluate running mechanics. PAL: Posture, Arm Action and Leg Action

- Posture: Run tall
- Arm Action: Opposes the leg action to assist with balance and propulsion during the drive phase
- Leg Action: Foot contacts the ground under the center of gravity

The goal is not to create a world class sprinter, but to improve his mechanics so he uses energy more efficiently and moves more quickly. Many kids move awkwardly because they do not move their arms; they run like a toy soldier. By correcting and emphasizing this detail with key cue words like "arm swing" or "top of the shoulders to the back pocket" during warm-up drills, the player's speed and coordination of movement improve.

> **Teaching Progression for Running**
>
> **March**: Kids mimic marching bands and exaggerate the high knees and arm swing, which are two keys to better running mechanics. The arm swing is opposite the leg swing: if stepping forward with the right leg, the left arm swings forward. Arms swing from the top of the shoulders to the back pocket.
>
> **Skip**: Step and hop. Check arm swing. Foot strikes on the ball of the foot. Drive knee up.
>
> **Sprints**: Check for the same arm swing and *front-side mechanics*: rather than kicking backwards as the foot takes-off from the ground, drive the knee up and forward. From the side, if the athlete is on his left foot, his right knee should be high and his heel under his butt with his foot dorsiflexed (toes up). The knee is in front of the foot, so as his leg extends toward foot strike, he strikes the ground with a positive shin/body angle to push forward.
>
> **Wall Running:** Stand facing a wall with hands shoulder height, bracing your weight. Stand on your right foot, with left knee high and left foot dorsiflexed under your butt (see Drills). Drive your left foot into the ground behind your center of gravity while the right foot drives up. Next, move to three steps at a time and then go for time, starting with 15 seconds.

Acceleration/Deceleration

This stage features the first critical period for speed development. "Linear, lateral and multi-directional speed should be developed and the duration of the repetitions should be less than 5 seconds. This is often called the 'agility, quickness and change of direction window.' Again, fun games should be used for speed training and the volume of the training should be lower," (Hamilton and Balyi, 2003).

In a 100m sprint, top runners reach maximum velocity around 30m. The first 30 meters are the acceleration phase. A regulation basketball court is 94-feet, or approximately 30m. Therefore, a basketball player never reaches maximum velocity. Instead, basketball is a game of quick bursts and changes of direction. A player's first two steps determine the fast break's success: the player who reacts to the change of possession and changes direction quicker has the advantage.

The same quick bursts and changes of direction determine success in many sports. Stopping a line drive up the middle, covering the tennis court, and rushing the quarterback require quickness, not speed. Training quickness – linear, lateral and reaction time – benefits athletes regardless of the sport they pursue. Incorporate quickness drills into the end of the Dynamic Warm-up.

When teaching kids to accelerate, imagine running up a flight of stairs. To run up the stairs, the body leans forward, the knees drive up and forward, the arms swing and the foot strikes behind the center of gravity. When accelerating, look for the forward lean and the front-side mechanics – many kids run slow because they fail to drive their knees forward and instead run like they are on a treadmill, shuffling their feet.

To decelerate, use two different methods: (1) a Hockey Stop or (2) a Lunge Stop. Use the lunge stop to go from a sprint to a back pedal (or from a back pedal to a sprint), and the hockey stop to change and run in another direction. In most cases, the final step of deceleration is the first step of acceleration (Lee Taft). Otherwise, one can slow down indefinitely, like a sprinter after completing a race. In shooting, the change from deceleration to acceleration is from horizontal to vertical.

Lunge Stop

- Use when running forward to stop quickly in the split stance (lunge position).
- Lower the hips and stop the lead leg knee over the foot, like a lunge.
- Shoulders should be more forward than a strength training lunge.
- Back leg bends close to 90-degrees.
- In live situations players do not hold the lunge position, but reactively push off to back pedal.
- The reverse lunge is done off the back pedal position with the rear or stopping leg much further back and the shoulders forward to accelerate quickly.

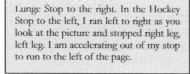

Lunge Stop to the right. In the Hockey Stop to the left, I ran left to right as you look at the picture and stopped right leg, left leg. I am accelerating out of my stop to run to the left of the page.

Hockey Stop

- Turn the hips, leg and feet so they are parallel with the end line, like when running line drills.
- Outside leg is the final decelerator and controls momentum to change direction.
- Inside leg begins deceleration because in a normal stride pattern (r,l,r,l,r) it touches down first as the body turns (Taft).

Acceleration drills like *Tennis Ball Drop, Red Light-Green Light* and *Get-up Tag* are fun ways to teach skills to young players. While these drills do not involve a basketball, especially at this stage, kids enjoy these games and they have value in terms of athletic development. As players develop better reaction time and first-step quickness, their basketball skills improve.

Beyond running and stopping, teach players to squat, skip, jump and land:

- **Squat** (right): Initiate movement at the hips; sit back and down with feet flat on the ground; shoulders over knees and knees over toes.
- **Skip**: Step and hop. Arm swing opposite leg swing, like running. Foot strikes on the ball of the foot. Work on the rhythm.
- **Jump**: Use arms and drive into the ground. Triple extension of the ankle, knee and hip.
- **Land**: Push hips back and land on the balls of the feet, sitting back to a flat foot with shoulders over knees and knees over toes. Land "like a ninja," soft and quiet. "Push the hips back in order for the shoulders to load forward. This action acts as a good shock absorber and also spring loads the athlete to explode again. This technique is a good first progression for teaching power jumping but if teaching reaction jumping the landing phase is much shorter and the re-jump is much quicker. The athletes will not bend as much but should keep vertical alignment with the knees over feet," (Taft).

Dynamic Warm-up

Once players understand these basic general skills, use a Dynamic Warm-up (See *Appendix*) to train and refine these skills. The Dynamic Warm-up (DWU) is neuromuscular training. As the neuromuscular system improves its efficiency, athletes move more quickly and explosively. For example, players run from baseline to baseline, use a lunge stop and back pedal to the baseline. Use the DWU to teach and emphasize skills. To incorporate the hockey stop, run from baseline to baseline, use a hockey stop and carioca back to the baseline.

In addition to a Dynamic Warm-up, play tag. Taft calls tag the best game kids can play and Boston Celtics Strength and Conditioning Coach Walter Norton, Jr. laments the absence of neighborhood games like tag and touch football due to early specialization, as players have lost the ability to make people miss. Norton says, "Because basketball practices are so structured, players become great at ball handling with both hands, but they are like robots and lack elusiveness. Teaching kids new skills takes a long time, because they have been doing the same thing for so long." Use tag to improve agility and evading skills. Dribbling with either hand is an important skill, but beating defenders is even more useful.

Balance

Beyond these locomotor skills, train balance. "Balance is essentially control of the center of gravity over the base of support and… is the basis for voluntary movement and control…Balance is the ability to reduce force at the correct time, at the correct joint, in the correct plane, in the correct direction, for the required activity" (Gambetta).

It is impossible to reduce and produce force without balance. Without balance, movement is awkward and may not be in the chosen direction. Essentially balance is the body losing and regaining control of its center of gravity. Therefore gravity and its control will facilitate movement. There is a continual reaction to gravity and external forces.

Inner Zone balance is balance where your body weight and center of gravity is balanced over your center of gravity: a stationary athletic stance. Outer Zone Balance is how far outside your inner zone you can reach or step and regain balance. The Balance Threshold is the point at which you lose control of your balance. Losing balance is lost balance. Using energy to regain your balance is using energy incorrectly (Gambetta).

Balance Progression
1. Bilateral Stance (Two-feet)
2. Unilateral Stance (One-foot)
3. Arms or legs as a counterbalance
4. No arms (hands on hips or head)
5. Eyes Closed
6. Varied Surface (Airex pad, wobble board)
7. Dynamic (with movement)
8. Increase range of motion (reach forward, backward and to the side with free leg)
9. Increase speed
10. Add Reaction (catch a tennis ball or a medicine ball)

Utilize Scientific Principles

Many coaches and parents misunderstand resistance training, plyometrics, aerobic/anaerobic training and nutrition. Many believe weight training is dangerous, though it is statistically safe. Many believe weight training stunts one's growth or that it is bad for a young person's bones, which is not scientifically valid; instead, resistance training may increase the bone density of growing children. Similarly, many believe a youngster should avoid plyometrics, though nobody tells kids to stop playing hop-scotch or jumping off the monkey bars (depth jump). Plyometrics (running, skipping and jumping) are a part of every active child's existence. Coaches who understand the physiology behind resistance training, plyometrics and nutrition enhance athletic development, which improves their on-court performance.

Understanding the body's mechanics and movement enhances a coach's ability to prevent injury and optimize performance. Possibly the three most important skills in basketball are running and stopping; jumping and landing; and shooting, and all depend on proper biomechanics. An athlete who continually lands incorrectly when jumping predisposes herself to an injury; a coach who understands the biomechanics of landing may prevent a devastating knee injury by teaching the correct mechanics and devising a program for the athlete to strengthen the necessary muscles and to learn the proper muscle memory (see *Appendix I* for more on ACL Prevention).

Coaches need not be scientists. However, the best coaches learn continuously. Coaches do not need an advanced understanding of biomechanical principles, but a general familiarity helps a coach notice major flaws, especially those which predispose an athlete to injury.

Fun Games

As stated by Barrett, "The aim of movement education is to create versatile, skillful movers in a variety of situations," (Barrett). Thus, coaches develop skills in an array of physically demanding activities and are mindful of skill acquisition and skill progression. Encourage players to explore, refine and practice skills through games and outside pursuits.

While coaching in Ireland, I visited an elementary school to conduct a basketball clinic. When I arrived, I learned that I had plenty of baskets, but we had about 80 kids at a time and only seven basketballs. My assistant took the older kids and the basketballs and did some ball handling and shooting. With the younger kids (6-10), I took a bag of tennis balls and played *Tennis Ball Drop*, *Get-up Tag* and catch. While each group only participated for 25 minutes, these kids loved the games and would have played all day if we had let them.

The P.E. teachers appreciated our ability to engage a large crowd and train skills. While the kids had a great time, I wanted to introduce skills and demonstrate simple games. A drill like *Tennis Ball Drop* teaches multiple skills:

- Acceleration: sprinting five to ten feet to catch the tennis ball
- Reaction time and visual awareness: reacting to a visual cue (the dropped ball)
- Hand-eye coordination: catching the ball
- Dynamic Balance: reaching to catch the ball below the knees
- Directional awareness: anticipating the ball's flight and speed
- Dexterity: catching the ball with one's weak hand

A child has no idea he is developing multiple skills, as his concern is catching the ball. This is the ultimate teaching tool for young children: an active, fun game with numerous repetitions and an individual challenge which teaches/trains multiple general athletic skills. While not specifically training basketball skills, five minutes of *Tennis Ball Drop* at practice hastens the player's overall athletic development, which ultimately makes for a better basketball player.

Stage 2: The Fundamental Stage
Training Goals: Coordination, sports skills, refinement of previously developed skills, additional exposure to various stimuli.
Emphasis: Adding stimuli to make games and drills more challenging.

During Stage 2, athletes broaden their basic movement skill foundation and incorporate more complex skills, more sport-specific skills and more strength skills. "Adding a variety of athletic skill development into the programs of young (especially pre-adolescent) athletes serves to (a) broaden the youngsters' athletic ability through an enhanced nervous system; (b) reduce the risk of potential injury by not making skill development one-dimensional; (c) enhance their potential ability in any particular sport via developing global skill; and (d) prevents emotional burnout, which is a highly problematic issue in North American youth sports," (Grasso). The defensive slide, for instance, is not just a basketball skill, but a sport-specific application of general lateral movement. Before teaching defense, athletes must learn correct lateral acceleration and deceleration.

"This is the window of accelerated adaptation to motor coordination," (Balyi and Hamilton). General basketball drills train sport skills and motor coordination. Players manipulate a ball, whether shooting, passing, receiving or dribbling; train spatial awareness while judging distances between oneself and another player; directional awareness when anticipating and chasing a rebound; visual awareness when sprinting down court and deciding whether to attack the basket or back out and set-up; temporal awareness in the shooting mechanics, especially at the free throw line and more. By using a skills-based approach, coaches develop better, more skilled basketball players and better overall athletes.

This is a sensitive period for developing balance, movement adequacy, kinesthetic differentiation, reaction to acoustical and visual signals and rhythmic motion (Grasso). Emphasize balance and coordination of movements and incorporate new stimuli into the Stage 1 drills to develop these skills.

- Balance: *RLGL*; on the red light, players stop on one leg, rather than two.
- Visual Signals: *Tennis Ball Drop* (start from different positions).
- Acoustical Signals: reaction to a coach's whistle (*Get-up Tag*).
- Rhythmic Motion: Skipping in the Dynamic Warm-up and two-ball drills from the Technical Section.

Add a basketball to drills like *RLGL* and *Tennis Ball Drop* to add complexity, train additional skills and make the drills more basketball-specific. *Tennis Ball Drop* with the player dribbling enhances the player's first-step quickness on a basketball move.

Beyond making Stage 1 drills more complex and basketball-specific, teach and train general strength and agility. Incorporate general strength, core strength and agility into the Dynamic Warm-up or use different drills as part of a warm-up station routine and/or give players homework.

General Strength

In *Movement that Matters*, Paul Chek discusses training movements, not muscles; rather than isolate the biceps with a preacher curl, train movements. Chek's six primal patterns represent the basic movements of life: twist pattern, pull pattern, lunge pattern, push pattern, bend pattern and squat pattern.

In this stage, start with body weight movements and progress to incorporate medicine balls and then dumbbells. Add some exercises to the DWU or assign players homework to train on their own. These six patterns provide plenty of different exercises to train general strength.

Twist: Medicine Ball (MB) Twist, MB Underhand Lateral Throw, MB Side Chop, MB Side Chop Throw
Pull: Pull-up, Chin-up, Horizontal Pull-up
Lunge: Front Lunge, Back Lunge, Side Lunge, Front-to-Back Lunge
Push: MB Front Throw, Push-up
Bend: MB Wood Chop
Squat: Body Weight (BW) Squat, MB Squat, Overhead MB Squat, MB Squat and Throw

Core strength

The core encompasses the muscles that attach to the spine and pelvis. Core strength is the first step toward overall strength, as the core initiates movement and stabilizes the body. Core strength, however, is more than training for a six pack; train all four muscles in the abdominal region (rectus abdominis, internal and external obliques and transverse abdominis) and the erector spinae (lower back). Focus on stabilizing the spine through *bridges*, *planks* and *side bridges* before moving to flexion exercises like sit-ups.

Lateral Movement

Lateral movement is the constant interplay between lateral acceleration and deceleration. Every change of direction requires a quick deceleration and an immediate acceleration. As players decrease the time required to decelerate and accelerate, their movement improves. The three primary skills for lateral movements are: (1) the lateral push or shuffle; (2) the crossover step; and (3) the hip turn. Also, because lateral movement applies directly to individual defense, teach the closeout as part of the skill progression, as it fits into the overall progression and builds on previously learned deceleration skills.

Lateral Push: In an athletic position, push opposite the direction of intended movement. To move to your left, push with the inside of your right foot. The left foot lifts slightly off the ground and, in slow motion, steps in the direction of the movement. However, the movement originates from the trail leg pushing, rather than the lead leg stepping. In slow motion, or one at a time, the distinction between the push and a step is small. However, as speed increases, the difference between the look and feel of the trail-leg push and the lead-leg step appears.

Crossover Step: When a player must move quicker than a push step (defensive slide), use the crossover step. The crossover step is the speed between the defensive slide and a sprint and it keeps the defender's hips squared to the offensive player. A crossover step is like half-carioca: when moving to the left, the right foot crosses in front of the left foot. As the right foot pushes down, the left foot steps and pushes.

Hip Turn: To change directions on an angle, use a quick hop and quarter turn. If starting with the right foot slightly forward, angling an offensive player to the defender's left (next page, left), the hip turn moves the left foot slightly forward to angle the offensive player to the defender's right (next page, right). Use the hip turn to add quickness and explosiveness to the change of direction, as it replaces a pivot and drop step. The traditional pivot and drop step is a slow, unnatural movement. On the hip turn, as the feet hit the ground, they reactively push in the direction of the desired movement, taking advantage of the plyometric effect to produce more force and quicker movements.

In the picture, to move to my right, as I hip turn, my left foot is positioned outside my knee to give the proper shin angle to push to my right.

Closeout: To teach a closeout, start with a line under the basket and the coach at the top of the key. Players sprint two-thirds of the way to the coach and then break down their steps. To break down, sit the hips back and down and keep head centered over your center of gravity. Either chop one's steps, like a stutter-step, or use several quick jumps to cover the last couple feet. When closing out, the first objective is to contest a shot and the second is to defend the penetration. Keep the hands up and butt down to contest the shot or a quick overhead pass and maintain the balance to defend against dribble penetration.

To train these skills, I start with the lateral push, or the accelerating movement, and then add the deceleration. The following is my entire defensive progression which includes lateral acceleration and deceleration, the hip turn, cross over step and a closeout, or the ability to sprint to an offensive player with enough speed to prevent an open shot and enough control to contain dribble penetration.

1) *One push.* To move left, stand on the right foot with the left foot three inches off the ground. Push-off the right foot and move left, staying low to the ground (not a hop) in an athletic position with shoulders over knees, knees over toes and toes pointed straight ahead.
2) *Three pushes and stop.* Push three times and stop on-balance in an athletic position; toes pointed forward with weight centered. Do not allow your shoulders to sway outside your base when you stop. If moving left, the left leg "meets the momentum" and stops with the foot outside the knee and knee outside the hip to create the proper push angle to move to the right. Taft says, "The last step of deceleration is the first step of acceleration." (Imagine standing on a subway with no rail to hold when the subway starts. Do you stand with a narrow base or a wide base? With a wide base, your body imparts force in the direction of the train's momentum to maintain your balance, while your upper body sways with a narrow stance, knocking you off balance).
3) *One change of direction.* Three pushes in one direction and a quick change of direction; push to the starting point. Emphasize a quick change of direction.
4) *Follow the coach.* While moving laterally, follow the coach's directions.
5) *Mirror Defense.* Two players face each other, one as the offensive player and the other as the defensive player. The offensive player leads. When the coach says, "Go!" the players slide laterally. The offensive player tries to create separation from the defensive player, while the defender tries to keep his nose on the offensive player's chest. Go for 15 to 30 seconds.
6) *Tennis Ball Shuffle.* Coach stands across from a player with two tennis balls. Coach tosses a ball outside the player's reach and he shuffles to catch it and pass it back to the coach. Go for 30 seconds.

7) *Hip Turn Drill.* To drill the hip turn, players start with a parallel stance (below, left) doing foot-fire (pitter-patter). When the coach points in a direction, players drop a quarter turn in that direction (below right) and then return to a parallel stance.
8) *Hip Turn and Chase.* Coach stands in front of a player with a basketball. Coach throws the ball over the player's shoulder. The player does a hip turn to drop his feet to move in that direction, allows the ball to bounce once and then uses a crossover step to chase and retrieve the ball. Do not turn your back all the way to the coach.
9) *Reaction Ball Closeout:* A player sprints toward the coach. As the coach drops the reaction ball, the player breaks down. The player reacts to the first bounce and attempts to catch the ball before it bounces a second time.
10) *Closeout and Hip Turn.* Player sprints toward the coach. The coach points as the player nears. When the coach points, the player does a hip turn in that direction.
11) *Closeout, Hip Turn and Chase.* Player closes out to the coach. As the player breaks down his steps, the coach tosses the ball over one of the player's shoulders. The player does a hip turn, allows the ball to bounce once and uses a crossover step to chase and retrieve the ball. He passes back to the coach and closes out again.

Finally, teach players to cut. Cutting is similar to lateral movement, except it happens at forward angles (transverse plane) rather than right to left (frontal plane). A cut involves forward and sideways motion. Most non-contact ACL injuries occur when the athlete cuts, plants or lands from a jump. Emphasize the proper body position: plant your foot outside the knee, the knee outside the hips and weight on the inside of your foot; the sharper the cut, the greater the angle of the leg. As Taft says, "Meet your momentum."

Use the step before the cut to lower the body's center of gravity. Players cannot control their momentum in a straight up and down stance as their upper body sways in the direction of their movement. At fast speeds, cutting with the hip, knee and ankle in a vertical line does not slow one's momentum and the force must be absorbed somewhere, which is one explanation for ankle sprains and ACL tears. "While the ball was in play, there was a change in movement category every two seconds. This resulted in more than 1,000 different movements during a game. This is very significant, because it indicated the high-intensity quick changes in movements demanded by the game" (Gambetta). Since the game involves many movements, incorporate as many as possible into a training session to prepare players for the competitive stress.

Practice the movement before incorporating other basketball skills. Use the *Ice Skater Drill* to teach the body position and lateral push and a *45-degree Bound* to teach a cutting movement. Incorporate change of direction training into the *Utah Line Drills*; emphasize straight, not curved lines. Do not rush fundamentals; take time to teach movements correctly and then add an element of reactivity through tag or a reaction ball.

Dynamic Warm-up

Use different agility drills and tools like the speed ladder and reaction ball to add variety to the DWU. A speed ladder is a flat ladder used to train footwork and quickness. Dozens of patterns exist; be creative. Incorporate the speed ladder into stations at the beginning of practice or use as part of the warm-up in conjunction with other skills. The Reaction Ball is a multi-sided ball that bounces in different, unpredictable directions. Use the Reaction Ball instead of a tennis ball to add agility to the *Tennis Ball Drop Drill*. Other drills for training agility and lateral quickness are the *T-Drill*, *Spoke Drill* and different games of tag.

An obstacle course is a fun way to train various skills; use a speed ladder, hurdles, cones, etc. Start by doing the *Icky Shuffle* through the speed ladder; sprint to half court and do a zigzag shuffle around cones to the baseline and do five push-ups; then, skip to half court and do 20 side-to-side hops; finally, pick up a basketball and drive to the basket for a lay-up. This course incorporates an amazing array of skills and kids love the competition and challenge.

Without athletic skill development players fail to reach their basketball peak. "It is amazing how kids today are so poor at making guys miss… They are like robots and lack elusiveness," writes Boston Celtics' Strength and Conditioning Coach Walter Norton, Jr. General agility and quickness training produce a more effective player.

Stage 3: The Training Stage
Training Goals: Strength, anaerobic conditioning, power
Emphasis: Interval training, resistance training, power training, separation of the recreational players and serious competitors.

The Training Stage links the learning stages with the forthcoming competition stage; incorporates the previously learned and developed skills; and increases the training load and intensity.

As players mature, they can handle more intense and different training. However, as the training intensity and volume increase, coaches must plan the training to avoid burnout and injury and to maximize the training benefits. Rather than planning one practice at a time, coaches must plan training sessions over a period of time, whether a week, month or season. As players specialize and play only one sport competitively, thus dedicating more time to one sport, coaches must incorporate some aspects of periodization to balance the training.

Periodization

Periodization, in short, breaks the year into different components or phases to maximize the benefits of training. Typically, the year divides into three seasons or phases: preparatory (pre-season), competitive (in-season) and transition (off-season). In previous generations, periodization was simple: boys played football in the fall, basketball in the winter and baseball in the spring, while girls played volleyball, basketball and softball/soccer. Nobody needed periodization: players played football during the pre-season and baseball in the off-season. No need to worry about overtraining or overuse injuries. At a micro level, each sport included its own brief pre-season period before the competitive season; a basketball team with its first game in the end of November would start around the first of the month with 2-3 weeks of pre-season training before the first game.

However, today's basketball players specialize early, ignoring the benefits of playing multiple sports and the research against early specialization. Due to the increased specialization, coaches must use periodization to train their athletes properly and maximize the benefits of their training.

> "The rate of improving and perfecting your athlete's technical and tactical skills, are directly dependent on how you periodize your training program. During the preparatory phase, where the stress of competitions is almost nonexistent, skill acquisition is maximal. Now is the time to teach your athletes new skills and to perfect the ones acquired in the past year. Your athlete's skill improvement during the preparatory phase will be most beneficial during the league games and/or official competitions. The longer the preparatory phase, the better your athlete's chances are to improve skill effectiveness," (Bompa).

Currently, many players and programs skip the Active Rest/Transition Period. AAU try-outs occur before high school play-offs finish and AAU Tournaments start before the State Championships conclude. Players move from one Competition Period to the next without any rest, transition or off-season because players, parents and coaches believe the constant competition is necessary to excel.

Basic Periodization

Pre-Season Period: first practice to first game

Competition Period: first game to last game

Rest/Transition Period: 2-4 weeks starting after the last game

Off-Season Period: spring and summer

Rest is not to be confused with laziness; it is an important part of the training schedule. "It's becoming more and more apparent in our care of adolescents and even preadolescents, there is a lot of pressure on young children to do more and more in sports," said Thomas Clanton, team doctor for the NBA's Houston Rockets. "They never get a chance to rest," said Clanton, who also is a professor of orthopedic surgery at the University of Texas-Houston Medical School (Dixon).

Players do their mind and body a disservice if they ignore this period and rush from one competitive season to the next. In the NBA, owners and players complain about the high incidence of injuries suffered by players who play international basketball during the summer. Players like Yao Ming, Brad Miller, Chris Paul and others suffered injuries during the 2006-07 NBA season after a grueling schedule with the 2006 World Championships sandwiched between the end of the 2006 NBA play-offs and training camp. If professionally trained athletes suffer from injuries due to lack of rest and regeneration, what happens to high school players who do not devote 2-4 hours a day to training, massages, regeneration, ice baths and more, not to mention the poor diets of most teenagers? The lack of rest manifests itself in overuse injuries like shin splints, or ACL tears and sprained ankles. Without proper recuperation, muscles and ligaments are tired and immune systems are compromised. A month of active rest after the season will not set a player back or cost a player a scholarship, but an injury might.

> "Influenced by professional sports, some coaches attempt to imitate their heavy competitive schedule, and as such accept the notion; the more games/competitions, the better my athletes will improve. In reality the opposite is true: the more you compete the less time you have for training. As demonstrated by sports science, well designed training programs and not high number of competitions led to higher adaptation, and as a result, to higher performance improvement," (Bompa).

The off-season runs through the spring and summer. The off-season is a preparatory period before the more intense pre-season and in-season training. During this time, players should devote time to skill development. During the competitive season, most players' skill level decreases because they spend more time working on strategic elements and conditioning. Teams lift weights less frequently, do less speed enhancement, less agility training, less shooting and ball handling. Just as these stages should not be rushed, athletes should not ignore these periods which are vital to their athletic and basketball development.

> "To play/compete more means in reality to have a longer competitive phase, a situation which is possible only by reducing the duration of the preparatory phase, with all its negative repercussions: less time to acquire / perfect skills, reduced time to improve general conditioning (such as during the general preparatory phase), and shorter time to work on improving the sport-specific speed, power and endurance. Reduced time to train but increased time to compete means in reality to train and over train just the same exercises, same specific parts of the body, joints and muscles, and as a result, increase the incidents of injuries. On a long-term basis, shorter duration preparatory phases will reduce training time, lower the rate of adaptation, and ultimately result in a stagnation of performance improvement," (Bompa).

Periodization breaks the training year or season into different periods and cycles, which prevents emotional and physical burnout and overtraining. Within each period, coaches use cycles to plan training and prevent players from hitting a plateau. The three cycles are:

- Macrocycle: a training season
- Mesocycle: 21-28 days
- Microcycle: a training week, or 7-10 days

Coaches use these cycles to plan the team's training. Over the season, which could be November to March or September to July, depending on the level and program, what goals do you want to accomplish? In what order do you want to accomplish these goals? Once you determine the season's objectives, move to smaller periods like the mesocycles. If the overall goal is to build lower body strength to prevent ACL injuries for a girls' basketball team, what happens first? The first mesocycle may focus on balance exercises and developing single-leg stability in static positions. Next, the theme may be to develop static strength through squats, lunges and single-leg squats as well as basic landing technique. The next theme may address dynamic balance and more intense jump training to prepare for the forces players face during the season.

Within the mesocycles are microcycles which change the training stimulus on a weekly basis. In the second mesocycle focused on developing static strength, the first week may center on the lunge, with the second week emphasizing more squats and the third week incorporating more single-leg squats. Rather than doing the same workout for three straight weeks, using different variations of exercises constantly challenges the neuromuscular system and prevents a plateau.

Coaches use the cycles to plan each period, alternate emphasis and gradually build the player toward a play-off peak. During the pre-season, for instance, work backward from the first game to the start of practice. For a team which plays its first game during the first week of December and starts pre-season conditioning at the beginning of the school year, the pre-season is roughly three months or 12 weeks.

Plan training sessions in advance and balance the intensity and volume. Intensity is the effort level; a game is maximum intensity while a jog might be 50% intensity. If an athlete lifts 70lbs, and his maximum lift is 100lbs, he works at 70% intensity. Volume is the amount of work; for instance, 3 sets of 10 repetitions. As intensity increases, volume decreases. The other variable is rest, which is determined by intensity, volume and goals. Power and speed work require a longer recovery (more rest), while speed endurance or circuit training requires a small recovery period between sets.

> **Periodized Pre-Season Training Schedule**
>
> **Cycle 1**: September
>
> *Conditioning*: Speed Endurance (Interval sprints between 100m-400m)
>
> *Resistance Training*: Stabilization (Balance exercises, core strength, base of strength, slow lifts)
>
> **Cycle 2**: October
>
> *Conditioning*: Speed (sprints between 20m-60m)
>
> *Resistance Training*: Strength (hypertrophy, sets of 8-10 reps)
>
> **Cycle 3**: November
>
> *Conditioning*: Quickness (Shuttle runs, speed ladders, 17s, Champions, tag)
>
> *Resistance Training*: Power (medicine balls, Olympic lifts, explosive, sets of 3-5 reps)

When conditioning, do not conduct back to back high intensity workouts without incorporating rest. After a high intensity workout, plan a low intensity workout. A high intensity workout might include sprint intervals, plyometrics, running stadiums, or heavy and explosive lifting. Use the light intensity workout to train form. While running and jumping seem like simple, natural skills, some form drills can increase speed and prevent injury. At the college and professional levels, I lost players to injury caused by incorrect running mechanics which resulted in overuse injuries like

Achilles tendon injuries, tight hamstrings and knee problems. One season, we designed a remedial running program for a player because her poor running form contributed to speed deficiency and persistent knee problems. While these drills appear simplistic, nothing is more important to basketball success than quick and efficient movement.

Most coaches equate conditioning with aerobic work. However, this training has minimal impact on basketball and "research has shown that sustained aerobic work significantly compromises explosive power" (Gambetta). "On average, play stops every 15-30 seconds during a competitive basketball game and ensues in that time frame. Why then are coaches continuing to engage their athletes in the traditional approach of endurance-type training? (Crowley)."

Use interval training for basketball conditioning. A 30-second work time followed by a 15-second rest mimics the game environment. Use these intervals for various exercises, not just running. Do a set of speed squats or push-ups for 30-seconds followed by a 15-second rest. Work up to 8-10 sets. This type of training is more basketball-specific than running long distances and utilizes different exercises, not just running.

"Interval training stresses energy systems in the body that aren't accustomed to being used," says Jeramie Hinojosa, M.S... "Blood supply to cells increases, the cells use oxygen more efficiently and the enzymes that help create energy also increase. This improves fitness" (Smith).

For conditioning with sprints, *Shuttle Runs* add a change of direction dimension to the training. Modify the distance and rest time to train different components; to train speed endurance, run a longer distance (300m) at a lower intensity (80%) with a shorter rest interval (1:1); to train acceleration, run a shorter distance (20m) at a higher intensity (95%) with a complete recovery.

Resistance Training

Many myths persist in youth weight lifting; people believe lifting weights stunts growth or weight lifting has a high injury rate. In fact, weight lifting is a statistically safe sport, especially with supervision and proper guidance. The possibility for injury exists if players lift too much weight or lift improperly.

To prepare a resistance training program for young athletes, start with general and core strength and progress to lifts for power. "There must be sufficient power-related training during an athlete's early years (13-17) to maintain the genetically determined level of white (fast-twitch or power-related) muscle fiber. Power-related work also promotes the shift of transitional fiber to power-related muscle fiber," (Boyle). Basketball is an explosive sport; therefore, promoting the development of fast-twitch muscle fiber is more important than training slow-twitch muscle fiber.

General and core strength training includes body weight exercises and stability exercises such as push-ups, pull-ups, bar-dips, squats, lunges, step-ups, bridges and planks. Core (the muscles which attach to the spine and pelvis) strength stabilizes the body; furthermore, the core transfers power from the lower to the upper body and originates movement. Core strength is vital to overall strength. Core training is not just sit-ups or six packs: a front squat activates the core more than a sit-up due to the gravitational force acting upon the weight to pull the weight forward and down, while the core stabilizes the body and maintains an erect posture through the lift. Other examples of functional core training include medicine ball throws, chops (med ball, plate or cables) and stability ball exercises.

Power training includes plyometrics, medicine balls and Olympic lifts like the hang clean, power clean, push press and snatch. To test if an athlete is ready for plyometrics, test his stabilization and eccentric strength. To test stabilization, do a single-leg balance test as well as a single-leg squat test. In each case, hold for 10 seconds and observe the ability to hold the position with minimum lateral movement. To test eccentric strength, judge the length of the amortization phase in repetitive jumps and check proper positioning when landing from a jump or a hop (Gambetta). The amortization phase is the time on the ground in between jumps – this should be as small as possible.

While players must learn the proper form of Olympic lifts to perform correctly, these lifts are among the best exercises for basketball players. Former UCLA Strength Coach Bob Alejo writes, "We know that the Olympic style movements are physiologically the most powerful movements man can perform…The erectors (low back), glutes, hamstrings and quadriceps work together (assuming the lift is performed from the ground) in much the same way as many triple-extension movements such as vertical jumping…There appears to be a correlation in regards to the power clean or pulls and vertical jumping, horizontal jumping and sprint speed. As performance (amount of weight lifted) improves in the clean, improvements in jumping and sprinting speed also occur." For coaches unfamiliar with the Olympic lifts, the United States Weightlifting Association offers a Sports Performance Coach certification course which teaches the physiology and the proper execution of the lifts in a two-day, hands-on format.

Beyond general strength, core strength and power training, athletes need resistance training to develop maximal strength and strength endurance. Regardless of the activity, whether jumping, running or a sport-specific skill, applying more force leads to more success. Olympic sprinters spend hours lifting weights because improving force production builds speed. In addition to the lifts mentioned above, basketball players should incorporate front and back squats, multi-directional lunges, step-ups, deadlifts, shoulder presses, bent over rows, bench presses, lat pull downs, rows and other multi-joint, big muscle movements.

A very generic resistance training workout includes:
- Full body power lift (clean, snatch, high pull)
- Upper Body Push (push-up, bench press, shoulder press)
- Upper Body Pull (pull-up, lat pull-down, row)
- Knee Dominant (front squat, back squat, single-leg squat, lunge)
- Hip Dominant (deadlift, straight-leg deadlift, good morning, reverse hyper, step-up)

This basic resistance plan emphasizes the core and body weight exercises, utilizes power-related lifts, teaches proper weight lifting technique and builds functional strength for young athletes as they prepare to enter the next stage with more intense workouts.

Stage 4: The Competition Stage
Training Goals: Power, acceleration, vertical jump, dynamic balance, functional strength.
Emphasis: Prepare for competitions, train for peak performance, and elevate one's training to the next level.

In the first three stages, athletes train to improve athleticism, as increased overall athleticism improves basketball performance. In Stage Four, training is basketball and position-specific; this stage transforms the foundation into basketball success through increased intensity and specificity.

Test athletes to measure progress and determine weaknesses. Testing includes physical attributes such as height, weight and body fat percentage, as well as physiological attributes like flexibility, vertical jump, broad jump, push-up test and shuttle run. Use a Functional Movement screen to identify weaknesses and tightness to address. Measure results against recognized norms to determine strengths, weaknesses and training needs.

> **Basic Training Exercises**
> **Balance**: Single leg balance, wobble board
> **Upper Body Strength**: Military Press, Push-ups, Pull-ups, Rows
> **Lower Body Strength**: Front and Back Squat, Lunge, Good Morning
> **Power**: Cleans, Jump Squats
> **Core Strength**: Plank, Side Plank, Diagonal Chop

Kinetic Chain

The body is a kinetic chain, and an athlete is only as strong as his weakest link. The muscles, joints and neural systems work together as one functional unit. For this reason, train movements, not muscles. Muscles do not move in isolation. When a person jumps, the quadriceps does not extend like in a leg extension exercise; instead, the body applies force into the ground to overcome gravity and the triple extension of the ankle, knee and hip, caused through the neuromuscular system firing the correct muscles in the correct order, creates the jump. While the quadriceps relative strength affects a player's vertical jump, jumping requires more than quadriceps strength or knee extension. While jumping is the most specific way to improve one's vertical jump, to increase force production, a back squat is more effective than a leg extension because the neuromuscular system fires in a similar pattern, so the squat trains the movement, not just the muscle.

An injury or tightness affects the performance of the entire chain. As an example, a previous ankle sprain may decrease or delay activation of the gluteus maximus (Janda, et al). Therefore, athletes must (1) fully rehabilitate injuries and (2) relieve muscle tightness. The repetitive movements associated with basketball cause tightness. Muscle tightness may affect the range of motion at a joint or lead to reciprocal weakness; for example, tight hip flexors lead to weakness in the glutes. "If one segment is not functioning efficiently, then the other components must compensate, leading to tissue overload, fatigue, faulty movement patterns, and finally initiates the Cumulative Injury Cycle," (Clark). Stretching, especially after practice, and using a Dynamic Warm-up help to alleviate muscle tightness. To correct muscle imbalances and prevent neuromuscular inefficiencies caused by the tightness or trigger points, use a foam roll on your calves, hamstrings, hip flexors and the IT band as self-myofascial release (See *Appendix*). Most high school players ignore the advice and believe the foam roll is not worth the time; they believe something must be hard for it to work. However, NBA players use foam rolls religiously.

Vertical Jump

The 40-inch vertical jump is basketball's magical number. Everyone wants to dunk. While dunking may or may not add value to a player's game, the vertical jump expresses lower body power, and a powerful athlete has a better chance to be a good player than a non-powerful athlete. Lifting weights aids power development: power equals force x distance divided by time. For a vertical jump, the higher one jumps and the quicker one elevates, the more powerful the jump. Lifting weights addresses force production; a jump training program improves the biomechanics of jumping (and landing) and movement efficiency.

A jump training program consists of three types of exercises: a jump is when one lands on two feet; a hop is when one takes off and lands on the same foot; and a bound is when one takes off one foot and lands on the other foot. To see results, exercises must be done at a high intensity (95-100%), which requires appropriate rest between sets and exercises and a proper, gradual progression. A novice athlete should not start with depth jumps from a 24-inch box.

Some basic jumping exercises:
- Ankle jumps (like jumping rope)
- Single-leg side-to-side hops
- Vertical jumps
- Squat Jumps (squat slowly and jump; no arms)
- Tuck Jumps (jump and tuck knees to chest)
- Front Obstacle Jumps
- Lateral Obstacle Jumps
- Long Jumps
- Bounds for distance
- Hops for distance

When beginning a program, do one jump at a time. Jump and stick the landing; re-set and jump again. As players illustrate proper jumping and landing form and develop a base of eccentric strength, do repetitive jumps where one jump leads to the next. When doing repetitive jumps, focus on shortening the amortization phase, the time on the ground from landing to take-off. The most explosive leapers (Shawn Marion) have a very short amortization phase, with a pogo stick-like quality.

Basketball Physiology

Basketball is an anaerobic sport requiring a high percentage of fast-twitch, Type II muscle fiber: basketball requires high force production (Type IIb) and high power output (Type IIa and Type IIb). Basketball is a running sport, but the running occurs in short, powerful bursts with quick starts and stops and repetitive jumps and landings. "Aerobic endurance demands…are minimal…a typical NBA game…in the first half the ball was in play for an average of 49.1 seconds before action paused for an average of 35.3 seconds. In the second half, the average time of non-stop action was 37.5 seconds, with the average pause being 58.9 seconds," (Gambetta).

The phosphagen system and anaerobic glycolysis supply the energy to meet basketball's metabolic demands. The phosphagen system provides energy for fast and powerful movements, as in a full court sprint, a quick change of direction or a maximum jump. As intense exercise extends beyond 8-10 seconds, anaerobic glycolysis provides the body's energy. In an up-tempo game, with few breaks and sustained maximum output, glycolysis supplies the energy. One characteristic of glycolysis is lactate acid build up; therefore, a basketball player must train his/her system to tolerate higher levels of lactate acid in the blood.

No single energy system provides all the energy for a specific exercise. "Integrating the two metabolic demands is also a vital training need because many athletes must be able to perform under fatiguing conditions in competition. Nevertheless, each metabolic component needs to be trained individually for optimal results, and then both need to be combined in sport-related training," (Baechele).

Long distance training is contraindicated because training slow reduces explosiveness: to excel in basketball, train fast to meet metabolic demands and develop Type IIa and IIb muscle fibers. "[Speed expert Charlie] Francis believed that not only can you make an athlete into a sprinter, but, more important, that you might negatively affect an athlete's ability to develop speed by focusing on endurance," (Boyle).

Basketball is a multi-directional game; linear training (running straight ahead) alone is insufficient; train for the metabolic demands of quick stops and starts and prepare the muscles, ligaments and tendons for quick changes of directions. When designing a basketball conditioning program, include short interval runs and shuttle runs which emulate basketball's demands. A well-rounded conditioning program incorporates all aspects, but emphasizes multi-direction skills, acceleration and short sprints (10-30m).

Athletic Drills

I. Foundation Stage

Wall Drill: Place hands against the wall to create a power position with body in a straight line, but angled toward the wall. Run in place, driving the knees up. Start with two strides and build.

Tennis Ball Drop: Stand five feet away from an athlete and drop a tennis ball from shoulder height; as soon as the ball is dropped, the athlete accelerates and tries to catch the ball on its first bounce. Increase the distance as appropriate. Train multiple directions; have player start facing forward in an athletic stance and a staggered stance; then have player start facing laterally; then, throw the ball from behind the athlete; finally, throw the ball over the athlete's shoulder so he must turn and chase.

Get Up Tag: One player stands and the other player starts lying face down; the standing player starts in front. When the coach says go, the standing player sprints while the second player stands up, runs and tags the first player within a certain distance (20 yards).

Box Tag: Create a small box with cones or use the lines on the court to create a confined area (like the key). An offensive player and a defensive player play tag within the area. The defensive player must tag the offensive in as little time as possible.

Knee Tag: All players are it and can tag anyone; if tagged on the knee, must do three push-ups outside the boundaries and re-enter the game.

Speed Tag: One team versus another. The tagging team sends one person out to tag one of the other players and then immediately back to the start so the next person goes and tags another player. Continue until all players are tagged and back to the start. Time it; then switch sides and see if the other team can beat the first team's time.

Boxing Tag: Players pair up, and partners face each other. When the coach says, "Go," the players attempt to tag each other on the shoulder or the stomach while avoiding the tag attempts of their partners.

II. Fundamentals Stage

Bridge (top right): Lay supine (on your back) with feet flat on the ground. Push through your heels to lift your hips off the ground, creating a bridge with the shoulders and feet on the ground. Slowly descend and then repeat.

Plank (middle right): Start in a prone position (face down) with weight supported by elbows and feet. Hold the position. Squeeze your bellybutton to your spine and keep your butt down.

Side-Bridge (bottom right): Lie perpendicular to the ground resting your weight on your elbow and foot. Hold your other arm high. Hold the position for the desired duration and switch sides.

Pull-up: On a pull-up bar, use an overhand grip (palms face away) with hand wider than shoulder width and pull up so your chin is over the bar. Descend slowly and repeat.

Chin-up: On a pull-up bar, use an underhand grip (palms face toward you) with hands shoulder-width apart and pull your chin over the bar. Descend slowly and repeat.

Push-up: Start in a prone position with weight supported by your hands and feet. Start with hands under your shoulders. Bend your elbows to lower your body until your chest is almost to the floor. Keep your body in a straight line and push your body back to the starting position.

Horizontal Pull-up: Use a fixed bar, like a Smith Machine. Lie under the bar and put your feet on the end of a bench or on a stability ball (below left). Use an overhand grip and grab the bar with hands wider than shoulder width. Keep your body in a straight line and lift your body until your chest hits the bar (below right). Descend slowly and repeat.

Body Weight Squat: Sit hips back and down; knees stay over the toes and not in front; put arms out in front to improve balance; weight on the balls of your feet, but feet stay flat on the ground. Squat until the top of your thighs are parallel to the ground.

Overhead Squat: Start in an athletic stance with hands holding a PVC pipe or a basketball overhead. Do a full squat, keeping hands overhead and sitting hips back and down. Keep torso tall rather than bending forward at the hips (See *Appendix*).

Medicine Ball (MB) Twist (right): Sit down with feet in the air. Hold a medicine ball in front and rotate your torso from side to side. Touch the medicine ball to the ground as far in each direction as possible. Keep your nose on the ball; rotate your torso rather than just reaching with your arms.

MB Underhand Lateral Throw: Stand perpendicular to a wall in an athletic stance holding a medicine ball at your waist. Rotate you torso away from the wall as far as possible. Explode forward and throw the ball at the wall. Catch the ball and repeat.

MB Side Chop: Stand with feet shoulder width apart and hold a medicine ball over your right shoulder with elbows extended (left). Bend and bring the medicine ball down to the outside of your left leg (right). Explode through your heels back to the starting position. Work both sides.

MB Side Chop Throw: Stand perpendicular to a wall with your left shoulder toward the wall and feet shoulder width apart. Hold a medicine ball over your right shoulder with elbows extended. Bend, twist to your left and throw the medicine ball at the ground, so it bounces and hits the wall. Initiate the movement with your torso and keep your elbows extended. Work both sides.

Front Lunge (left): Step forward and bend at the knees until each knee is at a 90-degree angle; keep torso tall – do not bend over at the waist; front knee stays over the front foot, not in front of the foot. At the bottom position, drive into the ground on your front foot and step forward into your next lunge.

Back Lunge: Step backward and bend at the knees until each knee is at a 90-degree angle; keep torso tall – do not bend over at the waist; front knee stays over the front foot, not in front of the foot. At the bottom position, drive into the ground on your back foot and step backward into your next lunge.

Front-to-Back Lunge: Step forward and bend at the knees until each knee is at a 90-degree angle; keep torso tall – do not bend over at the waist; front knee stays over the front foot, not in front of the foot. At the bottom position, drive into the ground on your front foot and step backward with the same leg. One leg remains planted and the other leg steps forward and backward. Do 10 repetitions and switch legs.

Side Lunge (below right): Step laterally with one leg; keep feet pointed straight ahead and feet flat on the ground. Bend so your hip, knee and foot are in one straight line and your trail leg is straight. Drive into the ground with your lead leg and return to the start.

MB Front Throw: Stand in an athletic stance with a medicine ball at your chest, elbows tight to your body. Throw the ball to your partner.

MB Wood Chop: Stand with feet shoulder width apart and hold a medicine ball overhead with elbows extended. Bend and bring the med ball down between your legs as far as possible. Explode through your heels back to the starting position.

MB Squat and Throw: Hold a medicine ball in front of your chest with elbows tight to your body. Squat. As you push through your heels to stand, push up through the ball and throw the ball to your partner. As your partner catches and squats, squat and return to an athletic position ready to catch your partner's pass.

Mirror Defense: Two players face each other, one as the offensive player and the other as the defensive player. The offensive player leads. When the coach says "Go," the players slide laterally. Offensive player tries to create separation from the defensive player, while the defender tries to keep his nose on the offensive player's chest. Go for fifteen to thirty seconds.

T-Drill: Use four cones to make a "T." Put the vertical cones five yards apart and the horizontal cones five yards apart with the vertical cone in the middle of the horizontal cones. Sprint forward to the middle cone; shuffle to the cone to the right, then to the left cone. Shuffle to the middle cone and backpedal to the beginning.

Spoke Drill: Place one cone in the middle and eight cones around the perimeter. Start at the middle cone and sprint forward to touch the first cone; back pedal to the middle cone. Next, move at a 45-degree angle to the right to touch the second cone and return to the middle cone. Next, shuffle laterally to the right to touch the third cone and back to the middle cone. Next, move backward at a 45-degree angle to the right to touch the fourth cone and return to the middle cone. Next, back pedal straight back to the fifth cone and sprint forward to the middle cone. Continue in the circle to the left side, touching the cone at a 45-degree angle to the left, laterally to the left and at a 45-degree angle forward to the left. Each time, return to the middle cone before moving to the next cone. This drill incorporates the crossover step, sprints, backpedals and shuffles.

Lane-line Slides: Start with both feet outside the lane-line on one side of the key. Shuffle across the lane, so one foot gets outside the key and then back. Go for 30 seconds and count the number of repetitions.

Ladder Drills (use your arms):
- *2-feet in*: Running through the ladder, each foot touches in each square of the ladder
- *1-foot-in*: Running through the ladder, only one foot touches in each square of the ladder
- *Icky Shuffle*: Start to the left side of the ladder facing forward. Step into the first square with the right foot and then the left foot. Step out to the right side of the square with the right foot. Next, step into the second square with the left foot, then the right foot and step out with the left foot. Continue with the "in-in-out" pattern.
- *Lateral 2-feet in*: Moving laterally, step forward into the ladder with one foot and then the other, then step out with the first foot and then the second foot, and then step forward into the next square of the ladder

- *2-in, 2-out*: Like hopscotch: start with both feet outside the ladder and jump into the ladder with both feet, then jump out so both feet are outside the ladder, on either side of the ladder. Move straight ahead.
- *180-jumps*: Start with one foot in the ladder and one foot out of the ladder and body perpendicular to the ladder. Jump and turn 180-degrees in the air, so the foot that was in the ladder lands in the same square and the foot that was out of the ladder lands in the second square
- *Lateral Scissors*: Start in a staggered stance, perpendicular to the ladder, with the lead foot in the first square. Jump and land in a staggered stance with the lead foot out of the square and the trail foot in the first square. Jump and land with the lead foot in the next square and the trail foot out of the square.
- *Slalom*: Start facing the ladder with the right foot in the ladder and the left foot out of the ladder. Jump and land with the left foot in the ladder and the right foot out. Alternate feet all the way.

Ice Skater Drill: Stand on the right foot with left foot slightly behind the right foot, like an ice skater's stance. Push-off laterally, landing on the left foot on-balance. Push-off on the left foot and land on the right.

45-degree Bound: Like the ice skater drill, however, the athlete moves at a 45-degree angle forward. Athlete starts on his right foot and pushes laterally and forward, landing on his left foot.

III. Training Stage

Partner Resistance Running: Partner places hands against the runners shoulders and the runner leans into the the partner to create the power position. As the partner provides resisitance, the runner drives his legs and runs down the court.

Shuttle Run: Place three cones five meters apart. Start at the middle cone; run to one cone, then to the far cone and to the middle cone to complete the 5-10-5 shuttle run.

17s: Start on one sideline and run to the other sideline: that is one repetition. Finish 17 repetitions under one minute.

Champions: Commonly called "Suicides" or "Liners." Start on the baseline, run to the free throw and back; run to half court and back; run to the opposite free throw line and back; and run to the other baseline and back. Use to train hockey stops: emphasize running in straight lines and making quick changes of direction.

Front Squat: Hold the bar on your front shoulders. Keep elbows up and parallel to the ground and the bar in your fingers. Start with your feet slightly wider than shoulder width and sit your hips back and down. Descend; then drive through your heels to explode to a standing position. Keep torso tall.

Back Squat: Rest the bar on your upper shoulders behind your head and support the bar with your hands. Start with your feet slightly wider than shoulder width and sit your hips back and down. Drive through your heels to explode back to a standing position. Keep chest and eyes up through the lift.

Step-ups: Stand with feet together facing a bench. Step onto the bench with one foot and drive through that foot to step onto the bench. Drive the trail leg so it finishes with the thigh parallel to the ground. Step down and repeat. Do 10-15 repetitions and switch legs.

Single-leg Squat: Stand on a bench on one leg (left) and sit hips back and down to squat (middle, right). Standing on your right leg, flex your left foot and squat until your left heel hits the ground.

Bar Dips: With each hand on a bar and your body in between the bars, lower your body until your elbows form a 90-degree angle. Push through the bars to return to the starting position.

Bench Press: Lie on a bench and press the bar (or dumbbells) overhead.

Shoulder Press: Start with a bar or dumbbells at shoulder level and press overhead.

Lat Pull-Down: Use a Lat-Pull Down Machine and pull the bar to your chest.

Row: Several different ways to do a row with a machine, barbell or dumbbells. With chest and back sturdy, pull into your body at chest level. A bentover row: Grab a bar with an overhand grip and shoulders over the bar. Bend at the knees and hips and keep your back close to parallel to the floor. With shoulders pulled back, pull the bar to just below your chest and return the bar to the ground.

Good Morning: Stand with a light bar on your shoulders. Bend forward at your hips, keeping your back flat, until your chest is parallel to the floor. Extend at the hips and return to a standing position.

Deadlift: Grab a bar with an over-under grip (one palm faces away and one faces toward you) with hands wider than shoulder width. Start with shoulders over the bar and hips back (left and middle). Drive through your heels and extend until your hips are extended fully (right). Keep the bar tight to your body. Knees and hips should work together, not in segments.

Straight-Leg Deadlift: Stand with a bar in your hands with an overhand grip (palms away) and a very slight bend in your knees (above left). Lower the bar by sitting your hips back. Keep shoulders pulled back: imagine your shoulder blades pinching a pen. Lower the bar to the knees (above right) and then extend to a standing position. For variation, use a dumbbell and do a Single-Leg Deadlift; put the dumbbell in your opposite hand (bottom left), pull your shoulders back and lower slowly until the dumbbell reaches your ankles (bottom middle and right). Drive through your heels and extend to the starting position.

Hang Clean: Grab an Olympic bar with an overhand grip (palms away) with hands shoulder width apart. Start with the bar at the knees and shoulders over the bar, with hips back. In one motion, drive through your heels, explode through your hips and shrug your shoulders. As the bars momentum slows, catch the bar with hands under the bar at the shoulders and hips back in an athletic stance. **For proper instruction, find a coach certified through USA Weightlifting as a Sports Performance Coach or a Level I Club Coach.**

Power Clean: same as a hang clean, but start with the bar on the floor. **For proper instruction, find a coach certified through USA Weightlifting as a Sports Performance Coach or a Level I Club Coach.**

Push Press: Start with an Olympic bar at shoulder level with hands under the bar and hands shoulder width apart. Bend quickly at the hips and knees and drive upward pushing the bar overhead and locking the elbows. **For proper instruction, find a coach certified through USA Weightlifting as a Sports Performance Coach or a Level I Club Coach.**

Snatch: Grab an Olympic bar with an overhand grip (palms away) with hands shoulder width apart. Start with shoulders over the bar with hips back. In one motion, drive through your heels, explode through your hips and shrug your shoulders. Finish with bar overhead and elbows locked out. **For proper instruction, find a coach certified through USA Weightlifting as a Sports Performance Coach or a Level I Club Coach.**

Chapter 3:
Tactical Skills

In the summer of 2005, I directed a camp in Skopje, Macedonia with Greek and Macedonian players. Every night, the groups played each other. The Greeks were older, bigger and stronger. However, the Macedonians played beautiful basketball. They spread the court and used very basic tactical skills to create open shots. They found backdoor cuts to the basket, used dribble hand-offs and pick-and-rolls and dribble penetrated when necessary. The players never stopped moving, but they always caught the ball ready to shoot or drive. The ball never settled in one position; no player ever took needless dribbles. They shared the ball and everyone made their open shots or passed to a player with a better shot.

Since Team USA's losses in the 2002 World Championships, many people have discussed the lack of skill development in the United States. Most people focus on technical skills, like shooting. However, in the 2004 Olympics and 2006 World Championships, I saw tactical flaws. Team USA's best players did not understand how to play basketball. These players possess amazing ball skills and athleticism, but are pedestrian when playing without the ball. International defenses exploited Team USA's lack of movement, team cohesion and offensive sophistication, as NBA stars repeatedly attempted to attack 1v5.

The kids in Skopje possessed very good technical skills. To play such a style, teams must have players who can pass, shoot and dribble. However, their understanding of player and ball movement made them impossible to defend, even against older, bigger, stronger players. They combined basic skills into a complex-looking offense to create open three-point shots or lay-ups.

Basketball combines three physical components: Athletic, Tactical and Technical skills. While one can practice each separately, on-court success requires the combination of the skills. There is no designated hitter that allows a great shooter to play offense, spread the court and knock down a three; there is no libero position (a designated back row passer in volleyball) that allows Ben Wallace to play defense and use an immediate and automatic substitute on offense. Basketball requires players to play both ends of the court and use the different skills in concert with each other to perform.

When I teach tactical skills, I want to develop players and teams like the kids in Skopje. The tactical skill progressions build slowly so players learn the skill concepts and incorporate each into competitive play before moving to new skills. Through the stage-by-stage progression, players learn to play, not run plays.

Many people confuse tactical skill development with the ability to memorize and run set plays. Set plays or continuity offenses are not inherently bad; however, their success does not equal basketball understanding. Vern Gambetta uses the term *Adapted vs. Adaptable* to describe athlete development, but the concept fits here. Players adapt to set plays and memorize the cuts or screens. However, this memorization does not ensure that they understand how to cut or how to screen. An adaptable player understands the basic concepts which allow him to play in any offense or any system. His skills adapt to the new system of a new coach, while an adapted player struggles with a new coach as he has to re-learn the system.

Developing tactical skills is challenging because young players lack technical ability, the strength to spread the court, spatial awareness and the cognitive skills required to transfer drills to live play. Therefore, to organize young players, most coaches teach a set offense and expect players to play within the offense; they teach a press break and expect players to move to exact spots. Because teaching general skills is difficult, and players often look unorganized, coaches use structure to help players perform better. However, players learn to play within the structure, but cannot function without it. They do not make decisions on the court, but follow directions.

We judge coaches by their team's game performance, which is unfair, as most teaching and coaching occurs behind closed doors at practice. While practice ideally carries over to the game, in youth basketball, games are unpredictable with wide gaps in talent and coaches are often judged unfairly. These unfair judgments lead coaches to organize their teams during games. If a team appears organized, we believe they are well-coached; a less organized team appears poorly coached.

The easiest way to organize a team is with a 2-3 zone defense and a structured, patterned offense. If players know their position or their movements, they can follow directions. Parents appreciate the discipline and the order. However, when we introduce too much structure, especially at an early age, we restrict freedom. Rather than teach players how to get open, we tell them where to go. When a teacher teaches a math student, he does not tell the student an answer to one question; he teaches the student how to find the answer so the student can solve similar problems. If the teacher tells the student the answer without teaching the student problem solving skills, the student relies on the teacher for subsequent answers.

Basketball players rely on coaches for the same reason. If a coach runs the Flex and tells his players to set the Flex screen, receive the down screen and run to the elbow, the players know one answer to one question. What happens when the opponent switches the down screen? What if the player, while playing on a different team, receives a down screen and automatically runs to the elbow, even though this coach runs a 4-out motion designed for the player to read the defense and curl to the middle or flare to the wing? Players rely on the coach to tell them where to go and cannot adjust to different defenses or different offensive sets.

Play is the best method for learning and developing tactical skills. At the Spanish Player Development Centers, "players are taught simple movements and situations and then move up to situations that are more complex." At the Center, "we think this part of the program [small-sided games working on collective fundamentals] is an essential step that allows the player to learn how to play together with his teammates and develop his strategic intelligence," (Sergio). This is the whole-part-whole teaching method; start with the game (the whole); teach simple movements and play small-sided games (part) and return to the full game with improved skills and understanding (whole).

In <u>The Art of Learning</u>, Josh Waitzkin writes about his chess instructor's method of starting his instruction from the Endgame, when he had only one or two pieces left, rather than from the start with a full complement of pieces. Similarly, soccer coaches use small-sided games and offensive advantage games, like 5v2, to work on possession passing and moving. Small-sided games also benefit basketball players, as they learn the basics in a game form with more space and repetitions before moving to the full game.

At the youngest ages, devote almost the entire training session toward play, not separate units for athletic, technical and tactical drills. Players learn the game through playing.

According to the *Journal of Experimental Psychology: Applied*, athletes who learn the intricacies of a game on their own perform better than those who are heavily coached. The group which was explicitly coached learned quickly but overthought each move, says study author Mark Williams, Ph.D. of the Research Institute for Sport and Exercise Sciences. In coaching a child, 'encourage him to solve problems, as opposed to providing all the answers,' says Williams, (*Men's Health*, November 2005).

Nurture and foster players' feel for the game to improve individual decision-making and court awareness. Through play, athletes enjoy the experience, learn the game and are motivated to improve and play more. As athletes age, coaches organize these skills and enhance their development. At the highest levels, coaches develop systems around the players' skill sets and ensure players develop a feel for playing with their teammates in a style which uses the team's strengths. Throughout the development process, use an athlete-centered approach and empower athletes to use their skills.

Dr. Istvan Balyi coined the term "Peak by Friday" to characterize the coaches who only prepare for the up-coming game with little to no thought given to the players' long term development. The following progression fits within a Long Term Athlete Development approach, as it is a gradual progression which builds upon previously learned skills.

Stage 1: The Foundation Stage
Training Goals: Getting open, passing under pressure, give-and-go cuts, dribble hand-offs, basic man principles, squaring to a Hard2Guard position.
Emphasis: Introduce basic basketball concepts through small-sided games.

Every play during a basketball game depends on the opponent; therefore, when teaching players basic fundamentals, we cannot get too removed from the actual game. While players require some teaching to understand new concepts, players learn best through playing. Small-sided games involve more players and create the best environment for fun, learning and development.

Build good habits from the beginning. Tactically-speaking, coaches want players who move without the ball rather than standing and watching the action, and players who read and react to the defense and make the right decisions. We must teach players the basic rules and not assume players understand the game because they watch games on television. For young players, traveling and reaching are probably the two most important rules. Tactically, the basic strategy is to get open to create a good shot.

With so much to teach and so little time, games provide the best method to teach the rules, develop skills and motivate players. Playing games does not mean ignoring practice to play in multiple tournaments. Instead, small-sided games at practice are the best way to develop basic skills and understanding. This training environment lacks the performance pressure associated with a real game with a crowd, officials and scoreboard, so players experiment and try new skills. In games, players do what they can already do, which does not lead to development or improvement. In a practice setting, players try new things and coaches can assist with the learning without the pressure to win.

> **Benefits of Small-Sided Games**
> - More time and space to practice moves.
> - Similar conceptually to 5v5 games.
> - More skill repetitions for each player.
> - Competitive learning environment.
> - More players involved rather than watching.
> - More fun than drills.
> - Incorporate team elements like getting open and passing to an open teammate.
> - Uses basic tactical skills like give-and-go cuts and pick-and-rolls.

Movement Concepts

The foundation of team games is keep-away. The offense attempts to keep possession and the defense attempts to gain possession. In team games, the difference is scoring. In basketball, the offense keeps possession until it creates a good scoring opportunity, while the defense attempts to steal the ball and prevent easy scoring opportunities. With this mindset, keep-away provides a learning tool to teach basketball's basic rules – traveling and basic fouls – and train passing and cutting skills.

In keep-away games like *Volleyball Passing, 3v3 Football, Americanized Net Ball* and *3v3/No Dribble*, players move to get open, protect the ball, pass to open teammates and try to steal passes by pressuring the ball and getting a hand in the passing lane. These passing and moving drills teach players to be strong with the ball, use a pivot foot to create space and make cuts to create passing lanes without dribbling – the main technical skills developed during this stage.

Players require basic technical instruction to play, like the pivot foot concept – front and reverse pivots – and chest and bounce passes. However, limit the instruction and allow players to discover skills through the game. Give players an opportunity to learn from and correct their mistakes. However, if the majority does not understand a concept or rule, briefly explain the concept. The goal is an active, fun practice and learning through game play, rather than monotonous instructions and drills.

The game's structure teaches players good movement habits. When players play without the dribble, as with the games listed above, they must move around and create open passing lanes to advance the ball and score. These games teach players to evade defenders and move to a spot where the ball handler can make a safe pass. If the players struggle to get open, stop the action and quickly go over the technical aspects of getting open, like V-cuts and L-cuts. While players eventually must learn the basic cuts and terminology, at the outset emphasize simply evading defenders and moving to open spots without encumbering players with too much technical knowledge. Learning to create space by "juking" their defender will make their L-cuts and V-cuts more indefensible when the time comes to add more structure.

From the keep away games, move to small-sided games. Again, use the structure of the rules to teach and reinforce skills without encumbering players with too many instructions or drills. At this age, the offensive object is to get open and square to the basket. Therefore, play small-sided games with two rules: (1) catch and square to the basket and (2) pass and cut to the basket. Use the game's structure and rules to encourage players to move.

Half-Court Offense Concepts

The two most important tactical concepts to teach are the give-and-go cut and spacing. In 5v5 games, nobody at this age should be pigeon-holed into a position and all players should be encouraged to develop and use all the technical and tactical skills. A basic 5-out offense emphasizes all-around skill development, and the give-and-go and dribble-at give players two skills to use.

Spacing: Spacing is critical to offensive execution. If two players want to execute a give-and-go cut, but a teammate is in the way, the skill breaks down. At this age, emphasize spacing between teammates and leaving the basket area open for players to cut or penetrate.

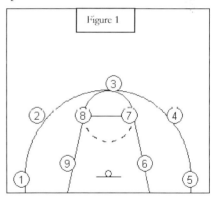

Figure 1

To teach spacing, use numbered spots. A common idea is to use five spots outside the three-point line and four spots inside the three-point line (Figure 1). The spots are the baseline, wings and top of the key beyond the three-point line and the blocks and elbows inside the three-point line. Any time the ball moves, either with the pass or dribble, all the offensive players move to a new spot. Nobody stands still when the ball moves. Players can move wherever they want provided they move. However, if they cut to the block, they post quickly and then cut to a new perimeter spot to leave the lane open. At this age, the easiest way to score is to get dribble penetration to the basket or an open basket cut.

In small-sided games during practice, the proper spacing creates good driving lanes for the ball handler and makes help defense difficult. When players stand close to the ball handler, they restrict the space the ball handler has to beat his man. Rather than stand close to the ball handler, the off-ball players should cut to open areas or space away from the ball handler. At this age, good spacing is about 10-12-feet, as this gives the ball handler enough space, but also keeps his teammates within range for a good pass. As players get older, good spacing moves to about 12-15-feet.

Give-and-Go: The give-and-go is just as it sounds. The first player passes to a teammate and cuts. The pass receiver catches the pass and passes back to the first player (F. 2). Defenders often relax when their man passes. When a player passes and cuts immediately, he catches his defender off-balance. This teaches players to stay active rather than passing and standing.

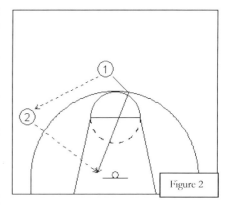

To teach the give-and-go, incorporate the concept into lay-up drills. Player 1 starts with the ball, passes to Player 2 and cuts to the basket. Player 2 passes back to Player 1 who finishes the lay-up. Next, emphasize the give-and-go in small-sided scrimmages. Rather than mandating the give-and-go, reward teams. When playing 2v2 or 3v3, score each basket as one point, but give an extra point for any basket scored directly off a give-and-go cut. Rather than spend extra time running 2v0 give-and-go drills, emphasize the concept through the small-sided scrimmages. Progress from 2v2 to 3v3, 4v4 and 5v5 and emphasize the give-and-go through this scoring system.

This progression builds quickly from teaching to training to competing with the concept. In later stages, teaching gains importance because precise skill execution is more important. However, precision is not vital at this stage, so quickly progress to the competitive games.

Dribble-at: The dribble-at is a basic tactical concept which offers two options: (1) backdoor cut or (2) dribble hand-off. To execute a dribble-at, the ball handler dribbles directly at his teammate's defender. The ball handler initiates the play to keep off-ball offensive players from flocking to the ball. If the defender drops under the level of the ball, his teammate cuts over top of the ball handler for a hand-off. If the defender plays between the ball handler and his teammate, the teammate cuts backdoor to the basket.

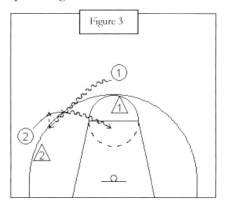

To hand off, the ball handler jump stops just short of his teammate's defender. The ball handler hands the ball to his teammate at waist level, much like a quarterback handing to a running back, and sets a screen for his teammate. Ideally, especially with older players with bigger hands, the ball handler holds the ball with his outside hand under the ball so his teammate has an easy transition from receiving the ball to the dribble (F. 3).

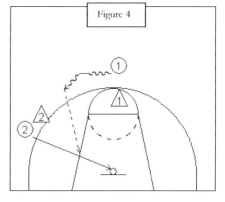

On the back door cut, the ball handler dribbles at his teammate's defender. If the defender moves to defend the hand-off, his teammate cuts to the rim. As he cuts behind his defender, the ball handler makes a bounce pass. The ball handler passes directly from the dribble and leads his teammate toward the basket with a bounce pass (F. 4).

To practice these skills, incorporate into lay-up drills. Player 1 dribbles at Player 2. P2 cuts backdoor and P1 makes the bounce pass for a lay-up. Next, P1 dribbles at P2. P2 cuts behind the dribble, receives the hand-off and continues for a lay-up. Next, emphasize the dribble-at in small-sided scrimmages. Rather than mandating the dribble-at, reward teams. When playing 2v2 or 3v3, score each basket as one point, but give an extra point for any basket scored directly off a dribble-at, either a backdoor cut for a lay-up or a hand-off that leads to a shot. Rather than spend extra time running 2v0 dribble-at drills, emphasize the concept through the small-sided scrimmages. Progress from 2v2 to 3v3, 4v4 and 5v5 and emphasize the dribble-at through this scoring system.

5v5 Concepts

Use 2v2 and 3v3 games in the half court and full court to train these concepts before moving to 5v5 play. 3v3 and 2v2 give players more space to practice their moves and shots and more time with the ball. 2v2 and 3v3 teach more effectively than 5v0 drills because they are conceptually more similar to the real action. "What a player does in a game is almost always influenced in some way by an opponent, who is not always predictable. This means that when youngsters try to apply what they have practiced in a drill to the scramble of a game, both technique and skill often breakdown because players cannot anticipate the defender's reactions," (Launder). Small-sided games train decision-making skills and the ability to handle defensive pressure.

Small-sided games create a competitive learning environment. Players practice individual skills with space to maneuver and incorporate team elements like finding a teammate who has a better shot, getting open and playing help defense. Small-sided games offer more space to offensive players to hone their technical skills. 5v5 games favor the bigger, stronger players who dominate defensively and go coast to coast for lay-ups. Technical offensive skills like passing, seeing the floor, shooting and dribbling develop slowly and small-sided games offer more repetitions and fewer stoppages. Small-sided games ensure more action, which equates to more fun for young athletes learning skills.

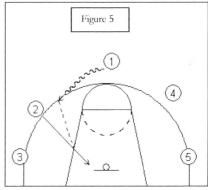

Using the three initial tactical concepts – spacing, give-and-go cuts and the dribble-at – creates a basic, generic motion offense. To create space for the cuts, either a give-and-go cut or the backdoor cut off the dribble-at, leave the post open. Start five players on the perimeter. However, anytime a player cuts to the basket, give the player the option to stay and post for a second, especially after a dribble-at backdoor cut when he does not receive the ball.

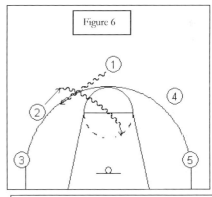

To use these ideas, a generic set is to start with five players around the perimeter. The ball handler (no positions at this point; players just fill spots) initiates with the dribble or a pass. If the ball handler dribbles at a teammate, the teammate reads his defender and cuts to the basket [F. 5] or cuts behind for a dribble hand-off [F. 6]. If he passes to a teammate, he immediately cuts to the basket [F. 7]. Either way, the other players fill new spots.

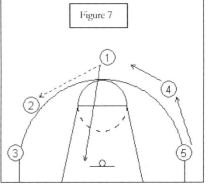

On a basket cut, another player fills the top or the ball handler can dribble the ball to the top. The players have many options of where to go and how to react. They will often make the wrong choice or look confused. This is okay. It is part of the learning process. For many coaches, this is frustrating, as coaches want to solve the players' problems so they know exactly where to go and when. However, if the coach solves the problems, the players do not learn, so the coach has to step in over and over again, until the motion becomes a set play.

At this age, the team's organization or the success of each possession is not as important as the players learning to think for themselves so they read and react to their teammates and their defender. This requires more patience and instruction than memorizing a set play. This forces players to adapt to the coach's offense rather than developing into adaptable players. However, if players memorize sets, their tactical foundation improves little throughout the season. When the players move to a new coach, he starts from the beginning or teaches new set plays to memorize, which is the *Peak by Friday* approach because it leads to better initial organization. By showing patience and allowing players to make and learn from mistakes, players improve through the season and begin to develop a basketball I.Q. which elevates their performance as they move to the next stage.

There are dozens of tactical elements and many coaches try to teach them all. However, over the course of a season, it is hard to master everything. Rather than introduce several things, concentrate on mastering one or two things. If teams execute fundamentals well, it does not matter if the defense anticipates the offense's attack. The offense is more effective if it confidently executes one or two skills than if it half-heartedly executes seven or eight. If you are fortunate to stay with one group of players for several seasons, and they pick up the skills quickly, flip ahead and introduce the beginning of the Stage 2 skills. However, few teams perform these skills well. It is better to approach learning and development gradually and progress with success rather than with limited understanding and mediocre results.

3v3 Development Leagues

These games offer more than just training aides; development-oriented leagues would replace standard 5v5 leagues with 3v3 leagues for this age group. English soccer academies wait until players are 11 to play full 11v11 soccer; in Italy, youth basketball players start playing in skill-oriented clinics at six, but formal competition waits until players are 12.

3v3 League Benefits

1. ***Everyone plays***. In a high school gym, a 5v5 game equals 10 players on the court. Using the side baskets creates four 3v3 games or 24 players playing.
2. ***No performance pressure***. Playing without officials and scoreboards reduces the performance demands.
3. ***No negative coaching***. Coaches at each basket help both teams, so there is more cooperation and learning rather than strict competition.
4. ***More action and fun***. No sitting on the bench equals more fun. With only three offensive players, everyone touches the ball more.

A 3v3 league promotes fun, learning and development rather than competition and winning. Players compete, but winning is not the end-goal. "Children thrive on challenges. Children are always in search of opportunities to gain skills and prove themselves," (Damon). This league challenges players like a 5v5 league, but is more age and developmentally appropriate. Rather than one or two players dominating the ball, all players handle the ball and players have more space to make a move or shoot. "The basic rule is…beginners need plenty of space to play effectively," (Launder). Rather than sloppy, bumblebee-ball, players play "real" basketball within a team environment with positive coaching and more emphasis on skill development and fun games.

Stage 2: The Fundamental Stage

Training Goals: Making cuts, setting and using an on-ball screen, help defense, basic team defense concepts.
Emphasis: Team basketball; player and ball movement.

When I played on a Swedish under-20 team, we played 2v2 or 3v3 during every practice. These games maximize time and create competitive situations, unpredictable environments and contested shots. While drills train new skills, drills cannot replicate game decision-making skills. Decision-making skills make or break the player, and players must learn to interpret and attack different situations. Small-sided games enhance individual instruction and transfer skills to the game.

At this age, continue with a global approach to teaching tactical skills. Rather than analyze every move, give players the objective and allow them to play and come to their own conclusions. Players require some specific instruction to develop more quickly, but the process is not a race. A global coach says, "This player has the ball, stop him from scoring," and then allows them to play, while an analytical coach tells the player which foot to put forward in his stance, how to react to a ball fake, where to influence the dribble and more. This is the art of coaching, as the most effective approach is somewhere along the spectrum from global to analytical, and the individual coach must decide how to balance instruction with play and repetitions. At this age group, however, continue to err toward the global approach as opposed to the analytical approach, especially with tactical skills. Allow players an opportunity to learn and make plays on their own.

Players have time to progress slowly through the different tactical skills and master each before moving to new skills. A team does not need every skill to play competitively. For instance, if players develop the give-and-go and dribble-at skills in Stage 1 and learn spacing in relation to dribble penetration and the on-ball screen during this stage, teams have plenty of offensive options to attack different defenses.

Players play a lot of basketball, but few players learn the game. Coaches tell players what to do, when to do it and how to do it, so they eliminate the players' learning. Coaches crave control; they attempt to minimize errors by making players robotic. However, these players never develop basketball awareness and rarely progress into good players. Those who survive this approach are typically the best players at this age and possess the ball for most of the game and practice, enabling them to develop by reading and seeing things. When coaches give players some responsibility and control – like running a true motion offense dependent on the players' reading and reacting to the defense – it increases the players' awareness, their ability to make decisions and their desire to take responsibility for their actions.

MOVEMENT CONCEPTS

Rick Majerus says that "offense is spacing and spacing is offense." The previous stage presented a five-out motion-oriented offense predicated on the give-and-go cut, the dribble-at and nine generic spots. In this stage, spacing evolves from filling spots to moving to more dangerous positions. Generally, the offense wants three players on the strong side and two players on the weak side. However, as the ball transitions to the weak side, the two players have extra room to execute a two-man play: a give-and-go, a backdoor cut, a dribble-at or an on-ball screen. If nothing develops quickly, at least one cutter is likely to cut to balance the floor with three players on the strong side.

The following are some generic offensive templates:

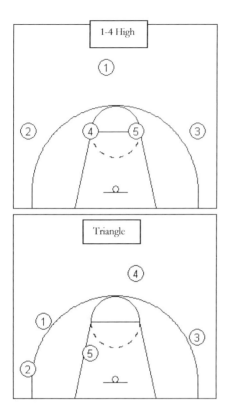

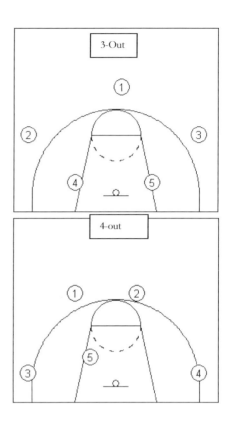

From these sets, players must know how to react to a cutter or dribble penetration. In general, as with the give-and-go, when a cutter cuts, the other players fill the open spots. However, when a player dribbles in a teammate's direction, the teammate has three basic options: (1) Flare, (2) Cut backdoor, or (3) Loop.

If the ball handler dribbles toward a teammate, the teammate flares [Figure 1]. However, if his teammate is along the sideline, he cuts backdoor or loops behind the dribble, depending on his defender. If his defender plays below the cutter, he loops [Figure 2]; if his defender helps above the cutter, he cuts backdoor [Figure 3]. If the cutter is wide open, and his defender leaves him to help on the ball, he holds his position and prepares to shoot [Figure 4].

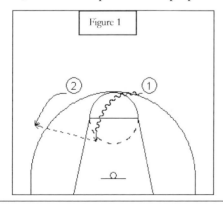

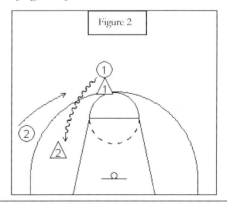

If the ball handler dribbles away from a teammate, the teammate loops behind the dribble [Figure 5]. If the teammate starts two passes away, he drifts to the baseline corner for a skip pass [Figure 5]. These principles maximize the ball handler's space and punish help defenders.

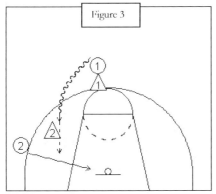

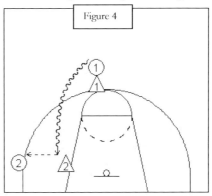

In Figure 5, Player 1 dribbles to the baseline; Player 2 loops behind the dribble and Player 3 drifts to the corner to give Player 1 two outlets if help defenders stop his drive and take away the post players.

The player movement requires reading the direction of the drive and the reaction of the defender. However, good players anticipate the movement and react immediately, while lesser performers take too long to make a decision and react late. The players who anticipate and react have a "feel" for the game, while the lesser performers do not. As evidenced by Team USA's offense in the 2006 World Championships, many players are great with the ball, but ineffective when playing off the ball. Use concepts, drills (*String Spacing*) and small-sided games to teach these skills.

When scrimmaging, emphasize spacing through the scoring system. Reward the proper cut with a point, or only count baskets scored directly from the proper movement. Teach players to play basketball and use these skills in games.

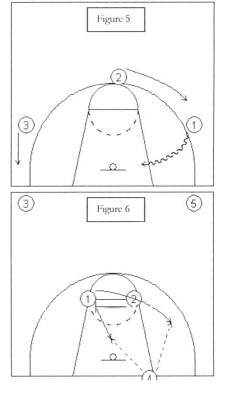

Half-Court Offense Concepts

Cross Screens: When moving from cutting to using a screen, cross screens and on-ball screens are the easiest screens to teach. When setting an on-ball screen, the defender is always in the same spot: defending the ball. Therefore, it is easy for the screener to headhunt and find the defender to screen.

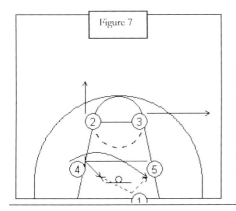

Cross screens are used as easy in-bounds plays. Some coaches go crazy with inbounds plays, but simple plays work when executed properly. If a team struggles to inbound the ball against a press, a simple cross screen gets one of the players open. One player sets a screen for his teammate who cuts; the screener rolls opposite the cutter [Figure 6]. The same screen works for an underneath out of bounds play, as one post screens for the other and then rolls to the basket [Figure 7]. If executed, one player is almost always open.

On-Ball Screens: In drills, the coach dictates the action and players follow directions. In live play, a player's decision-making skill determines his success. When introducing a skill, like an on-ball screen, a drill teaches the different options and enables players to train their technical skills – ball handling, shooting and passing. For instance, if a coach wants to teach a side on-ball screen, he could use two different shooting drills to initiate the lesson. In the first, players use the on-ball screen and hit a pull-up jumper off the dribble. In the second, the ball handler passes to the screener who picks and pops for a jump shot. The ball handler goes shoulder to shoulder with the screener and as the ball handler dribbles away from the screen, the screener rolls open. To roll, use a reverse pivot and open to the ball: the screener's eyes follow the ball and he opens his chest in the direction of the dribble, making a reverse pivot on his bottom foot.

While these drills illustrate the basic options, they fail to teach the skill's tactical components. Players must read and react to the defense. Play 2v2 as the next step in the learning progression. 2v2 gives the offense a huge advantage when using an on-ball screen because there is no help defense. However, the ball handler reads the two defenders and the screener decides whether to pick-and-pop or pick-and-roll to the basket. After playing 2v2, play 3v3 and progress to 5v5.

During these games, the coach can tell the defense how to defend the on-ball screen. If players constantly switch or go under the screen, the offense never really reads the defense. To mix things up, tell the defense how to play, but do not let the offense know. If playing *3v3 Cut Throat*, where the teams change on every possession, an assistant coach can tell the defense how to defend the screen before they take the court each time. This way, teams face different defenses and learn to read and react.

On-Ball Screen Situations

Defense	Offense
Traps the ball handler	Space the trap with a protect dribble to create a passing lane to the wing or to the screener popping.
Hedges to force the ball handler high or to take away the shot	Extend the hedge with a second hard dribble past the hedger. Try to turn the corner or force the defense to switch or leave the ball handler open while the hedger retreats and the on ball defender recovers.
Switches	Exhibit patience. A switch creates two mismatches. Drive a big on the perimeter or find an open passing lane into the post using a teammate to enter the ball.
Goes underneath the screen	Look for the shot, the drive or the crossover to use the screen again.
Moves to take away the screen	Go away from the screen. If the defender anticipates the screen and moves in that direction, punish him by driving the open lane. Some teams, especially NBA teams, send the ball handler toward the baseline on a side pick-and-roll to trap the ball handler. On the dribble attack, stay off the sideline and attack the basket the screener slips into a passing lane between the two defenders.
Screener's defender moves high early to hedge or trap the ball handler.	"Slip the screen:" rather than setting the screen, the screener cuts toward the basket, leaving his defender on the high side, away from the basket.

These are six ways to defend an on-ball screen; the location changes the defense slightly. Offensively, keep the dribble alive and extend the defense, forcing it to make a decision. See the entire floor and do not get tunnel-vision on the screener.

HALF-COURT DEFENSE CONCEPTS

Figure 8

Start the defensive instruction with one help defender. While playing 2v2, use the games to teach the proper positioning of the off-ball defenders in relation to the ball. If the ball is on one side and his man on the other, the help defender plays with one foot in the key and points to the ball and his man [Figure 8]. If the weak side offensive player cuts to the ball, the help defender denies the pass. Emphasize defensive communication: in 2v2, if the help defender moves from a midline help position to deny a flash to the elbow, he must tell his teammate defending the ball, as the on-ball defender no longer has help to the baseline side. With two players on the floor, it is easy to know who should be talking to whom. Develop these habits early, as the best defensive teams and players communicate loudly and clearly.

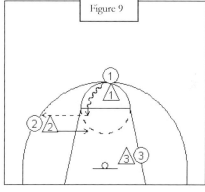

Figure 9

As games move to 3v3 and 5v5, focus on the initial help defender. At this age, do not allow ball handlers to split defenders. The next defender must be ready to help the on-ball defender and not allow the penetration between the on-ball defender and the nearest help defender [Figure 9]. Defensively, help over, not up. Usually, when a post player helps up to stop the ball, nobody rotates behind him to take his man on the pass [Figure 10]. However, when players rotate over to help, they leave open a jump shooter, not a lay-up. At higher levels, teams may adjust this strategy to take away open three-point shots, but at this age, teach defenders not to get split.

Once the team understands the first help defender, start to teach the secondary help [Figure 11]. Once a team helps or doubles on the strong side, the weak side defenders zone the weak side and help the helpers. If the post stops penetration, a

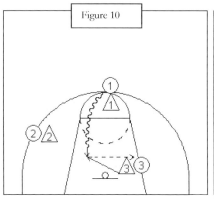

Figure 10

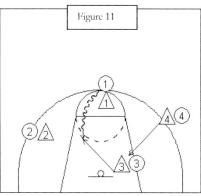

Figure 11

weak side defender slides in front of the offensive post player to take away the easy lay-up.

PRESSURE CONCEPTS

Transition play dominates youth basketball. Many teams press and presses create numbered advantages in one direction or the other: if the defense steals the ball, they have an immediate offensive advantage, but if the offense breaks the press, they have an advantage attacking their basket.

As with half court skills, players need some basic instruction to play against pressure and in transition, and they need to play in these situations to learn from their mistakes. The basic principle to use against a press or any type of trap is Diamond Spacing.

Diamond Spacing: When the defense traps a player, his teammates form a diamond: one teammate is ahead of the ball, behind the ball and diagonal through the trap [Figure 12]. If the defense traps and covers these three players, the fifth offensive player runs to the rim and is open for a lay-up. Without this spacing, the ball handler does not know where to find his teammates and the spacing breaks down. This basic principle organizes the attack and defeats pressure.

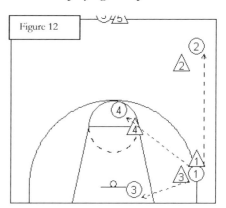

TRANSITION CONCEPTS

In the open court, create a 2v1 opportunity. When the offense has a 2v1 advantage, finish with a lay-up; the second player is there in case the shooter misses. In transition, force the defense to stop the ball and find the open man.

To work on the beginning of the press and the end of a fast break, play *2v2 Rugby*. *2v2 Rugby* creates 1v0, 1v1 and 2v1 lay-up opportunities, and players train open court ball handling and ball handling versus back court pressure. Use small-sided games rather than drills because drills train players to be good at the drill. They adapt to the drill, but do not always develop adaptable skills. In 3v2 transition drills, players play the drill: they jump stop at the top, pass to the wing, receive the return pass and shoot. However, in games, transition play is dynamic with more offensive players and defenders trailing. Players must practice attacking the basket as they would in a game. Otherwise, the drills fail to transfer to game skills.

5V5 CONCEPTS

In a 5v5 offense, an on-ball screen can be very difficult to stop. If a team runs the screen well, knows its options and plays unselfishly, an on-ball screen could constitute the entire offensive strategy during games. There are several ways to run an on-ball screen and several basic sets to use to implement on-ball screens which are diagrammed below.

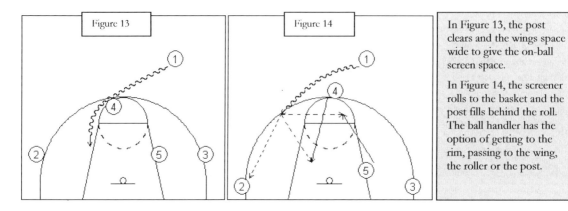

In Figure 13, the post clears and the wings space wide to give the on-ball screen space.

In Figure 14, the screener rolls to the basket and the post fills behind the roll. The ball handler has the option of getting to the rim, passing to the wing, the roller or the post.

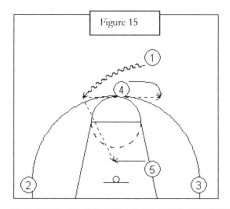
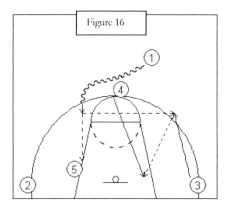

In Figure 15, the screener pops rather than rolling to the basket. The post dives into the key, looking to seal his defender as the ball handler passes to the screener.

In Figure 16, the low post moves to the ball side and tries to seal as the ball handler dribbles off the scr The opposite wing fills behind the screen as the screener rolls to the opposite block to post.

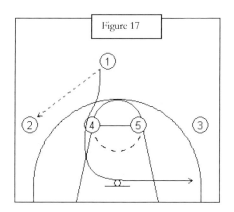
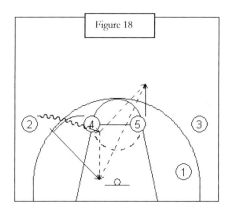

In Figure 17, the PG passes to the wing and clears to the opposite corner to isolate the side pick-and-roll.

In Figure 18, the post sets an on-ball screen and the wing drives middle. The opposite post steps high as an outlet if the defense traps or hedges hard.

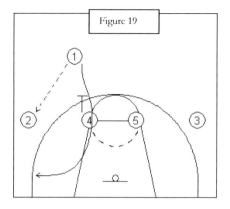
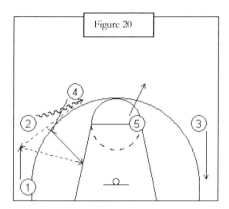

In Figure 19, the PG passes to the wing and uses a back screen from the post. He cuts to the strong side corner to leave the block open.

In Figure 20, the wing uses the screen and the screener rolls to the rim. The PG fills behind the screen for a shot or post entry pass.

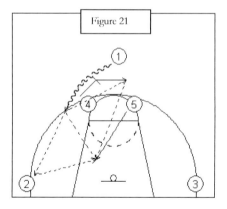
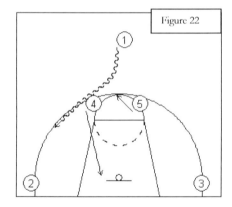

In Figure 21, the offense uses the Horns set; the screener screens and rolls to the basket while the opposite post flashes high.

In Figure 22, the offense uses the Horns play but the screen pops high and the opposite post cuts to the rim for the direct pass or the high-low.

Stage 3: The Training Stage
Training Goals: Open court decision-making; attacking defenders; off-ball movement; defensive rotations.
Emphasis: Transition basketball; decision-making.

In Stage 3, coaches organize the attack to create a more developed system of play and to balance development with competition. Building on the previous skills, the major new skill is screening away from the ball, now that players have an understanding of playing the game, cutting and spacing the floor. When players learn to use screens first, they never learn to get open on their own and the screens become less dynamic, as players move from Point A to Point B without regard for the defense. Now, players fully realize the value of a screen and react to the defense rather than running from spot to spot.

When I started to coach, I worked a camp that taught "motion." However, it is not a motion offense. A motion offense is more than an offense which involves activity; a motion offense requires the offense to read and react to the defense and to teammate's cuts and screens without a set pattern. At the camp, posts set down screens for the wing [Figure1]; the point entered the ball to a wing and screened for the opposite post [Figure 2]. No deviation or thinking allowed. Players ran to spots and if they ran to a different spot, the coaches stopped the action to tell them the correct spot. This is a continuity offense, like the Flex, where players go spot to spot and coaches eliminate players' decision-making. This is not a motion offense.

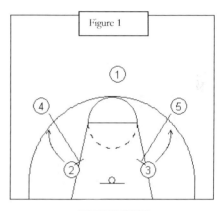

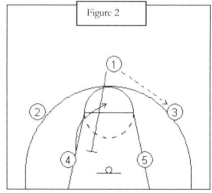

MOVEMENT CONCEPTS

Teams use screens in the half court and the full court. To be effective, players must react to the situation and make the correct play. Good players anticipate their decision. If receiving a screen, a shooter anticipates curling off the screen. However, if his defender runs under the screen, he recognizes the defense, adjusts his cut and flares. If he runs to a spot, the defender knows where to go and can defend the screen easily. Screens are only effective if the offensive player uses the screen appropriately and moves to the open spot. When a screen is set, read the situation, react to other players and make a decision. Majerus says, "It's better to be late than early." If the offensive player is patient, the defense shows the offense where to cut:

Screen Away from the Ball

Defense	Offense
Beats offensive player to the screen	Cuts Backdoor
Follows the offensive player around the screen	Curls off the screen toward ball and basket
Goes underneath the screen	Flares or fades away from the screen
Fights through the screen	Straight cuts away from the defense

The basic objective is to create as much distance from the defender as possible. This is the general rule offensively. Against a zone, players away from the ball position themselves at the point of an equilateral triangle with the two nearest defenders to create the maximum distance for the defenders to close out and to create indecision between the defenders [Figure 3]. Creating space is the off-the-ball objective.

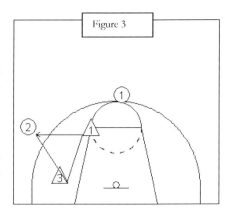

When using a screen, the screener and cutter read each other. One player cuts high and one cuts low. If the cutter curls high, the screener rolls to the rim [Figure 4]; if the cutter curls to the rim, the screener flashes high [Figure 5]. The screener moves opposite the cutter, unless he feels his defender cheat and slips the screen to the basket. Regardless, a screen creates two cuts: one from the cutter and one from the screener.

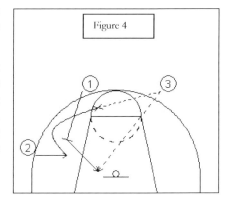

Initially, when teaching screens, players call out their cut so the passer anticipates the pass, and the cutter thinks about the cut. Move from this drill to a drill with one defender where the cutter reads his defender. Next, use a 2v2 drill with a screener and cutter on offense and defense and a coach or player passing the ball. Finally, move to live 3v3 games before transitioning to 4v4 and 5v5 games.

TRANSITION CONCEPTS

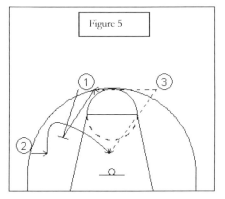

Transition basketball separates average teams from well-coached teams. Well-coached teams create good shots and make the right decision when they have an advantage, while average teams make mistakes. University of Tennessee Women's Basketball Coach Pat Summit says, "Basketball is a game of transition and transition basketball must be practiced." Whether a coach stresses a sideline break or a middle break, advance the ball down court quickly to take advantage of the defense. Great transition teams commit to running, pass the ball unselfishly, make good decisions, space the court and attack aggressively.

Drills with static defenders fail to replicate the dynamic game environment. Instead, use the following drills to train transition offense and defense: *1v2-2v1, 2v1 Breakdown, Rabbit, Transition Progression, San Diego Transition D, Army Drill and Numbers Transition Drill*. The guidelines below offer a few teaching points, which build on the simple lessons from Stage 2.

1. 2v1 is the desired break; try to turn every transition situation into a 2v1.
2. Finish all 2v1 breaks with a lay-up.
3. Ball handler attacks with a scorer's mentality, not a passer's. In a 2v1, the ball handler finishes at the basket unless the defender stops the ball completely; in a 3v2, the ball handler must be prepared to shoot the three if the defense stays back or penetrate past the first defender.
4. Make the play early. Many players take one or two dribbles too many.

5. Spacing is critical. In a 2v1, attack wider than the lane-lines; in a 3v2, wings get wide; in a four or five-man break, space in width and depth – one or two players trail beyond the initial rush and cut to gaps in the defense.
6. Always be the second man; if a teammate has a break away, never take the lay-up for granted. Be the second man down court in case he misses.

TRANSITION DEFENSE CONCEPTS

When faced with a numbers disadvantage, protect the basket first, then stop the ball, then find the shooters and finally match up. Make the offense take more time to give your teammates a chance to recover. In a 2v1 break, the defender jabs at the ball handler and then backs into the passing lane, never completely committing either way. The more the offensive player thinks, the more time he takes and the more he is likely to make a mistake or a tentative play. As the second defender recovers, he talks to the first defender so the first defender knows to match up and stop the ball, as the second defender takes the other offensive player. The retreating defenders are the eyes of the defense in transition because they see the entire play and can direct teammates.

In a 3v2 break, the first defender protects the basket and the second defender slows the ball. If the defender turns the dribble toward one side or forces an early pass, he takes the player who receives the first pass and allows the first defender to protect the basket. In a numbers disadvantage, force the ball to one side and keep the ball on the side to shrink the amount of court to defend. The trailing defenders sprint to the weak side and match-up. *Army Drill* is the transition drill I use virtually every practice, as I believe transition defense is the most important part of defense.

HALF-COURT OFFENSE CONCEPTS

Soccer teams do not use plays; instead, players use guidelines or principles to anticipate a teammate's moves. If an offensive player dribbles toward the end-line, he expects one teammate to make a near-post run and one to run to the far-post, and he crosses the ball accordingly. Likewise, basketball players need organization – a set of expectations. The following principles organize players and create expectations which are enhanced through training in competitive situations.

1. Pass and Move. An athlete's best opportunity to get open is as soon as he passes, as his defender follows the ball and/or relaxes.
2. A player is most open for a shot or move to the basket when he first receives the pass.
3. String Spacing. as a dribbler dribbles toward an offensive player, the offensive player flares away from the dribble forcing his defender to decide whether to help on the dribbler, leaving the offensive player open, or not help, leaving the ball handler's defender on an island; if the offensive player cannot flare any further (already near the sideline) he either loops behind the offensive player or cuts backdoor. As a dribbler one position away dribbles away from the offensive player, he follows to the vacated spot to maintain a passing angle.
4. If the ball goes to the baseline, either with a pass or dribble, the opposite wing drifts to the baseline corner to give a passing lane.
5. If a ball handler dribbles toward a post player, the post circles away from the ball keeping shoulders squared to the ball.
6. Diamond Spacing. If a ball handler is trapped, his teammates form a diamond. One player is to his right (up the floor); one to his left (retreat pass/horizontal) and one straight ahead (splits the trap).

7. When intending to set a screen, communicate with the teammate. Show a fist, call his name or use another pre-arranged signal to communicate.
8. Guards screen for posts and posts screen for guards to prevent easy switches.
9. When using an off-ball screen, curl if the defender trails; flare if the defender goes high side/ball side; cut back door if the defender gets between the cutter and the screener; make a straight cut if the defender tries to fight through the screen. Screener rolls opposite the cutter; if the cutter goes to the basket, the screener goes high; if the cutter goes high, the screener rolls to the basket.
10. When using an on-ball screen, use two dribbles to spread the defense unless the ball handler turns the corner to the basket. If the defense hedges, traps or switches, and the ball handler cannot split the defense, use two dribbles to extend the defense.
11. Little offense on big defense is a better mismatch than little defense on big offense.
12. Triangle spacing. Against a zone, position oneself in a triangle with the two nearest defenders to add indecision as to which defender closes out.

HALF-COURT DEFENSE CONCEPTS

Defensive instruction depends on a coach's system. Some teams pressure the ball, others contain; some deny all passes, others emphasize help. The *Shell Drill*, *Scramble* and *Seminole D* are three drills used to teach and train team defense as a whole, especially the important rotations when an initial defender gets beat off the dribble or due to a double-team in the post. Beyond these general principles, each coach decides his defensive system, and defensive instruction varies accordingly. However, some general defensive principles are constants.

1. Head on a swivel; see ball and man at all times.
2. When the ball moves, everybody moves. When your man moves, you move.
3. Communicate. Every player needs to communicate. Use small catch phrases.
4. Influence sideline-baseline in the half court. Weak side rotation must step in front of posts to eliminate interior pass and offensive rebounds if the post leaves to help.
5. Contest every shot. Force players to dribble into their shot: do not allow a catch and shoot.
6. Possession does not end until defense gets the rebound. Everyone blocks out and rebounds.
7. Do not get split. Do not allow the ball handler between his defender and the help defender.
8. Deny cutter outside the paint. Step from a help side, pistol position into denial position and bump the cutter before he enters the paint. Never let a player cut towards the ball without being denied.
9. In transition, retreat to the key keeping vision on the ball. Build the defense from the inside, out.

Conclusion

In every situation, follow a drill with competition. Drills are teaching tools; however, live play is like a pre-test. In math class, the teacher does not explain a concept, give homework and then give the graded exam; the teacher explains the concept (instruction), gives homework (drills/repetitions), gives a pre-test or end of chapter test (live play) and then the exam (game). The live play can be a small-sided or full scrimmage, depending on the skills emphasized and the time available. 3v3 remains the optimal game and a useful component to simulate the game and transition players from drills to 5v5 play with additional repetitions against live (unpredictable) defense.

Many players know when and what to do; however, when forced to read the defense and make a split-second decision, they fail. Experience and making decisions in an unpredictable environment will improve analysis. Small-sided games eliminate the robotic, well-drilled player who cannot react to new situations during competition.

Too much instruction and not enough play or too much play and not enough instruction hamper Stage 3. Balance is the key. Use drills to introduce specifics and teach skills. When teaching a defensive closeout, teach the movement, the small steps with weight back and hands high, and use a drill to train this skill. However, once the skill is learned, use competitive repetitions incorporating the skill. Many teams drill several skills without defense and then scrimmage 5v5. Instead, use a 1v1 drill to train decision-making and anticipation. In games, skills do not break down; decision-making and communication break down. Players need repetitions to train all aspects of the skill.

> **10-Week 3v3 Break Down**
>
> **Week 1**: Two Rules: (1) Every time you receive a pass, you must square all the way to the basket; (2) Every time you pass, you must cut to the basket.
>
> **Week 2**: Any basket scored on a give-and-go cut is worth 2 points; all other baskets worth 1 point.
>
> **Week 3**: Any pass completed counts as 1 point; any basket scored counts as 3 points.
>
> **Week 4**: Offense cannot shoot until it runs one pick-and-roll.
>
> **Week 5**: A basket scored as a result of a pick-and-roll is worth 2 points; all other baskets worth 1 point.
>
> **Week 6:** No dribble.
>
> **Week 7**: Any player who properly reads and uses a screen away from the ball earns 1 point. All baskets are worth two points. Therefore, a basket scored by a cutter properly using a screen is worth 3 points.
>
> **Week 8**: Two dribble maximum.
>
> **Week 9**: Offensive rebounds count as 1 point; all baskets scored count as 2 points.
>
> **Week 10**: Two rules: Every time you receive a pass, you must square to the basket; (2) on every pass, you must make a basketball play (cut or screen).

Stage 4: The Competition Stage
Training Goals: Mental skills, strengths/weaknesses, team strategy, competitiveness, skill application.
Emphasis: Refine and enhance skills, utilize players' strengths and capitalize on technical skill development.

Stage 4 transitions from developing players to developing a team system. Through the LTAD model, players develop a wealth of basketball skill and knowledge. Stage 4 grows more specific and sophisticated as coaches concentrate on several areas which complement the team's strengths. For instance, some teams attack quickly, while others show more patience. Teams like the New Orleans Hornets rely heavily on Chris Paul to run the pick-and-roll and find open teammates, while the Utah Jazz run Flex screens and tight pick-and-rolls designed to get the ball to the basket. The Hornets concentrate on an athletic post setting screens and running to the rim and wings who shoot the three-pointer, while the Jazz requires physical post players and wings that can finish in traffic and make free throws. The coach determines his team's system, which determines the practice drills and emphasis. A Hornets' practice and a Jazz practice emphasize different concepts and incorporate different drills, sets and shots because of the teams differing styles, strengths and personalities.

HALF-COURT OFFENSE CONCEPTS

In Stage 4, players develop the instincts and rolls to play against zone defenses. Most high school teams rely on a set play and shooting three-pointers against zones. At the varsity level, players must learn the tools to attack zones with motion-oriented concepts so they read and react to the defense much as they do against a man-to-man defense.

Attacking Zones: The *Dribble Drag* creates open perimeter shots and post entry passes. Using a three-guard front against a 2-3-zone, pass from the point to the wing. After passing, the point shallow cuts behind the front of the zone and replaces the wing [Figure 1]. The wing receives the pass and dribbles middle [Figure 2]. The ball handler drags the top defender to the middle. When he passes back to the wing, the outside bottom defender must close out [Figure 3], leaving the baseline open for a cutter [Figure 4] or creating a 1v1 match-up on the low block [Figure 5]. If the bottom wing defender does not close out, the player is open for a shot. The toughest place for a zone to defend is the area where the dribble drive originates, as the dribble drags the defender out of the area.

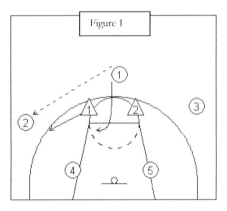

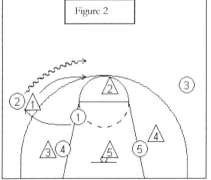

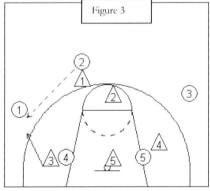

Great zone defenses communicate, as players alert teammates to cutters entering their area. When offensive players *cut from behind the zone*, the offensive player "gets lost" and finds a hole in the zone. Defenses react slowly to baseline cutters if the interior defenders fail to communicate. The slow reaction leads to an open shot or a distorted zone for another pass and a shot.

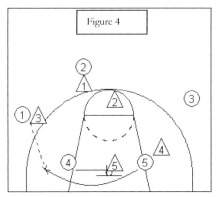

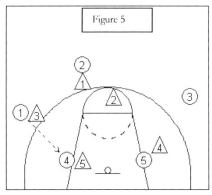

When a wing cuts along the baseline, the bottom defenders shift [Figure 6]. If the cutter cuts from behind the defense and the defense fails to communicate, the defenders react too late. As the guard passes to the wing on the baseline [Figure 7], the wing defender closes out late. Even worse, the middle defender is late to move to the low block. The offensive post can seal for good position [Figure 8] or step into the middle to screen the middle defender while the other post cuts to the open block for a lay-up [Figure 9]. If the defense sees the original cutter and talks, the defense's transition is much easier. However, all three defenders must work together. If the wing defender anticipates the cut, but the middle defender is late, the guard passes directly to the post [Figure 10].

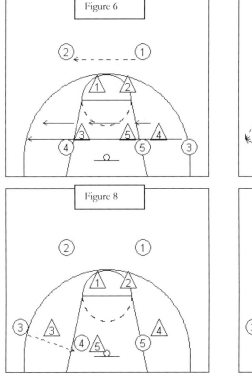

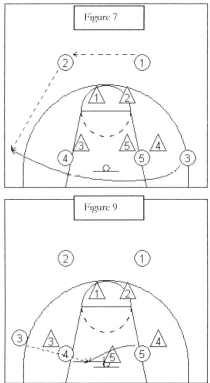

For some reason, few teams screen against zones. Zones turn otherwise active players into passive players. To force a defense to shift, *throw a skip pass using a flare screen*. The more the defense moves from side to side, the more likely the defense is to make a mistake and leave the offense open.

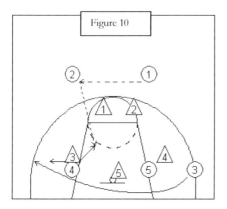
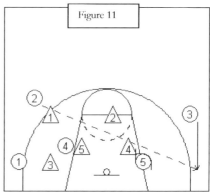

On a skip pass to the corner, the post screens the outside of the zone [Figure 11] and then shapes up in a gap before the middle defender recovers. On a wing to wing skip pass, the post screens the top defender, forcing the bottom defender to close out to the wing [Figure 12]. The post dives into the vacated space before the middle defender recovers [Figure 13].

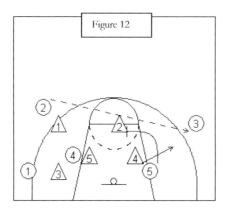
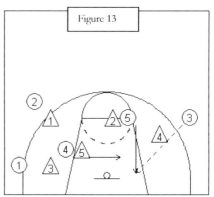

Another option is to use *diagonal cuts to drag the defense*, like the dribble drag, and create openings for the second cutter. As the first cutter cuts across the middle defender [F. 14], the second cutter cuts to the open space [F. 15]. If the weak side defender follows the second cutter [F. 16], an offensive wing cuts to the rim [F. 17]. The diagonal cutter to the middle draws the attention of two players, which leaves the second or third cutter open if the timing is right. Teams use this idea to run a lob play: the first defender attracts

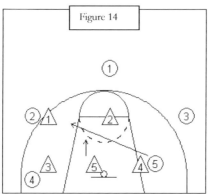
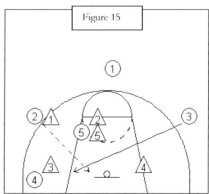

attention, the second sets a screen and the third receives the lob [F. 18 and 19]

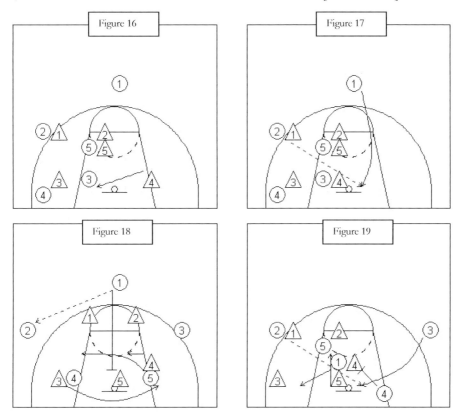

Post Spacing: When the offense passes into the post, the game stops, as players stand and watch. Just as teams must practice how to read and react to dribble penetration when a play breaks down, players must learn how and where to move when the ball enters the post and the post player does not score immediately.

Teams have different philosophies, but at minimum the passer must relocate. If the passer enters the ball to the low block from the wing, he can drift to the corner or toward the guard spot (outside the three-point line, lane-line extended) [Figure 20]. The passer can clear 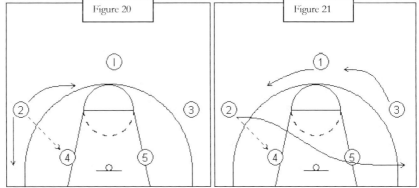 the area and cut to the basket and through to the opposite corner with the other players rotating one spot [Figure 21]. Finally, the passer can set or receive a screen. On any pass from the wing to the low block, I teach the passer to cut toward the elbow. A teammate can use the screen and cut to the wing or cut backdoor [Figure 22]. The screener can set the screen and pop high or if his man doubles, cut to the front of the rim [Figure 23]. I teach players to cut to the elbow because players have options to screen or dive to the rim, and they give the post enough space to make a move. To isolate the post, we send the wing to the opposite corner and let the post work.

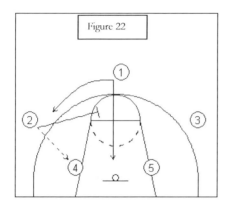

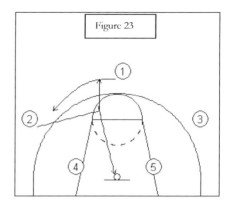

Post Splits: Offense boils down to three-man basketball on the strong side. If the ball is passed to the weak side, the two players use a two-man game, like a dribble-at or pick-and-roll, or someone cuts to the ball side to create the three-man game or triangle.

One three-man series is the post split. On the strong side, the wing passes to the low post, mid-post or high post, depending on the team's personnel [F. 24]. On the pass, the two guards cut together. The options from this position are numerous: (1) post hand-off on the cut [F. 25]; (2) guard screens the wing for a hand-off [F. 26]; (3) guard screens the wing who flares for a three-pointer, while the guard cuts to the rim [F. 27]; and (4) guard screens for the wing who cuts backdoor while the guard pops to the three-point line. The options off this set are too numerous to list.

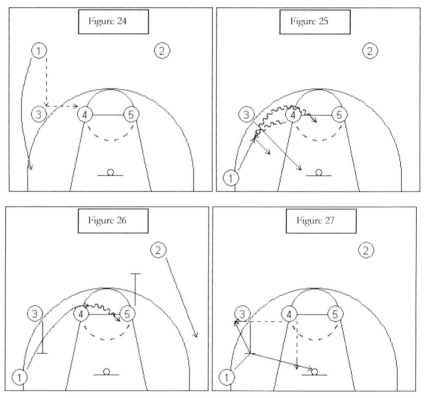

On option #4, for instance, when the wing cuts backdoor, he clears the strong side for a two-man game between the post and guard. The offense continually shifts from the three-man series to two-man series either through ball reversal or cuts.

While the strong side runs the post splits, the weak side can set back screens, flare screens, down screens or just space the floor. The key to this offense is spacing and timing, as screens set too early free players when the passer is not ready. When timed correctly, the spacing and the different cuts are very difficult to defend, which is one reason Phil Jackson and Rick Adelman-coached teams typically are near the top of the league in offensive efficiency, as they use these principles in their offense.

High-Low Game: Another way to create space for a post player in the low post is to run high-low plays. One easy way to enter into a high-low is through a high on-ball screen with the floor spread. In a Horns' set, the point guard can dribble off a high screen to either side. The screener can roll to the basket with the other post filling high [F. 28], or the other post can dive to the rim while the screener pops high [F. 29]. On the pass to the cutting post, the low post seals in the lane for the high-low entry pass. If someone helps on the low post, his offensive player is open for a three-pointer or to receive a pass and enter it into the low block.

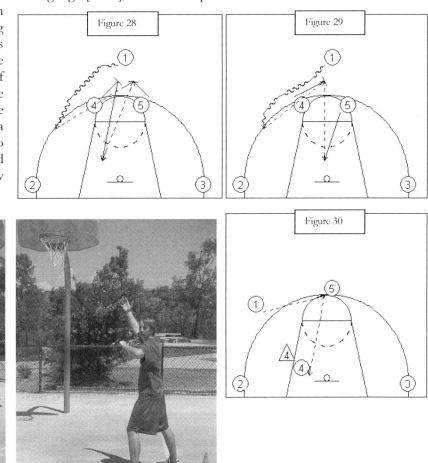

To succeed in the high-low game, posts must understand how to reverse pivot and seal. When the post rolls to the basket, the defense (cone) is often caught on the high side [above left], which is why the ball handler is unable to pass the ball directly to the post [F. 30]. On the reversal to the top, the post holds his position and reverse pivots with his top foot. As he pivots, he calls for the ball with his outside hand looking for the lob pass over his defender [above right]. If the defense plays below the post player rolling to the basket, he uses a "Don Nelson Move" to seal the defender under the rim. As he rolls to the rim, he walks into the defender and puts one foot between the defender's legs. As the pass reverses to the top, he reverse pivots on this foot and sits on the defender's leg, sealing the defender and creating a clear passing lane for the man at the top.

Mental Skills

Beyond these few tactics, tactical skill development during this stage is mental. Players read and react rather than thinking. They play on instinct rather than at a conscious level. The more they practice in small-sided games and scrimmages, the more they refine their skills and hasten their decision-making. When a mistake occurs, use questions rather than answers to help players develop a better basketball I.Q. Ask high order questions which force the player to think rather than nod his head or give a one word reply. Low order questions are factual and often lead to yes/no responses. High order questions require abstract or higher-level thinking and challenge athletes to apply, analyze, synthesize, evaluate and create knowledge.

An example of a bad question is: "Do you know what you did wrong?" This question allows the player to answer yes without thinking. A low order question is: "Where did the ball go?" This question is fact-based, as the player answers "Left" without thinking. A high order question is: "Why did the ball go left?" A "why" question forces the player to explain his answer, which requires thinking and analysis.

The best approach is a series of questions which start easy, grow more difficult and force the player to analyze the entire situation: "What defense were they in?" By starting with an easy question, the coach checks the player's read of the situation. If the defense played zone and the player answered "man," the coach knows the first problem to tackle. If the player correctly answers "a zone," a follow-up might be to ask, "How do we attack a zone?" or "Where are the gaps in the zone?" These are fact-based questions. When the player illustrates the gaps in the zone, then ask, "What caused the turnover?" The player knew they were in a zone, he knows the gaps in the zone, so why did he throw the ball to the other team? Maybe the player admits that he did not see the defender move to take away the cutter. The coach could follow up and ask the player why he thought the defender anticipated the pass and the player might realize that he had tunnel vision on the cutter.

If the coach simply asked, "What happened?" from the beginning, and the player answered "I didn't see him," and the coach accepted the answer, no teaching occurs. Maybe he did not see him because he thought they were playing man-to-man. Maybe he does not know the gaps to attack. Maybe he had tunnel vision on the cutter. Maybe he failed to move the defense with a pass fake before making the pass. Who knows? By probing with questions, the coach evaluates the player's understanding and can teach appropriately, giving the player the tools he needs rather than simply making abstract suggestions like "pass fake next time." If the coach simply tells the player that he made a bad pass, the coach re-confirms the result and frustrates the player, as the comment points out the obvious rather than teaching or helping the player improve.

Game Preparation

This is the Competitive Stage, so teams prepare for game situations and opponents during practice. The first three stages concentrate on developing the player within the team game, while Stage 4 emphasizes the team system. Practice game scenarios: end-game situations, how to hold a lead, how to come from behind, how to foul if needed, how to set up a game winning shot and what to do in a tie game. Scrimmaging with different situations (up three with 30 seconds to play; down two with 15 seconds to play; down five with one minute to play) prepares players for competition; secondly, the in-practice competition builds the competitive fire.

Stage 4 uses the same drills as earlier stages; however, the speed and intensity increase. Use competitive play (1v1, 3v3 or 5v5) to measure players and build mental toughness. Training depends on the coach's system, the player's maturity, the player's prior development and the team's personnel.

The varsity level requires teaching and coaching, while prior levels are predominantly teaching. Even in pursuit of victory, do not ignore individual development, learning and fun. Players seeking to play at the next level must improve and diversify their games; others need continued improvement to increase confidence. While practices increase in intensity, training should be challenging so players approach practice with a positive mindset; players should not dread practice nor feel bored. While there are ebbs and flows, challenge players to maintain motivation.

Tactical Drills

I. Foundation Stage

Americanized Net Ball: A full court, 4v4 game played with two basic rule changes:
1. No dribbling. The ball must advance with a pass.
2. No blocking an offensive player's shot or stealing the ball from an offensive player. A defender may contest a shot or steal a pass, but it is a foul if the defender reaches or blocks, whether the reach or block is "all ball" or not.

Volleyball Passing: Two four-man teams play within the volleyball court lines between the 10-foot line and the end line. No dribble. Teams cut to get open and pivot to improve passing angles. Teams complete passes until one team reaches 100. On a turnover, the player who committed the turnover runs out of bounds and does two push-ups, giving the new offensive team a brief man advantage. The score is continuous; teams pick up where they were when they last had the ball.

3v3 Football: Play 3v3 with no dribble. Objective is to pass the ball the length of the floor and across the baseline (end zone). If a pass is intercepted, or if the ball goes out of bounds, the opponent attempts to pass the ball into its end zone.

3v3/No Dribble: Play 3v3 without the dribble. Objective is to pass, move and screen to get an open shot and make a basket. Depending on numbers, play to one basket (younger) or three baskets (older).

II. Fundamentals Stage

2v2 Rugby: Works best with eight players: four teams of two. Two teams play while two teams rest. A team remains on the court until scored against; if they score, they pick up full court against a new offensive team. Only the dribble advances the ball in the backcourt; all passes must be backwards. Work on the trap and recover defensively and proper spacing offensively: receive the pass and advance quickly up court with the dribble. Play to five.

The Gauntlet: Divide the court into 4 zones – baseline to foul line extended; foul line to half court; half court to foul line; and foul line to baseline. Place two defenders in each zone. They defend only their zone. Two offensive players work through the Gauntlet to score. On any defensive rebound, steal, turnover or out-of-bounds, the offensive pair sprints to the beginning and tries again. If they score, the eight defensive players run. Each offensive pair goes for 2:00.

3v3: Manipulate rules to teach different aspects of the game and keep games short (3-5 baskets). Reinforce good habits and punish bad habits through the rules.

3v3 Cut Throat: Play 3v3. If offense scores, they stay on offense. If defense gets a stop (rebound, turnover), they move to offense, and the offense exits. New team enters on defense. Every time an offensive player receives a pass, they must square to the basket or it is a turnover. Every time an offensive player passes, he must cut or it is a turnover. On any change of possession (basket, defensive rebound, turnover), outlet to the coach and the coach enters the ball into play as a live ball.

String Shooting (Flare): Passing line (with balls) starts on the wing beyond the three-point line and shooting line starts at the top of the key. Passers penetrate middle, jump stop and pass to the shooter. The shooter flares away from the dribbler to create space. Shooter follows his shot and players switch lines.

String Shooting (Follow): The first wing dribbles to the baseline, jump stops and passes to the shooter. The shooter follows to the wing (keeping good spacing) and shoots. Again, shooter follows his shot and the players switch lines. The shooter must keep enough distance between he and the dribbler. Passers reverse pivot to pass out, protecting the ball from the defense.

2v2 Penetrate and Pitch: Confine the court to a certain area to create a penetrate-and-pitch and help-and-recover situation. The offense gets two passes and unlimited dribbles to score. The initial ball handler penetrates to the basket to score; if he cannot beat his man or if he draws help, he kicks to his teammate and creates space for his teammate to penetrate. If the offense scores, they stay on offense and new team enters on defense. If defense stops the offense, they move to offense and new team enters on defense. Play to five.

Arizona Penetrate-and-Pitch Drill: Start with a player on each wing and one at the point with the ball. Point passes to a wing, cuts to the rim and fills the weak side corner. The wing penetrates middle and kicks to the other wing. Wing catches, shot fakes and passes to the point in the corner who catches and shoots.

Wildcat 3v3 Penetration Drill: Play 3v3. Offense must receive the pass outside the three-point line or on a backdoor cut to the rim. Emphasize dribble penetration, reading the defense and finishing at the basket or kicking to a shooter at the three-point line. Keep the floor spaced. If the offense scores, they stay on offense; new team always enters on defense.

Pick-and-Pop Drill: Guard starts with the ball and sets up the screen by taking the defender below the level of the screen. Screener sets the screen and pops wide. Use a second passer to pass to the screener for a jump shot on the first four moves.

- Guard turns the corner on the screen and penetrates into the lane for a floater.
- Guard takes the ball wide with two dribbles and shoots.
- Guard takes the ball wide with two dribbles, hesitates and penetrates into the lane for a jump shot.
- Guard takes the ball wide with two dribbles, hesitates, crosses over and penetrates for a jump shot.
- Guard takes the ball wide with two dribbles and passes to the screener for a shot.

2v2 Pick-and-Pop Drill: Start with the ball on the wing. Offense starts with an on-ball screen. Defense chooses how to play the screen. For practice purposes, coach can change up the defense and tell the defense how to play the screen, but do not tell the offense. Force the offense to read the defense and make the right decision to get a good shot.

III. Training Stage

Utes Shooting Drill: Set up a chair where the player typically receives a screen within the offense and use the screen. Call out your cut as you use the screen: Flare, Curl, Tight Curl or Backdoor. After the players learn the footwork for each cut, the passer calls out the type of defense as the shooter nears the screen, so the offense reacts and makes the appropriate cut.

Utes 2v2 Shooting Drill: P1 starts at the guard spot on offense defended by D1, and P2 starts on the wing defended by D2. Designated passer (DP) starts at the opposite guard spot. P1 passes to the DP and cuts to set a screen for P2. P2 v-cuts. If D1 cheats high to help on the screen or turns his back to P1, P1 cuts to the basket. Otherwise, P1 sets the screen and P2 uses it. Once DP enters the ball, the offense has one pass to score. P2 or P1 can catch and shoot or catch and drive to the basket. If the offense gets an offensive rebound, the ball is live. Possession ends when defense secures the ball or the offense scores. If offense scores, they stay on offense; new team enters on defense; defense must get a stop to play offense.

Foster 1v1 Drill: Offensive player starts on the baseline and the defensive player starts at the free throw line with the ball. Defensive player passes to the offensive player, sprints to half court, turns and picks up the offensive player, attempting to keep him away from the paint. Defensive player must force the offensive player to change directions and not just run right past the defender. Offensive player receives the pass and attacks the basket.

1v2-2v1: One player starts on offense and two players start on defense. The offensive player attempts to advance the ball up court and jump stop in the key for a shot; the defense traps and prevents the offensive player from advancing the ball. On a change of possession (made basket, rebound, steal, violation), the two defenders move to offense and attack 2v1 against the original ball handler.

Rabbit: Teams line up along opposite sidelines. Team A starts with two offensive players at half-court and its first defender protecting its basket; Team B starts with one defender protecting its basket. As soon as Team A crosses half-court, the second Team B player sprints to the center circle and then retreats to help his teammate: the 2v1 fast break becomes a 2v2 game. Offense remains on offense until the defense rebounds or steals the ball; if the offense scores, they rebound and score again. Once Team B gets the ball, Team A's offensive players exit and Team B attacks 2v1 against Team A's first defender; the second Team A defender enters when Team B crosses half-court. Play to seven points.

2v1 Breakdown: Defense starts at the free throw line with the ball and offensive players start on the baseline. Defensive player passes to one of the offensive players and back pedals to half court. The offense advances the ball with the pass until half court and then attacks 2v1 from half court.

Numbers Transition: Players start on the baseline in a single file line. The coach tosses the ball toward the other basket. P1 runs for the ball and attempts to score a lay-up at the opposite basket. P2 tries to stop P1. P3 sprints to the half court circle and then to the opposite free throw line-extended to become an outlet. P4 sprints to the half court circle and then to the free throw line-extended on the opposite side from P3. P5 sprints to the half court circle and then back pedals as a defender. After P1 scores, P2 inbounds to P3 or P4.

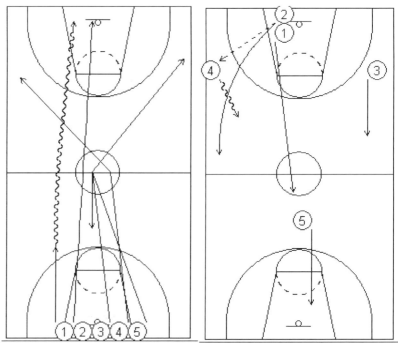

P1 sprints back on defense to team with P5. P2, P3 and P4 attack 3v2. Once the play finishes, the sixth person in line starts as P1 and the drill continues; if there are fewer than 10 players, players jump into line and join the drill immediately.

Army Drill: Drill starts with 3-5 offensive players across the baseline and 3-5 defensive players across from them along the free throw line extended. Throw the ball to one of the offensive players: the offense takes off toward their basket on a fast break. The corresponding defensive player (player across from player who received the ball) must touch the baseline and then get back on defense. All other defensive players must get back to stop the fast break and slow offense until the defensive player recovers.

Transition Progression: Nine players start in the key; five blue offensive players and four red defensive players. Coach tosses the ball to a Blue player and the Red defenders retreat while the Blue offensive players attack 5v4. Once the Blue team shoots, the shooter and the passer step off and the other Blue players sprint back on defense; the four Red defenders secure the rebound and attack offensively 4v3. Once again, the Red passer and shooter step off to create a 3v2 advantage for the Blue and then the Blue passer and shooter step off to create a 2v1 for the Red. Each team starts with the ball. This is a quick drill and forces the offense to communicate as soon as they shoot.

San Diego Transition D: Team A starts on offense with A1 shooting a free throw and A2 on the lane line. Team B has three players along the lane line to rebound. A1 shoots, and Team B rebounds the miss or inbounds the make and attacks 3v2. After Team B scores or Team A rebounds or steals the ball, A3 and A4 join A1 and A2 and attack the three Team B players in a 4v3 break. After Team A scores or Team B rebounds or steals, two new players join the three Team B players and attack in a 5v4 fast break. After Team B scores or Team A rebounds or steals the ball, the A5 joins Team A and the two teams play 5v5 until someone scores.

Shell Drill: Start with four offensive players around the perimeter and four defensive players matched up against each one. As the offensive players swing the ball, defenders sprint and adjust positioning; when the ball is moved, every player must move and position himself in relation to the ball: defenders one pass away should have a hand in the passing lane and those two passes away should be in help position. After players understand proper positioning in relation to the ball, allow offensive players to cut to the basket. Defenders now must deny the basket cuts and then assume proper positioning. In the third stage, allow dribble penetration baseline, so defenders must stop the ball and rotate to protect the basket and force the pass back to the three-point line. After players master the rotations, add a fifth offensive and defensive player in the post. Teach defense positioning (whatever the particular scheme, front, behind, three-quarter front) for the post defenders and also the wing defenders; how to help, how to double, rotations out of the double team. Eventually play the drill live.

Seminole D: Build enthusiasm and pride in getting defensive stops. In a normal scrimmage, score offensive points normally, but give the defense five points (or more) for a stop. If and when either team leads by more than five points, give the trailing team the choice of playing defense or offense. If teams continue to stay on offense (and some will because they know they can't stop anybody defensively), increase the amount of points for a defensive stop. The idea is to reward the stronger defensive team and illustrate how defensive stops can win games, regardless of offensive output.

Scramble: This is a defensive 5-on-4 drill with no offensive restrictions. Defense must hold offense without a shot for a period of time (10 seconds). Drill works mini-transition and also team defense when a player is beaten off the dribble and play does not go into the "shell" form. The top player must cover the ball; the next two players match-up with the next most serious scoring threats and the fourth defensive player plays the weak side, shading towards the basket.

IV. Competition Stage

1v1: Play from different angles with different rules: play full court; start with defense in help and a skip pass; start with a point to wing entry pass; start with ball checked at half court, the three-point line, the block; limit the number of dribbles. Use the rules to emphasize instruction.

50-Point Game: Play 5v5 full court. Count one point for every completed pass and five points for a made basket. Subtract five points for a missed shot and return the score to zero if a player dribbles. The first team to reach 50 points wins.

Chapter 4:
Technical Skills

While technical skills and tactical skills work simultaneously, technical skills are the basketball-specific skills: shooting, ball handling and passing. These skills are easily drilled and instructed in isolation, though their worth is measured in concert with tactical skills because the defense's presence changes everything. Through the different stages, we introduce these skills as part of the game, then work to perfect the skill execution and finally focus on the integration of the skills in the game environment. However, we never want to move too far from the actual game.

Basketball, as a sport, is accessible because Technical Skills dominate the game and anyone can practice these skills on his own. Even an individual sport like tennis requires someone or something to send balls over the net. Basketball players simply need a ball and a basket to train basketball's most important skill: shooting. However, one's technical success depends greatly on his foundation of athletic skills and his tactical awareness.

1. The Foundation Stage

Training Goals: Teach basics (stopping, starting and pivoting), lay-ups, ball handling, and passing.
Emphasis: Fun, teaching skills to enable small-sided competition and modified rules games.

Novice players require basic technical instruction to play small-sided games. However, keep instruction simple and the drills to a minimum. Use small-sided games, especially 2v2, to increase ball handling and shooting repetitions. However, teach the following skills:

- Lay-ups: right and left hand
- Ball handling: speed dribble, protect dribble and a change of direction
- Passing: chest and bounce pass
- Stopping: Quick stop and stride stop
- Pivots: front and reverse
- Protecting the ball: Hard2Guard position, diamond the ball, and space step

> **Lay-up Progression (right-hand)**
>
> **Step 1:** Start just beyond the block facing the basket with feet together. Step and jump off the left foot. Lift the ball into shooting position and follow-through all the way to the basket. Imagine a string running from the elbow to the knee; if the right elbow extends up, the right knee drives up.
>
> **Step 2:** Start one big step away from the block. Step right foot-left foot. Jump off the left foot, lift and follow-through.
>
> **Step 3:** Start from the elbow. Use three steps: step left-right-left. Dribble the ball on the first step and pick-up the dribble with the right hand; bring the left hand to meet the ball. Jump off the left foot, lift the ball and shoot. Eliminate baby steps; use three full strides. Increase speed and move further from the basket.

Lay-ups

Teach players to shoot lay-ups with both hands. In elementary school, my team won two Parochial League Championships. We made 20 right-handed and 20 left-handed lay-ups in a row to start each practice. The lay-up practice made us better players, and the requirement inspired us to practice on our own.

When teaching a new skill, isolate the skill. Rather than start players at the three-point line with a couple dribbles, start near the basket and eliminate dribbling. Once the player improves, train the skills together. Start with the hand behind the ball and aim for the near top corner of the square. Protect the ball from the defense: many players rock the ball across their body to get momentum. Keep the ball outside of the body and use the legs to get the ball to the backboard.

Use the *Extension Lay-up Drill*, *X-Lay-ups*, *Full Court Lay-ups* and other drills to practice shooting lay-ups at game speed from different angles. After mastering the basic technique, increase the speed of execution.

Ball Handling

Dribbling is the easiest skill for young players to master. While we use dribbling and ball handling synonymously, dribbling refers to the action of bouncing and controlling the ball, while ball handling incorporates decision-making abilities, vision, anticipation and other skills players develop as they gain confidence and experience.

While dribbling ability is somewhat overrated – the best ball handlers (Jason Kidd, Steve Nash and Chris

> **Dribbling Technique**
>
> • Dribble with the finger pads and calluses, not the palm.
>
> • Pound the ball: extend from the elbow, not just the wrist and follow-through on the dribble.
>
> • Use an appropriately sized ball.

Paul) rarely use anything more than a change of pace, a crossover or through-the-legs dribble – confidence is instrumental in ball handling development and overall offensive success. Court vision is paramount to a guard's success, and the more confidence the player has dribbling, the more his vision improves. "As a simple rule, the more complex and demanding the centrally performed task, or the more stressed the athlete, the narrower will be the functional visual field size, resulting in errors that coaches often describe as tunnel vision," (Meir). Developing one's dribbling ability early in his career gives a player more confidence, increasing his vision and leading to more success, which increases motivation and confidence.

Use stationary drills like the *Pistol Pete Series* to build the feel and control with the ball. Create challenges with these drills to make the drills more game-like and fun. For instance, do the *Figure-Eight Drill* for 30 seconds and count the number of repetitions. Developing quickness and control with the ball is the primary goal, but ball handling drills also develop hand-eye coordination, rhythm and hand quickness.

In addition to general ball control and quickness, focus on three primary dribbles: Speed Dribble, Protect Dribble and Crossover Dribble.

- Speed Dribble: Use the speed dribble in the open court to go from Point A to Point B as fast as possible. Dribble the ball waist-high. Push the ball out in front and cover as much distance as possible on each dribble.
- Protect Dribble (right): Use a wide stance and an arm bar to protect the ball. Dribble the ball low (mid-thigh) and near the back foot. Put chin to the inside shoulder to keep eyes up the court.
- Crossover Dribble: In the open court without defensive pressure, change hands with the ball by pushing slightly toward the middle of the body. Near a defender, dribble the ball low (knee level) and snap the ball across the body. Bounce the ball toward the foot in the direction of the drive. Receive the dribble at knee level.

Beyond basic drills, like racing up and down the court, use *Red Light-Green Light* to train the speed and protect dribbles: use the speed dribble on a green light and protect dribble on a red light. To train other skills, incorporate a drill like the *Baby Crossover Drill* on a yellow light. Modify the game to train visual cues, not just verbal cues. To ensure players dribble with their heads up, use visual cues to represent the verbal cues: a palm up equals a red light. The *Cone Workout* is another drill to teach players to drive hard and turn the corner on defensive players, and obstacle courses are fun ways to incorporate ball handling.

Passing

Introduce the basic passes, but use games to train the skill. Once players learn the form, throwing the ball is not the weakness; instead, passing problems occur in the tactical execution, the decision-making, the pass' location or the timing. Keep Away games train passing skills; also, *Monkey in the Middle* is a good segue between stationary passing drills and the Keep Away games. The basic basketball passes are:

- Chest Pass: Elbows out, hands on the side of the ball, extend straight from one's chest, aiming for teammate's chest and finish with thumbs down, chest over thigh.

- Bounce Pass: Similar to a chest pass, but bounce the ball one-half to two-thirds of the way to your teammate. The ball should bounce up to the receiver's thigh.
- Overhead Pass: Pass from the forehead, not behind one's head. Aim for teammate's throat. Follow-through and finish with thumbs down. Use as an outlet pass or a skip pass.
- Wrap-around Pass (Air and bounce pass): Extend around the defense with your hands and feet. Step to the defender's side with two hands on the ball; follow-through with your outside hand. Use as a post entry pass.
- Hook Pass: Pass off the dribble. Hook the ball over head and follow-through. Use on a pick-and-roll.
- Push Pass (air or bounce pass): Pass off a dribble. One hand behind the ball and push the ball with arm extending like a horizontal shot. Most commonly used pass, as it protects the ball from the defense by using the outside hand to throw the pass. Quickest pass off the dribble.
- Baseball Pass: A one-hand overhead pass like a baseball player. Finish with thumb down to control the pass.

Stopping

Stopping is an athletic skill and a basketball skill. As an athletic skill, without a ball, two ways to stop are a Lunge Stop (a one-two stop with a staggered stance, like a lunge) and a Hockey Stop (a small hop and 90-degree turn, like an ice skater or a skier). With the basketball, the two stops are a 1-2-stop and a jump stop; I teach two types of jump stops: a quick stop and a jump stop or NBA pro hop and use the quick stop in Stage 1. Teaching the proper way to stop improves basketball skill and injury prevention, as stopping (along with landing and cutting) is where serious knee injuries occur most commonly.

On the stop, emphasize the head and butt; imagine the butt as the anchor. To stop, drop the anchor: sit the hips back and down into a half-squat position with shoulders over knees and knees over toes. Keep your chest and eyes up and head centered over your center of gravity: if the head moves forward, the body falls forward and knocks the player off-balance, leading to a travel.

- Quick Stop (commonly called a jump stop): A two-foot stop on a one-count, either when receiving a pass or off the dribble, with feet shoulder width, knees bent and butt down to stop under control. On the quick stop, the player does not jump into the air, but hops off one foot and lands on two feet. The hop is small, quick and controlled. Land like a ninja, without a sound.
- 1-2-Step: A quick step-step stop off the catch or the dribble. The first step becomes the pivot foot. Sit the hips back and down; flex the ankle, knee and hip to diffuse the force over a larger area and reduce the impact on any one joint. Stop with the shooting foot forward. When a right-handed player stops right-left, he stubs his left foot rather than take a full step to keep his right foot forward.

Pivots

For young players, the pivot foot is difficult. However, using the pivot foot is essential to offensive execution. Too many times, when the defense pressures a young player, he twists and turns with two feet firmly planted. Or, worse, he moves both feet.

The pivot foot is an offensive player's tool to combat pressure. If he has a live dribble, the threat of the dribble is his other tool. However, he always has a pivot foot to create space, turn away from pressure or create a passing angle. A front pivot is when the player pivots in the direction he is facing (leads with his toe); a reverse pivot is when he pivots opposite the direction he is facing (leads with his heel). The pivot foot stays on the floor while the lead foot (free foot) moves. When pivoting, keep 60-70% of one's weight on the pivot foot. Stay low and keep head level; when players rise as they pivot, they slow their pivot.

Players use a permanent pivot foot, an inside pivot foot or a combination. With a permanent pivot foot, the player uses the same foot as their pivot foot, regardless of situation; a right-handed player uses his left foot, and a lefty uses his right foot. With an inside pivot foot, the player uses the foot closest to the middle. A combination uses the permanent pivot foot and the inside foot; when moving toward the basket or when quickness matters, he uses an inside pivot foot; however, when moving away from the basket or when standing and waiting for the pass, he uses his permanent pivot foot. At a young age, teach the inside pivot foot so players learn to use both feet.

Protecting the Ball

Traveling violations and jump balls mar youth games. Training the pivot foot reduces traveling violations and the following concepts alleviate jump balls.

Many coaches teach the triple threat position. I love the concept, but dislike its execution. In fact, the triple threat is so pervasive, rather than correct its execution, I changed the name. I use the Hard2Guard position, which makes players a true threat to pass, shoot or drive. When players learn the triple threat position, they put their pivot foot forward and tuck the ball on their hip, away from the defense. These players are a half-step from turning their back on the defense and "turtling." Turtling is the common position in youth basketball where the player turns his back to the defense and bends over to protect the ball.

Because triple threat position (above left), in practice, is so close to "turtling" (above right), I teach the Hard2Guard position (right). In the Hard2Guard position, the player starts with the ball cocked into shooting position in the shot pocket (roughly the armpit). Body is squared to the basket, eyes toward the basket and lead foot forward. To protect the ball from the defense, keep the ball active using pass fakes, ball fakes, shot fakes and pivots.

Another concept to use with young players is The Box. When defended closely, do not bring the ball through your mid-section, the area between your knees and chest. When sweeping the ball from one side to the other, rip through low with wrists below the knees or rip through high leading with elbows across the hairline.

While the Keep Away games test these skills, use *Utah Line Drills* to train quick stops and pivots. Developing good footwork at an early age improves one's ability to acquire new and more advanced skills later. At this age, playing is more important than fundamental execution. Teach the skills to improve play during the small-sided games and give players the tools to protect the ball.

2. The Fundamentals Stage

Training Goals: Introduce basic skills, teach proper shooting mechanics, increase individual moves, practice basic defensive concepts.

Emphasis: Skill acquisition, general skill development, skill execution and playing against defenders.

Skill acquisition is a process. Nobody exits the womb running. Similarly, players acquire skills gradually: they master a part of a skill, gain confidence and motivation through the mastery, and move to more complicated aspects of the skill. Break learning into pieces and progress through a series of learning stages rather than attacking the whole skill at once.

> **Suggestions**
> - At this age, eliminate the three-point line because players lack the strength and coordination to shoot correctly from behind the arc.
> - Use an appropriately-sized basketball.
> - Emphasize man-to-man defense to prevent teams from playing lazy 2-3 zones.

Emphasize the proper skill execution and encourage players to practice on their own. Nobody masters these skills during this stage; experts agree it takes 10 years to master a skill at an elite level (Balyi, Ericsson). "During this time, children are developmentally ready to acquire general overall sports skills that are the cornerstones of all athletic development," (Balyi and Hamilton).

Shooting is the most important technical skill, and field goal shooting percentage is the number one determining factor in the outcome of games (Oliver). Beyond shooting mechanics, expose players to more ball handling moves, live ball moves, defense, passing and post play. Develop the basic coordination of movements: proper execution is more important than speed of execution.

Shooting Form

Teach players to be makers, not just shooters. A player's range extends as far as he can shoot without a break down in form. The goal is to make shots, and shooting from too far away makes a player a worse shooter. It may hurt the player's ego to shoot close to the basket, but this prepares

> **BELIEF**
>
> **Balance**: Make sure players squat properly; many mistakes result from an improper bending movement. Shoot with shoulders over the knees and knees over the toes in an athletic position.
>
> **Eyes**: Fine center on the basket. Choose a spot (front, back, middle), but be consistent every time.
>
> **Line** (alignment): Straight line extends from the ball, through the hand, wrist, elbow, knee and foot.
>
> **Index Finger**: Center the ball between the index and middle fingers.
>
> **Extension**: Extend from the ankles, knees and hips to power the ball. Elbow extends overhead, so the elbow finishes above the eyes.

him to progress, while a player developing poor mechanics must re-learn to shoot in the future.

I use the BELIEF method to teach proper shooting mechanics, and the *Three in a Row Drill* to restrict a player to his range. The most important ingredient for successful shooting is belief or confidence.

Teach the mechanics from a stationary position and eliminate as many variables as possible. Focus on the starting position (balance and alignment) and the finish (follow-through). Start in an athletic stance with the ball in the Hard2Guard position (next page). When players learn to shoot from the triple threat, they start their shot from their hip and develop a dipping motion. When they start without instruction, they often start in the middle of their body and have a sideways motion. Start from the Hard2Guard position to develop the correct form from the start.

Many kids develop flaws in their shot because they shoot off-balance. Some players do not realize they favor one leg over the other or bend forward with their knees to an off-balanced position. Ensure players bend properly into an athletic position to enable proper power transfer through the shot. Shoot up and through the ball emphasizing the power from the legs rather than pushing the ball to the basket.

From a stationary position, work on shooting off a catch. Pass to a stationary player and train a step-in shooting method. The player steps in to the catch and shoots. Work on stepping in with both feet. Start with his strong foot as the pivot foot; for a right-handed shooter, use the left foot as the pivot foot and step with the right foot on the catch. As the player steps in to his shot, ensure his hips stay flexed and he remains in a crouched position; many players stand upright as they step in and change their body posture to a more erect stance. Once he feels comfortable stepping in with his right foot, use the right foot as the pivot foot and step in with his left foot, which is a half step, as a right-handed shooter shoots with his right foot forward.

In addition to the step-in footwork, work on moving the ball from the catch to the set position. From the catch, sweep the ball to the right side of his body and shift the hand position so his hand is under the ball and the ball, hand and elbow are vertically aligned as the player rotates into his shot. Experienced shooters take this movement for granted, but if the player fails to get the correct hand placement before he gets to the set position, he reduces his accuracy as he lacks consistency. The shot from the set position to the finish is always the same. However, the shot preparation differs for each shot. Emphasize the shot preparation, which finishes at the same point – the set position – every time.

As the player shoots more consistently and successfully, add forward movement. When moving toward the basket, the player must acquire balance and decelerate properly. These skills should be trained during the athletic skills training, but many players need to re-learn habits as part of their shooting instruction. If a player cannot decelerate on balance, he cannot shoot successfully. Many players fall forward as they shoot which limits their upward drive and creates a flat shot. When moving forward to the catch, train the 1-2-step and practice a right-left and left-right step-in. Emphasize the chest and eyes up and the hips down on the catch and teach players to anticipate the stop, so they decelerate on the first step of the 1-2-step, rather than waiting in between their steps to initiate their deceleration.

Catch the ball at the depth of your shot in an athletic position: shoulders over knees and knees over toes. Sit the hips back and down. While most focus on the degree of knee flexion, hip flexion and extension is more important. Rather than instruct players to bend their knees to get more lift on the ball, sit the hips back and down and make sure the shooter fully extends his hips during the shot. The triple extension of the ankle, knee and hip should drive the player straight up, finishing with an erect posture (right), not out with a slightly bent forward posture.

Next, shoot off the dribble while moving straight to the basket. The shot mechanics remain the same. If dribbling with the right hand, a right-handed shooter brings his left hand to the ball as he picks up his dribble. If dribbling with his left hand, he sweeps the ball across his waist to his right hand to pick up his dribble. The right hand stays on the right side of the body, ready to rotate in a straight line into the shot. Step in with a 1-2-step, using the inside foot as the first step. Start in the middle of the court and dribble straight at the basket working on a right-left and a left-right step-in. Then move to different angles, but keep the movement straight to the basket.

Finally, work on curling toward the basket. Use the 1-2-step with the inside foot and square all the way to the basket. Get low on the step-in to stop all momentum and shoot in one plane. Once the player gets the ball to the shot pocket, every shot is the same. However, the beginning of the shot, from the catch to the deceleration to moving the ball to the shot pocket differs. Players cannot practice every possible shot, but if they build good habits with general shots, they can adapt to specific shots during games. Use the *Circle Drill* to teach players the proper footwork and *Elbow Shooting Drill* to practice shots off a curl.

Proper footwork facilitates better balance and a quicker shot; instruct, train and emphasize footwork and balance when shooting, as correct lower body execution ameliorates correct upper body mechanics. Practice game shots from game spots at game speed.

Finishing

When I coached in Europe, a coach told me that American basketball differed from European basketball because European drills finish with a shot. They emphasize scoring or making the basket. In the U.S., players do not spend enough time making shots.

Finishing drills fail to simulate game action. In today's game, with long, athletic defenders, players must be creative finishers. One untaught and unpracticed skill is making shots. Coaches drive out players' creativity through mindless drills. Players get in the lane and do not have a perfect shot or the perfect angle and they get stuck. I teach kids to shoot different shots, but they lack imagination. They struggle when asked to imagine a defender and shoot any shot they want or to jump from five feet out not two or to shoot over me when I stand on a chair. They want to shoot the textbook lay-up. They lack diversity and imagination.

I practice the following shots with players and encourage them to use their creativity once they understand and execute the basics:

- Crossover Lay-up: Start the move on one side of the basket and finish on the other by going across the front of the rim (use the rim to protect the shot). Finish off the backboard with a "hook-like" motion with the hand and wrist. If the move starts on the right side of the court, the player drives across the front of the rim, jumps off his right foot and finishes with his left hand on the left side of the basket.
- Reverse Lay-up: Start the move on one side of the basket and finish on the other by going under the rim (use the rim to protect the shot). Finish off the backboard with the palm to the target. On the shot, turn your shoulders toward the middle of the court. Starting on the right side, drive under the basket, jump off your left foot and finish with your right hand on the left side. "Wave good-bye" as you release the ball and put the ball high off the glass.
- Floater: Use when attacking toward a defender, especially a shot blocker, rather than protecting the ball from your man. The floater is a quick "push" shot: with hand under the ball, shoot the ball as soon as your feet leave the ground and get the ball high so it falls into the basket.

When doing a drill, no cone, trash can or stationary defender can replicate a game situation; however, putting players into game-like situations where they must finish against bigger players, stronger players or quicker players readies the players for similar scenarios in an actual game.

Basketball is not a robotic sport. In baseball, which is less spontaneous, a pitching machine falls short because a hitter must learn to read the pitch. If the player knows what to expect, he can work on his swing mechanics, but he cannot fully experience batting. Basketball, which is more fluid and dependent on external variables, requires players to play to improve; they have to make shots in game-like situations. Simply playing an endless string of games is not the answer, as a player may get only three or four shots in an entire game. Smaller scrimmages provide the repetitions and live defense needed to develop the feel for the game, eliminating the mechanization of the modern player.

Live Ball Moves

The offensive player's greatest advantage is when he first receives the ball, as he is open to shoot or he receives the ball with his defender moving toward him: a quick move against the defender's momentum is more effective than a move against a defensive player who is set and ready. The other important concept is: "A fake is not a fake if it looks like a fake," (Dave Hopla, Washington Wizards' Assistant Coach).

- Drive Step: The first step in an attacking drive. Attack the defensive player's top foot to force the defender to turn his hips. Attack directly past the defender with nose over toes; put your shoulder on the defender's hip, going *body up, body in*. Knock away the defender's hand and keep your inside shoulder low. Extend with the dribble. Keep head and eyes up to see the floor.
- Jab Step: A small step used to set up a move, create space or keep the defender off balance. The jab step must be long enough to make the defender believe it is a drive step, but short enough to keep the offensive player well-balanced. Make a quick, hard step. Rip ball to knee. Keep 60-70% of one's weight on the pivot (push) foot to avoid the travel.
- Space Step: Step your lead leg between the defender's legs; if the defender does not move, sweep low and attack. If the defender gives ground, sweep to a Hard2Guard position to find a teammate, an open shot or an opportunity to attack. Use the space step to clear space and square to the basket when receiving the ball with back to the basket. A quick space step clears space to reverse pivot into a Hard2Guard position or for a sweep-and-go move. The space step is like a jab step, which is more commonly taught, but is a bigger step used to create space and relieve ball pressure, not necessarily to set up an attacking move.
- Shot Fake: Utilize only the upper body; the lower body remains low and ready to explode. The eyes sell the fake and must look at the target. A good fake includes no wasted motion. Make an explosive fake to the hairline.
- Pass Fake: Use to move the defense or hold the help defense, similar to a quarterback faking a hand-off to hold the linebackers. As a rule, the pass fake is used to fake the player who is covering the pass receiver or to freeze scrambling defenders.
- Ball Fake: A smaller, quicker fake used against the player guarding the passer to create a passing angle. Fake low to make an air pass or fake high to throw a bounce pass. The pass follows directly from the fake with no wasted motion.

Play 1v1 to train these skills: (1) Start on the wing with the defense checking the ball; (2) Start at the top of the key with the defense rolling the ball and closing out; (3) Start with offense on a wing, defense in help position and a passer making a skip pass; (4) Start with the offense and defense on the block and passer at the top of the key: offense cuts to get open.

Ball Handling

Train different ball handling moves like a crossover, space dribble, hesitation dribble and fake crossover. Finish ball handling moves with a lay-up, reverse lay-up, crossover lay-up or floater.

The *Number One Rule of Good Ball Handling* is to direct head and shoulders toward the offensive basket to enhance court vision. When the defensive player directs the offensive player to the sideline or forces the offensive player into a protect dribble, the defensive player wins the battle. These four moves enable an offensive player to control the defensive player, to attack the basket and to maneuver out of bad situations.

- Crossover Dribble: Use to change directions. Set-up the defender in one direction and execute a low crossover to go in the opposite direction.
- Space Dribble: Use to create space from the defensive player and square shoulders to the basket; essentially it is a backwards dribble in a protect dribble stance, using the width of the body to protect the ball. Push off on the inside foot and shuffle backward for one to two dribbles.
- Hesitation Dribble: A basic change of speed dribble used to keep the defense off-balance or set up an attacking move.
- Fake Crossover: Use to move the defender in order to maintain a straight line drive. To execute the move, the hand makes a "C" on the downward flight of the dribble, bringing the ball to the middle of the body and then to the outside for the next dribble. To accentuate the ball fake, take a small jab step in the direction of the fake and lean the inside shoulder into the fake.

Stopping

Stage 1 emphasizes the quick stop, but one may also use a true jump stop. The jump stop is a two-foot stop on a one-count usually off the dribble. While a quick stop is quick and controlled, use a jump stop to cover ground and create space away from a defensive player. When stopping on the dribble, the player steps as he picks up the dribble and jumps into the air off his step. He continues moving forward in the air and lands on two feet simultaneously. When receiving a pass, the player steps as he catches the pass and jumps into the air off that step. He lands on two feet simultaneously – in this case, he does not have a pivot foot.

An advanced jump stop is the Bust-Through Move. When the defender is on the offensive player's hip as he penetrates, he uses a big jump stop to explode through and past the defender. Use the Bust-Through Move to split between your own defender and a help defender. When penetrating down the lane for a right-hand lay-up, jump to the left to cut off your defender and make a quarter turn to turn your back to the help defender. Finish with your left hand at the front of the rim. Protect the ball by ripping the ball from your right hand dribble across your hairline to your left shoulder. Land on balance and finish with the left hand.

Post Play

Effective post play relies on the four P's: Positioning, Pivots, Pump Fakes and Patience. Every player, regardless of size or position, benefits from post play instruction and practice because these four factors translate to every area of the court. While perimeter players evade defenders, post players use their footwork and body to create shots. The same skills help a guard fight through a trap or get open against an aggressive defensive player.

Before moving to the four P's, teach players to finish with a power lay-up or a baby hook.

- Power Lay-up: Stop with shoulders squared to the backboard and jump off two feet. Use the outside arm to shoot and the inside arm to protect the ball. Keep the inside hand on the ball until the release of the shot. Keep the inside hand's palm to the ball and use the arm to find the defender's arm and protect the ball.
- Baby Hook: Rather than squaring shoulders to the rim, the front shoulder points to the rim with the feet perpendicular to the basket. Turn your chin to the front shoulder. Keep both hands on the ball until the release to use the body to protect the ball. Take the ball directly from the shoulder/chest in a straight line to two o'clock for a right-handed hook shot or 10 o'clock for a left-handed hook shot. The arm extends straight up from the shoulder through the elbow and the wrist, with the wrist and hand pointed toward the target. With the shooting elbow locked, the hand and wrist-snap propel the ball to the basket. The follow-through finishes toward the target, very similar to the finish of a jump shot.

To get players started, teach players some basic moves. The three easiest moves are:

- Drop Step Power Lay-up: Drop the bottom foot toward the basket, sealing the defender. Use one dribble, gather with shoulders parallel to the backboard and finish with a power lay-up.
- Step Middle Jump Hook: Step to the middle with the top foot to seal the defender's top foot. Dribble and gather on two-feet with inside shoulder pointed to the rim. Shoot the baby hook.
- McHale Up And Under: Step to the middle with the top foot, dribble, gather with two feet with front shoulder to the rim, show the ball high and then step through and past the defensive player to the basket. Can also make the same move to the baseline.

When receiving the ball in the post, whether from a pass or an offensive rebound, use the Diamond Position (right). This position replaces the traditional "chin it." Rather than get a rebound and chin the ball, diamond the ball: protect the ball by the back ear with elbows out, forming a diamond with the ball and body. This position protects the ball from a defender, while positioning the player for a put back off an offensive rebound or to outlet the ball off a defensive rebound.

These are the basics. To teach positioning, have players post with their bottom foot above the block. This gives the player room to attack to the baseline or the middle with a good angle. Square feet to the ball and create a line running from passer to post player to the basket removing the defender from the play. Do the work before the catch: work to receive the ball with two feet in the paint to facilitate an easy score. Make contact with the defender and use a front or reverse pivot to turn toward the ball. Sit on the defender's knee to eliminate his quickness. Once the player receives the pass, diamond the ball and look over the opposite shoulder. Do not rush the move. Feel the defense, find the help defender and make a move accordingly.

Once a player learns the basics, he can use any combination of pivots and pump fakes to get the defender off-balance and create the space needed to score. From the low post, players should aim to use no more than one dribble to score. Use drills like the *Mikan Drill, Peth's Post Positioning Drill* and basic *Block2Block Post Move Drill* to teach basic footwork and finishing in the post and use 1v1 and 2v2 games to prepare players to use the moves in a game.

A player who uses his body to create separation, utilizes pump fakes to keep the defender off-balance and uses front and reverse pivots consecutively without traveling is a well-rounded and effective player. In the NBA, point guards Tony Parker and Steve Nash use these concepts in the paint as well as any post player. The great scorers in recent NBA history used fakes, pivots and spins like a post player: MJ created space for a fade-away jump shot and then for his step-step counter move by getting into the defense and spinning away; Kobe does similar things; Paul Pierce uses spins, fakes and pivots to get to the free throw line.

Individual Defense

Individual defense largely depends on a player's lateral quickness, basketball intelligence and desire. However, there are some defensive concepts to teach to help defenders improve. Once players learn the lateral movement through the athletic drills, combine the skill with the proper positioning and play 1v1 to train individual defensive skills.

Defensive positioning depends on a team's defensive strategy. Some teams force players to their weak hand, while some force to the sideline-baseline. I teach players to close out to force to the sideline-baseline. When playing against a shooter, make the shooter dribble to a shot. Do not allow a catch-and-shoot shot. However, if the player is not a great shooter, contain the dribble and force him to be a shooter. The difference is the degree of one's closeout. Against a shooter, the defender closes out so he can touch the shooter. Against a non-shooter, the defender leaves separation on the closeout and inches closer if the offensive player does not attack.

To teach positioning, start from a live ball position in different areas of the court. Above the free throw line, the defender's backside is toward the baseline; below the free throw line, his backside is toward the opposite sideline. As the offensive player holds the ball, the defender's nose stays on the ball: the defender cheats a half-step in the direction of the ball rather than playing nose to nose. When defending a stationary offensive player, use a wide stance. The best way to defend a player is to dissuade the player from making a move. With a wide stance, the offensive player has to go around the defender, not past the defender, and the driving lanes appear smaller. Keep the feet active: as the offensive player moves the ball, the defender's positioning constantly changes. Also, use active hands to distract the offensive player. Force the offensive player to devote his attention to protecting the ball. When defenders keep their hands by their side, they make it easy for an offensive player to play with confidence, see the floor and make positive moves. If the defender jabs at the ball or traces the ball with one hand, he forces the offensive player to protect the ball which reduces his aggressiveness.

Most coaches focus on stopping the first dribble. However, the offensive player gets to say "Go!" The offensive player moves first and stopping the first step is almost impossible. Instead, focus on the second step or dribble. Defenders must defend the drive step and the jab step in the same way because the defender risks getting beat if he anticipates. Defenders must honor fakes, but not over-commit. If a defender fails to honor the first move, and the offensive player makes a move not a fake, the defender has no chance to stop the offensive player. As the offensive player makes his move, give ground with the hip turn on the first step and use a crossover step to recover. Recover with the nose on the ball by the second dribble.

When defending a ball handler attacking with speed, never stand flat-footed and never square all the way to the dribble. Use a narrower stance and keep your feet moving. Contain and slow the dribbler; as he reaches the scoring zone, force the player in one direction – preferably to his weak hand – and play the drive. If the player is on the sideline, keep him there and do not over-commit and allow him back to the middle. Contain the straight-line drive to the basket by keeping your nose ahead of the ball on his inside shoulder. If he is in the middle of the court, do not allow a straight-line drive to the basket. Force the player to change directions and play the crossover, trying to force the player as wide as possible on his change of direction.

3. The Training Stage
Training Goals: Create attack-minded players, advance previously learned skills.
Emphasis: Creativity, training skills for game-play, adding intensity to the drills and speed of skills.

The Training Stage advances previously introduced skills, nurtures attack-minded, aggressive players and incorporates basic skills into game-specific situations. Offensively, cultivate the Hard2Guard Mentality. Defensively, develop aggressive, smart defenders who understand situations and take advantage of the offense's weaknesses. Skill development complements the tactical, decision-making training by developing the skills and confidence to exploit these mental skills.

The Hard2Guard Mentality

A great pitcher controls a baseball game unless he makes a mistake (gets behind in the count, hangs a curveball). All pitchers are hittable, but a great pitcher dominates hitters. A Hard2Guard player maintains similar control. The pitcher initiates the action. The hitter can anticipate and start his swing early when facing a fastball pitcher or step up in the box against a knuckleballer, but if he guesses wrong, he gets beat. Similarly, the offense initiates the action: the offensive player says, "Go!"

When playing 1v1, we give the advantage to the offense. However, when we add players, we favor the defense. While basketball is a team game, 1v1 action occurs on every play. One defensive player cannot stop a player like Kobe Bryant, Chris Paul or Dwyane Wade; they have the ability, but, more importantly, the mindset. They force the defense to stop them. Most players catch the ball and believe they are guarded.

This is not an invitation for selfish play, frivolous dribbling or dominating the ball. However, players must look to create scoring opportunities and attack the defense. They must possess the mindset that an individual player cannot stop them. This attitude, confidence and mindset separate the good players from the great players.

Hard2Guard is an attitude. The confidence to make a move or take the shot is the most important attribute. Wade, Kobe and Paul separate from the pack because of their mental approach, their fearlessness, and their confidence. An aggressive, attacking attitude puts fear in the opposition. A strong understanding of how to defeat various defenses and a strong mental preparation lead to a successful Hard2Guard player.

Shooting

In Stage 3, start with the same shooting skills as Stage 2, but add intensity, speed, volume and distance. Shoot game shots from game spots at game speed.

Early in this stage, players develop more strength and move from a set shot to a true jump shot. Players adjust their set point and their release to shoot from a higher point. Through these improvements, players often take a step backward before moving forward. As they add the jump to their shot, they struggle with their coordination. Manage a player's confidence and encourage the learning process.

When moving to a jump shot, the problem is shooting on the way down or floating in the direction of the pre-shot movement. Emphasize the footwork to acquire balance before the shot, which leads to balance throughout the shot. Some players – like Kobe – can shoot off-balance shots because they acquire balance in the air. Kids at this age cannot. Shoot early in the jump and shoot the ball high. When players elevate their set point, they flatten their shot. Shoot the ball up then out, like shooting out of a telephone booth.

In this stage, work on game-type shots, especially shots off a cut away from the basket. Emphasize the square to the basket and balance. If players do not acquire balance, they fade away as they shoot. Work on shooting off flare cuts, straight line cuts away from the basket and flashes to the baseline corner.

Finishing

Beyond the basic finishes, there are several other finishes for players to learn and add to their repertoire:

- Inside Hand Lay-up: Jump off the outside foot and shoot a lay-up with the inside hand. Extend with the ball and turn your back toward the defender.
- Duck-Under (Steve Nash Hook): Attack the basket like a lay-up. Use the last two steps as a stride stop – for a right-handed lay-up, stop right-left. Show the ball on the stop and do not lift the right foot. Front pivot on the right foot away from the defense and finish with a left-handed hook.
- Duck-Under Step-Through: Attack the basket like a lay-up. Use the last two steps as a stride stop – for a right-handed lay-up, stop right-left. Show the ball on the stop and do not lift the right foot. Front pivot on the right foot away from the defense and fake the hook shot. Step through with the left foot and finish with a lay-up.
- Runner: Shot like a jump shot, but jump off one leg and continue moving forward on the shot to "run" away from your defensive player. Shoot around the free throw line when you beat your man, but the lane is congested.
- Running Hook: Shoot like a lay-up, except keep your inside shoulder toward the defender and use the width of your body to protect the ball. Finish with a hook-like motion over your head, rather than in front of your body.
- Spin: Use against body contact. Plant your inside foot on the final dribble; keep ball in the same hand and reverse pivot to the basket, sealing the defender; as your foot steps down, pick up the dribble with both hands, front pivot so both feet are squared to the baseline and finish with a power-lay-up.

Ball Handling

As players develop better moves, quickness and control with the ball, increase their ball handling arsenal. The four additional change of direction moves are:

- Spin Dribble: Use against body contact. While dribbling from right to left with your left hand, plant your right foot and reverse pivot. Take the ball with you: spin with your left hand on top of the ball. Dribble while the ball is protected from the defense. Seal the defender and explode towards the basket.
- Through-the-Legs: Like a crossover, except the front leg protects the ball from the defender's reach. If dribbling from right to left, step forward with the left leg and bounce the ball behind your left foot. Point your left foot in the direction of the drive to open your hips.
- Behind-the-Back (pull back): To protect the ball, crossover behind the back. Quick stop and sit down in a low stance. Dribble the ball under your butt. Body and ball move together; if dribbling from right to left, the player moves slightly to the left to protect the ball.
- Around-the-back (open court): Wrap the ball around the back, bouncing the ball on the side of your foot and pushing the ball forward, not straight down. If going right to left, pull the ball around your back with your right hand to the left side.

Challenge players to handle the ball under pressure and make decisions off the dribble. Ball handling encompasses more than dribbling; players must use the dribble to make a play.

Incorporate ball handling moves into shooting drills, so players shoot directly off the move. This trains the reception of the dribble, which is where most moves break down.

While players need continued development of their ball control and quickness, add defense and use1v1, 1v2 and 2v2 drills to train ball handling. 2v2 penetrate-and-pitch drills teach players to beat their man and read the help defender, either finishing at the rim or kicking to their teammate for the open shot.

In games, players often make the wrong pass/shot decision. In penetration, we condition players – especially point guards – to think pass first. Instead, penetrate to score. Passing is the second option, not the first. To create the passing lane, a player must force a help defender to defend the ball. Otherwise, a pass goes to a more defended player. When a player draws the help defender, he has done his job to get a teammate open and should pass to the open teammate.

Often, the player penetrates and with no defensive pressure, he gets his head up to see the floor. He makes the pass because a teammate appears open, even though he did not draw the help defender, so the defender can recover and play the pass receiver. Then, when he penetrates and draws a help defender, he shoots because the ball pressure diverts his attention away from finding the open player. He shoots because he knows where the basket is, but not his teammates. The ball pressure forces his attention to protecting the ball and away from finding the open player. Ball pressure creates the indecision which leads to a bad shot, while the passive mindset leads to a bad pass. Practice the principles of penetration for times when the play breaks down or a player makes an aggressive move to the basket. Confidence with the ball increases a player's field of vision under pressure, and awareness of his teammates' tendencies helps a ball handler find the open player when facing a split-second decision under pressure.

Post Play

Practice a go-to move and a counter to each shoulder and increase a player's repertoire of moves and speed of execution. Train moves against contact, finishing through a defensive player. Focus on finishing with shoulders squared to the baseline, not the basket to protect the shot from the defense. Learn to fend off defenders with the inside hand without extending to draw a foul call. Train moves from a step off the block, the short corner and high post; work on passing out of a double team and splitting defenders to get to the basket. Three additional basic moves are:

- Quick Spin (against an aggressive defender leaning on the offensive player): Make a quick front pivot on the baseline foot and step to the basket; extend with the dribble. Use the elbow on the turn to nudge the defense away from the basket. Finish with a power lay-up or a reverse lay-up.
- Quick Spin Duck Under: Make a quick front pivot on the baseline foot and step to the basket; extend with the dribble. Stop with a stride stop under the basket and front pivot for a reverse lay-up or baby hook. On the left block, pivot on the right foot. Step with the left foot and dribble. Keep the left foot on the ground and step with the right foot. Pick up the dribble and fake a shot, like jumping for a reverse lay-up on the right side of the basket. Front pivot on the left foot and finish with a right-handed hook on the left side of the rim.
- Reverse Move off Dribble: Player steps with top foot into the middle of the key. As the defender moves to cut off the move to the middle, the offensive player dribbles and drops

his bottom foot to the basket, making a reverse pivot with the top foot, sealing the defender's bottom foot. He gathers on two feet and finishes with a power lay-up.

In addition to the detailed moves, a post player can simply pivot to the basket and attack, especially if the defender plays behind the offensive player. Since most instruction starts on the right side of the court, and most right-handed players favor their left foot as their pivot foot, most reverse pivot moves sweep and attack to the baseline. Many times, players get stuck on the baseline with nowhere to go.

I teach an inside pivot because it creates consistency between the low post, mid-post and high post. In the high post, I demand an inside pivot because most high post plays involve a backdoor cut, and the inside pivot creates a better passing lane and protects the ball from the defender. On the right side of the court, the inside pivot uses the right foot. The player opens to the middle of the court and creates more space for a drive to the baseline side or to the middle. The basic moves off the inside foot reverse pivot are:

- Sweep and Go: Reverse pivot and sweep the ball low, driving past the defensive player with a quick, long first step. On the right side of the floor, with the right foot as a pivot foot, make a half turn reverse pivot and extend with the left foot to the basket dribbling with the left hand.
- Sweep and Shoot: Same move, except this time the defender retreats on the aggressive sweep move creating space to shoot.
- Sweep-Jab and Go: Reverse pivot and sweep the ball low. Step aggressively on the sweep and rip ball to knee. Use a crossover step to attack. On the right side with the right foot as the pivot foot, reverse pivot and step to the middle with the left foot. As the defender reacts, step past the defender with the left foot while dribbling with the right hand.

Players can use these three moves anywhere on the court when they receive a pass with their back to the basket. Post players can use these moves in the low post, high post and short corner, while perimeter players can use the moves on the perimeter when they cut to receive the pass and use their body to protect the ball from their defender on the catch.

Use 2v2 post drills. Post players develop slowly because they do not receive enough competitive touches. 2v2 helps post players adjust to defenders and make game moves just like 2v2 on the perimeter for guards.

4. The Competition Stage
Training Goals: Enhance and refine skills; prepare for game execution.
Emphasis: Competitive skills, playing to one's strengths and peak performance

In this stage, most technical skill development occurs during the off-season, as players dedicate time and effort to deliberate practice, which is necessary to elevate a player's skills to another level. If players develop properly, skill development is small changes and tweaks to make good skills into great skills.

The major focus is perceptual skills – reading the situation and the cues of defenders and teammates to make quicker decisions and faster moves. Players do not have time to think. They must notice subtle cues and take advantage. When a defender leans forward on a shot fake, the player must attack immediately. Many players make a fake, and it works, but they notice too late and do not take advantage. Use dynamic and variable drills rather than static drills and include an offensive and defensive player in most drills.

During the season, develop skills within the team's system and refine skills. Use small-sided games, 1v1, 2v2 or 3v3 to train technical skills at game speed against live defense. While players need continued practice on the basics, their ability to perform skills against defense determines their success.

Technical drills serve as conditioning drills and train multiple skills. A partner shooting drill like *Interval Curls* trains game-like shooting, conditions the athlete and works on passing and receiving skills. Full court ball handling drills like the *Logger Drill* and post footwork drills like *Tap-Outlet-Finish* train game-specific conditioning.

During a training week, or even every practice, use the basic instructions and drills from the initial stages: players never outgrow fundamental training. Even when coaching professionally, I used the *Three in a Row Drill* every practice and started every post breakdown with the *Mikan Drill*.

University of South Carolina football coach Steve Spurrier believes there are Everyday Drills, which train basic fundamentals. Players never get too old or too good to practice the basics and those who spend the most time practicing fundamentals are typically the best players. During a San Antonio Spurs game, the analyst was surprised to see Tony Parker working on lay-ups with an assistant two hours before tip-off; he said players typically practice only jump shots. But, Parker was rewarded with a trip to the All-Star Game.

Make technical drills competitive to ensure maximum effort and speed. Shooting drills like *30* train multiple shots from different spots and test shooting accuracy and speed.

Shooting

In Stage 4, players fill various roles within their team. Some players are shooters, and some are not. Some developed the skill according to the model, while others pick up bad habits along the way and struggle with their shooting consistency.

For those with well-developed shot mechanics, expand their range and introduce different shots, like a step-back and shooting off a spin. Work on shooting intensity and maintaining solid mechanics through fatigue. Raise the level of expectations and focus on tactical aspects of shooting, like shot selection and creating space to take a shot. Make the shot fake into a real weapon.

For those with poor shot mechanics, the approach depends on the player. Some players understand their competitive careers are nearly finished and lack the motivation to re-learn proper shooting habits. Others have enough other tools to move to the next level and have the motivation to change their shot.

For those who lack motivation to change, focus on shot selection and taking shots within their range. Concentrate on free throw shooting and developing consistency from the line. Put them in a role which does not require a lot of outside shooting and allow them to play to their strengths.

For those with a chance at the next level and the motivation to change their mechanics, start at the beginning and dedicate time to the basic form. Start close to the basket and concentrate on the mechanics, not the makes. Shooting development is a process, not an overnight event, and players need patience to re-learn their mechanics.

Other technical skill training involves position breakdown; use breakdown sessions to reinforce the team's system and general position-specific skills.

Point Guard

The point guard is the floor general and an extension of the coach. Beyond basic ball handling and shooting skills, point guards need a high basketball IQ; the position requires a thorough understanding of the game and the coach's philosophy. Use drills to work on handling traps (*1v2/2v1*); train penetrate and kick (*String Shooting, Berkeley Pass and Finish*); use the pick and roll; make decisions in transition (*3v2*); shoot off the dribble (*One Dribble Pull-ups*) and finish shots in the key.

Focus on mental skill development with the point guards. They need to understand the coach's system to become an extension of the coach on the court. The mental skills transition a good ball handler into a true point guard. As the games get faster, point guards must slow the action to make better decisions. Point guards need to understand the opponent's defense. The best way is to see how they defend the low post:

- Do they front? If so, is the lob available? If the help defense cheats for the lob, is the skip pass available?
- Do they play behind? If so, can your post score 1v1? Will they double team? If so, will they double off the passer, post to post or from the top?
- Do they ¾ front? If your post can hold position, dribble to create a passing lane. If defense plays high, dribble to the baseline and feed the post. Or look to drive baseline, as post can act as a screen on the help defender.

Put point guards in challenging situations: in a scrimmage, use an extra player to pressure the point guard in the back court, effectively playing 5v6 in the back court into a 5v5 scrimmage. Concentrate on changing speeds to control the defense and keep the defense off-balance rather than allowing the defense to speed up the game and get the point guard playing faster than he wants.

Point guards must develop on-court leadership skills to be an extension of the coach. They need to learn to use stopped clock time to urge, encourage and instruct:

- Make sure everybody knows his man, especially on a substitution.
- Point out mismatches.
- Let teammates know how the opponent defends the post and what is available.

Wing

Wing breakdown sessions train ball handling, creating one's own shot, shooting off cuts within the offense and passing into the post. Breakdown the proper way to set up and use screens (straight cut, flare, curl, backdoor, etc.), as well as creating space without a screen. Work on individual live ball moves and creating space for a shot (step-back jumpers). Train passing into the post with a *Block Passing Drill*. Work on the footwork on the reception of the pass off different cuts in the offense and attacking directly off the catch or pivot. Use live defenders to practice reading defenders and reacting to slight cues.

Post

Post breakdown reinforces the general footwork and trains posts to get open and provide a passing lane for the wings. Practice moves from spots where players get the ball in games, whether off offensive rebounds, on the low block or in the short corner. Incorporate defense into post drills as few interior shots occur without a defensive presence and reading and taking advantage of the defense is the most important post skill to learn and the most difficult to teach.

Keep the instructions and moves simple. Find them, feel them and seal them: create and keep contact. Many post players learn new move after new move and suffer paralysis from analysis. Focus on positioning, patience, pivots and pump fakes, not mastering 101 different moves.

When fronted, seal toward the baseline to protect a lob pass from help defenders (right). Call for the ball with both hands and use your hip to hold off the defender. Do not release for the ball until you can see the ball through your hands. Do not spend energy fighting for position. If the defender pushes you away from the basket, relax for a second and then re-post. Use the Don Nelson Move rather than wrestling for position: Stick foot between the defender's legs and your knee into his crotch. Pivot and seal the defender. Sit on his knee to take away his mobility.

When a teammate penetrates, make yourself a threat. If your teammate drives to your bottom foot, circle up the lane line or under the basket to the opposite block. If your teammate drives at your top foot, circle toward the short corner. Square shoulders to the dribbler at all times and keep hands up to receive the pass.

Post players need to read the defense and make quick moves. Work against double teams and practice passing in tight spaces, like block to block.

Beyond position breakdown, skill refinement and conditioning, additional technical practice occurs through tactical training. Once technical skills reach a satisfactory performance level, the next step is game application, which requires practicing skills in a game environment with multiple repetitions.

To elevate your technical skills to the next level requires an off-season commitment to deliberate practice. Deliberate practice requires a specific goal, concentration, immediate feedback and sufficient repetitions. In-season practices lack these qualities because of the group dynamic. Therefore, for real skill improvement, off-season deliberate practice with a coach or trainer is necessary.

Chapter 4B
Technical Skill Progressions

The followings skill progressions break down the basic technical skills into easy to use descriptions with common mistakes and teaching points. The Skill Progressions are a review of the different skills covered in Chapter 4 combined with some new and more specific information to assist with feedback and instruction.

Progressions

Ball Handling Progression	p. 110
Finishing Progression	p. 114
Passing Progression	p. 119
Post Play Progression	p. 122
Shooting Progression	p. 126

Ball Handling Skill Progression

Skill Progression	Demonstrated Ability	Common Flaws	Teaching Points
Stationary dribbling	Maintain control of ball with both hands in a stationary stance.	Slapping at the ball Dribbling with the palm Looking down at the ball; Poor posture; Ball controls the player.	Keep hand rounded, but fingers remain firm Pound the ball – make the ball noisy Follow-through Push from the elbow, not just the wrist Dribble with the fingers and the calluses; Sit down in an athletic stance - chest and eyes up.
Stationary high-low dribble	Maintain control with hand on top of the ball and "kill" the dribble to a low dribble (shoe strings) and pound the ball to a high dribble (waist level).	Scooping the ball rather than pounding it Tapping the ball with the weak hand	Keep hand on top of the ball; move the body position, not just the ball height; use the full arm to pound the ball from a low to high dribble.
Stationary crossover	Maintain control of the ball while pounding the ball from one hand to the other. Keep the ball out of the palm and wrist – receive the ball with the fingers and push back immediately.	Ball too high Lack of control Eyes looking at the ball Poor posture	Hand on the side of the ball Push across your body Fingers point to the floor Bounce the ball at least in the center of the body Receive the ball low
Walking/jogging with the dribble	Maintain control of the ball while moving forward in a straight line.	Tapping the ball with the weak hand Bouncing the ball straight down rather than pushing it ahead Carrying the ball.	Make contact with the ball toward the back of the ball with the palm slightly lower than the fingers to push the ball forward
Running with the dribble	Maintain control of the ball with eyes up while running forward.	Ball in the palm of the hand Hand under the ball (carrying) Slapping the ball with a flat hand Ball controls the player	Keep ball in the fingers and calluses Push the ball in front
Stopping with the dribble	Stop quickly and maintain control of the dribble.	Ball in front of the player	Sit hips down Chop steps

Skill Progression	Demonstrated Ability	Common Flaws	Teaching Points
	Protect the dribble or come to a jump stop on-balance.	Exposing the ball to the defense Standing too tall Off-balance	Dribble the ball by the back leg Lower the dribble Control the ball with the fingers
Protect dribble	Turn inside shoulder toward the defense, protect the dribble by the back foot and maintain control with eyes forward (chin on the inside shoulder).	Expose ball to defense; fail to look up the floor; slap the ball; dribble too high.	Keep chin on the front shoulder to see the floor; look at the offensive basket; keep an arm bar up; dribble low and by the back foot; change the rhythm of the dribble.
Shuffling with the dribble	While maintaining control of the ball, shuffle forward, pushing off the back foot, and shuffle backward, pushing off the front foot.	Expose ball to the defense; switch hands with the ball when stopping; stand too tall; eyes down; crossing feet.	Stop quickly; create space on the first push; keep hand on top of the ball; push ball in the direction player is moving.
Retreating with the dribble	To move away from the defense or create space for an offensive move, pull the dribble back, stay low and push away from the defensive player with a backward gallop (push off the inside foot and keep the inside foot forward rather than a normal stride).	Exposing the ball to the defense Tiny steps – too slow Off-balance.	Use the push to create space but keep shoulders squared to the basket and stay prepared to make the next move; keep chest and eyes up to see the floor.
Changing hands with the ball	In the open floor, change hands with the ball on each dribble so the defense cannot steal the ball from behind.	Carrying the ball Keeping the ball too close to the body	Push the ball out in front Use a hip-high dribble Remain under control and prepared to make a move or stop quickly Attack at 80% speed
Changing speeds with the ball	While attacking with the dribble, change speeds with a stop-and-go, skip, stutter-step or simply slowing down and accelerating by pushing the ball out in front.	No acceleration Head down Not enough variance between fast and slow Carrying the ball.	Change body posture on the acceleration Inside shoulder down Use the change of pace to keep defender off balance or to set-up a move Sell the fake Do not rush
Change of direction w/stop or	Change pace to set up a change of direction. Off the hesitation, use an over	Fail to protect the ball No acceleration	Sell the fake Crossover toward the leg in the direction you are going

Skill Progression	Demonstrated Ability	Common Flaws	Teaching Points
hesitation	the top, waist-high crossover, and protect the dribble with the body while moving past the defender.	Insufficient fake Eyes down Carrying the ball.	Push ball out in front Inside shoulder down
Change of direction with attack	Set up the defender in one direction, plant, push with the outside foot and crossover toward the foot in the direction of the drive. Explode past the defender with the next dribble.	Too high Ball in the palm of the hand Bounce ball in the middle of the body No push-off Stop before the move Stand-up after the move Fail to protect the ball	Plant your foot outside the body Receive the dribble low and push the ball forward Keep the ball in the fingers Be quick with the ball Get the crossover dribble toward the foot in the direction of the drive Inside shoulder down Drive directly past the defender
Pass off the dribble	Use a quick motion to take the ball directly from the dribble to the push pass.	Ball to the middle of the body; pass with the inside hand; travel; one-hand pass; too much wasted motion.	Bring the off-hand to the ball; use the outside hand; follow-through, much like a shot; quick pass from the hip; pick-up the dribble with hand behind the ball, not on top.
Behind the back dribble	Use a jump stop off a speed dribble to create separation from the defender and put the ball behind the back to protect the dribble; move in direction of the dribble.	Bounce the ball too far forward Stand-up on the dribble Push hips forward Receive the ball too high Allow the ball into the palm and the wrist	Pound the ball behind the back, just like a crossover Move with the ball – body and ball together Keep the ball tight to the body Use body to protect the ball
Through the legs dribble	Execute the through-the-legs dribble just like a crossover, except the ball bounces behind the heel of the front foot.	Wasted movement Ball in the palm Unnecessary skip or shuffle Stand-up on the dribble No follow-through Lack of control on the reception of the dribble	Open the hips in the direction of the move Change directions on the move, not after Point toe in new direction Pound and sweep the ball low Receive the ball low and keep the ball in the fingers
Around the back dribble	On the run, put the ball all the way around the back and use the body to protect	Ball bounces behind the player, not in front	Attack the defender Wrap the ball all the way around the back – ball

Skill Progression	Demonstrated Ability	Common Flaws	Teaching Points
	the ball while blowing past the defender with little hesitation.	Wrong situation – not a half court move or a move when tightly defended Loose with the ball Ball too far away from the body or too high	bounces next to your foot, not behind it Hand follows through to the opposite hip Keep the ball tight to the body Stay low
Spin Dribble	Against body contact, plant the inside foot, protect and pull the ball through, pivot and extend with the dribble away from the defender.	Change hands with the ball too soon Change hands too late Palm the ball Travel Stand-up too tall No body contact with the defender No seal No extension	Use the dribble to lead in the direction of the drive Hand on top of the ball Use against body contact – never in open space Lead with the ball Stay low to absorb contact and maintain line to the basket Seal the defender Never expose the ball to the defense
Double moves	Combine different moves. Use the first move to set up the defender and explode past the defender with the second.	Unnecessary hesitation Not fluid with the ball Ball in the palm Lack of control Ball too high between the first and second move	Use a hesitation if intentional, as one of the two moves – otherwise, avoid unnecessary skips or shuffles Change the cadence of the dribble Read the defense Stay low Explode past the defender – do not belly-out.

Finishing Skill Progression

Skill Progression	Demonstrated Ability	Common Flaws	Teaching Points
Form Lay-up	Begin at the block with feet together; step with inside foot, jump and shoot the lay-up with the outside hand underneath the ball and off-hand supporting the ball.	Throwing the ball Jumping off the wrong foot Using two hands Not practicing your weak hand Off-hand not supporting the ball Ball in the palm	Jump up like a rocket, not out like an airplane Isolate the skill - no dribble Keep ball in the fingers and calluses Follow-through Extend arm all the way to the basket.
Two-step Lay-up	Step away from the basket; for a right-handed lay-up, step with the right foot (outside foot) then the left foot (inside) and jump off the left foot and shoot the right-handed lay-up with right hand under the ball and left hand supporting it.	Stutter-step Twisting body Ball in the palm Shooting underhand Shooting out, not up Shooting too flat Aiming too low.	Be prepared to jump on the second step Shoot the ball early in the jump Push up and through the ball Aim for the top corner of the square on the backboard.
One-dribble Lay-up	Start outside the elbow; step with the inside foot first, dribble with the outside hand, step outside foot, inside foot; jump off the inside foot and shoot the lay-up with the outside hand.	Stutter-steps Rock the ball across the body Swing the ball up to the basket; pick up the dribble with the inside hand, not the outside hand	Extend with the dribble Jump up, not out Shoot high off the glass Get low on the first step Bring the off-hand to the ball Protect ball from the defender.
Speed Lay-up	Start at half court (and progress to full court) and dribble with the outside hand as fast as possible to the basket and finish a lay-up with the outside hand, jumping off the inside foot.	Jump off wrong foot Rock the ball across the body Pick up the dribble with the inside hand Slow down into the shot	Extend with the dribble Jump up not out Get low on the last dribble to control your jump Shoot the ball softly

Skill Progression	Demonstrated Ability	Common Flaws	Teaching Points
		Shoot the ball too hard.	Hit the glass on the ball's downward flight High off the glass.
Inside Hand One-dribble Lay-up	Start outside the elbow; step with the outside foot first, dribble with the outside hand, step inside foot, outside foot; jump off the outside foot and shoot the lay-up with the inside hand, extending with the ball and turning back toward the defender.	Wrong foot Expose ball Only use strong hand and avoid the weak hand Fail to understand when to use Stutter steps.	Extend with the ball Shoot with hand under the ball Use body to protect the ball Get underneath and inside the defender, rather than protecting the ball high and wide Use to stay in stride, avoid taking an extra step and to surprise a shot blocker Extend with your last step into the defender's body.
Crossover One-Dribble Lay-up	Start outside the elbow; use a crossover step with the outside foot to go across the front of the rim and finish off the backboard on the other side of the rim. Finish with a "hook-like" motion, with the hand and wrist.	Too many steps Stutter steps Poor angle Use too much English, rather than the proper angle.	Finish with both hands high Wide shoulders: use the width of the body to protect the ball Bring off-hand to the ball.
Reverse One-dribble Lay-up	Start outside the elbow; step with the inside foot with a crossover step and attack under the basket with an outside hand dribble; open toward the middle of the court on the jump off the inside foot. Shoot over the head while traveling away from the rim; finish with the palm toward the target. Finish with right hand on the left side of the basket and vice versa.	Use wrong hand Look over the outside shoulder Finish across the body Do not extend with the jump Try to spin the ball in the basket.	Look over the inside shoulder Turn toward the center of the court Wave good-bye with the follow-through Palm to the target High off the glass

Skill Progression	Demonstrated Ability	Common Flaws	Teaching Points
			Extend on the last step and with the jump – move away from the trailing defensive player.
Power Lay-up	Stop with shoulders squared to the backboard and jump off two feet. Use the outside arm to shoot and the inside arm to protect the ball. Keep the inside hand on the ball until the release of the shot. Keep the inside hand's palm to the ball and use the arm to find the defender's arm and protect the ball.	Expose the ball Face the defender, rather than turning inside shoulder to the defender Finish small Lack of balance on the jump stop.	Get big on the jump stop Sit hips down to maintain balance Keep the ball high Protect the ball with your inside hand Turn the width of your body to the defender Elevate on the shot.
Open Court Lay-ups	Start at half court or the length of the floor, attack the basket, make a move at the three-point line and finish with one of the different finishes.	Slow down into the shot Jump off wrong foot Rock the cradle Finish short.	Shoot high off the glass Accelerate into the shot Get low on the move Game speed Protect the ball Imagine the defender.
Floater	Quick "push" shot used when attacking toward a defender, especially a shot blocker. With hand under the ball, shoot as soon as the feet leave the ground and get the ball high so it falls into the basket.	Shoot too late Shoot like a jump shot Rush the shot Off-balance Not squared Out of control.	Shoot off two feet Control momentum Release quickly Finish high Stay squared to the basket Eye on the target.
Runner	A quick shot much like a jump shot, but shot off one leg to "run" away from a trailing defensive player when there is no room to get to the rim.	Rush the shot Jump straight up Flat shot Ball behind the head Shoot too close to	Extend on the jump Acquire balance in the air Protect from the trailing defender

Skill Progression	Demonstrated Ability	Common Flaws	Teaching Points
		help defense.	Shoot like a jump shot once on balance Shoot high.
Finger Roll	Shoot like a "lay-up," except the hand is under the ball to soften the release when moving quickly or shooting close to the rim. Use when players' hands are near the rim on the release, not with younger players playing below the rim.	Jerk hand back and miss short Push too hard Get stuck in between	Let the ball roll off the fingers Shoot at the peak of the jump Only use when close to the rim Explode up.
Running Hook	Shoot like a lay-up, except the offensive player keeps his inside shoulder toward the defender and uses the width of his body to protect the ball and finishes with a hook-like motion over his head, rather than in front of his body.	Turn body to expose ball to defense Poor angle on shot Shoot too far behind the head, not over the ear	Point inside shoulder to the defense Use width of body to protect the ball Follow-through like a jump shot, except hand goes to the side Both hands high Must account for momentum Shoulder to the ear on the shot.
Up-and-Under	After a jump stop, use a shot fake and step-through with a crossover step and finish with a baby hook or power lay-up.	Travel Step with wrong foot Fail to protect the ball Forget to shot fake Anticipate the move rather than reacting to the defense Too slow Drop the ball after the fake.	Big step Jump off two feet Ball to eyes on the fake Ball across the hairline on the step-through Get the defender on your back Finish away from the defender Both hands high to protect the ball.
Spin	*Only used against body contact*. Plant the inside foot on the final dribble; keep ball in the same hand and reverse pivot to the basket, sealing the defense; as you step, pick up the dribble with both hands, front pivot to	Pick-up dribble too soon Switch hands with the dribble when turning back to	Rip the dribble to the opposite shoulder Point toe toward the rim to open

Skill Progression	Demonstrated Ability	Common Flaws	Teaching Points
	square both feet to the baseline and finish with a power-lay-up.	defense Expose the ball.	hips Both hands high on the finish Seal and maintain contact Get low to absorb contact and blast through it on the move.
Duck Under	Start like a lay-up, but stop with a stride stop on the last two steps (outside-inside). Front pivot on the outside foot to create space away from the defense and finish with a baby hook.	Lift the pivot foot Fade away No pump fake Shoot a shot rather than a hook Small pivots – move inside a telephone booth rather than covering ground	Pivot away from the basket Get balanced before shooting Pump fake on the stop Cover ground – use a big stride stop and a big pivot to create the space for the shot
Duck Under Step-Through	Start like a lay-up, but stop with a stride stop on the last two steps (outside-inside). Front pivot on the outside foot to create space and pump fake to get the defense leaning. Step past the defense and finish off two feet.	No pump fakes Fake away from the basket rather than using a believable fake Don't drag your pivot foot	Sell the fake, don't rush Cover ground Balance Quick pivots Protect the ball

Passing Skill Progression

Skill Progression	Demonstrated Ability	Common Flaws	Teaching Points
Form Pass (Chest)	Two hand chest pass. Finish with thumbs to the floor. Hit the receiver in the chest.	Favor the strong hand Pass too low or too high. Pass too slow. Fail to step-in to the pass.	Extend to the pass receiver. Follow-through. Step-in to the pass.
Form (Bounce)	Two hand bounce pass that hits the receiver about the waist.	Bounce too close to the passer, which creates a slow pass. Favor the strong hand.	Follow-through and bounce the ball about two-thirds of the way to the pass receiver.
Form (Overhead)	Quick pass from the forehead that hits receiver in the chest.	No follow-through, so the ball sails too high. Bring the ball behind the head like a soccer throw-in.	Make the pass from the forehead. Snap the pass and follow-through with thumbs down.
Form (wrap-around)	Step away from the defender and make a one-hand bounce pass, usually as a post entry pass.	Fail to protect the ball. Fail to create space from the defender's hands. Try to spin the ball to the receiver Off-hand comes off the ball too quickly.	Big step to create space. Use a quick ball fake to get the hands up for a bounce pass or down for an air pass (preferable). Keep two hands on the ball but follow-through with one.
Stationary passer to moving target	Execute all the passes to a moving target. Enable the receiver to catch and do something rather than leading the teammate into a turnover.	Pass too hard. Pass at a downward angle which makes for a more difficult pass to catch. Pass behind the moving target. Pass into traffic.	Step in to the pass. Pass to where the player is going, not where he is. See the whole floor, not a narrow target.
Off the dribble pass to stationary target (push pass)	Quick, one-hand pass off the dribble. Pick the ball up with two hands and follow-through with one hand, like a shot.	Make the pass with one hand only. Travel on the pick-up of the dribble	Get hand behind the ball and follow-through. Keep two hands on

Skill Progression	Demonstrated Ability	Common Flaws	Teaching Points
		Pass across the middle of the body.	the ball, but follow-through with one. Make the pass straight off the dribble. Use the outside hand.
Off the dribble to moving target	Quick, one-hand pass off the dribble. Pick the ball up with two hands and follow-through with one hand, like a shot; lead the receiver with the pass.	One hand pass. Pass behind the target. Pass at target's feet. Pass across the body. Travel.	Use outside hand. Always use a bounce pass on a backdoor cut. Use an air pass for a wing entry pass. Quick pass; no extra movement.
Stationary passer and receiver vs. on-ball defender	Use a ball fake to create a passing lane to pass the ball to teammate.	Slow pass. No fake. Telegraph the pass. Weak pass. No step in to the pass. No effort to move away from the defense. Fail to protect the ball.	Quick ball fake and pass. Get defender's hands high, throw low. Get the hands low and pass high. No wasted motion. One quick fake and pass. Use pivot foot to step outside the defender. Be active with the ball to protect from defender. Use a push pass, wrap-around pass or overhead pass.
Stationary passer vs. on-ball defender to receiver with a defender	Maintain Hard2Guard position and be active with the ball and pivots to protect the ball and remain poised to make a pass as soon as teammate makes a cut to an open area; lead the receiver away from the defense.	Pass to the receiver, not where he is going. Not ready to make a pass when he gets open. Turn back to the receiver. Fail to protect the ball. Forget a ball fake to open a passing lane.	Hard2Guard with the ball. Pivot and sweep to protect the ball. Ball fake to open a passing lane. Pass fake to move the receiver's defender if he is staring at the ball. Lead receiver with the pass.

Skill Progression	Demonstrated Ability	Common Flaws	Teaching Points
Passing versus a trap	Keep the ball active; fake high to get hands up and split the trap by stepping through to make a pass up the floor. Alternately, fake away from the receiver and use a big step to create a passing lane to the trailer. Receivers cut to an open position within the ball handler's vision and create a diamond formation with the ball handler.	No fakes. Turtle with the ball. Turn back to the court. Get caught with the ball too high. Stand upright. Get caught on back foot which leads to a weak pass. No fakes.	Stay in an athletic stance. Keep the ball active to protect the ball. Keep eyes up the floor. Use a pivot and fakes to create a passing lane. Get defender's hands up and tuck between them to split the trap. Do not expose the pivot foot – stay strong with the ball.
Passing versus a zone - use of pass fake to move the zone	Use a pass fake to move the zone and create a passing lane to a teammate. Use an overhead pass to make a skip pass or a wrap-around pass to enter the ball into the post.	Stare at target. Do not look defender away. Tunnel vision. Ignore on-ball defender. Do not step in to pass. No follow-through on a skip pass and the ball sails.	Never pass to the person when using a pass fake, except on a backdoor cut.
Passing from penetration in the paint to the right man	Off the dribble, find the most open man and deliver the appropriate pass.	Out of control. Off-balance. Pass with inside hand. Pass too low or too high. Fail to anticipate receiver's motion. Tunnel vision.	Receiver relocates to create a passing lane without a defender in the way. Pass with outside hand. Under control and on-balance. Understand when to stop and draw defense all the way and when to deliver the ball before the help arrives. Attack to score, not to pass.

Post Play Skill Progression

Skill Progression	Demonstrated Ability	Common Flaws	Teaching Points
Baby Hook Finish	Point the front shoulder to the rim. Keep both hands on the ball until the release and use your body to protect the ball. Take the ball from your shoulder in a straight line to 2:00 o'clock for a right-handed hook shot or 10:00 o'clock for a left-handed hook shot. Extend from the shoulder through the elbow and the wrist, with the wrist and hand pointed toward the rim. When the shooting elbow locks, your hand and wrist-snap propel the ball to the basket. Follow-through toward the target like a jump shot.	Squaring to the rim Exposing the ball Inside arm down Narrow base Poor balance Push-off with inside hand Avoid contact Fade away No follow-through.	Low body base of support: feet wide, knees bent and butt down Shoulders to the baseline Finish high off the glass Protect the ball with the inside hand Chin on your front shoulder. Keep palm to the ball.
Power Lay-up	Stop with shoulders squared to the backboard and jump off two feet. Use the outside arm to shoot and the inside arm to protect the ball. Keep the inside hand on the ball until the release of the shot. Keep the inside hand's palm to the ball and use the arm to find the defender's arm and protect the ball.	Expose the ball Face the defender, rather than turning inside shoulder to the defender Finish small Lack of balance on the jump stop.	Get big on the jump stop Sit hips down to maintain balance Keep the ball high Protect the ball with your inside hand Turn the width of your body to the defender Elevate on the shot.
Post Positioning	Establish proper post position with shoulders squared to the passer and feet above the block with a wide stance at the feet and shoulders.	Narrow stance Narrow shoulders Post too low Fail to get defender's hands out of the passing lane.	Get big and wide Take up space Provide a target Aim for the first hash mark with the top foot Call for the ball Diamond the ball upon reception – elbows out, ball by the ear opposite the defense.
Drop Step	Drop the bottom foot toward the basket,	Small step	Point toe to the

Skill Progression	Demonstrated Ability	Common Flaws	Teaching Points
	sealing the defender. Use one dribble, gather with shoulders parallel to the backboard and finish with a power lay-up.	Release seal Fail to protect the ball Dribble too high Dribble outside the body Stand up on the step.	rim to open hips Use body to protect the ball Low, quick dribble Dribble in between your legs, not outside your body Wide base.
Up-and-Under	Step to the middle with the top foot, dribble, gather with two feet with front shoulder to the rim, show the ball high and then step through and past the defensive player to the basket. Can also make the same move to the baseline.	No shot fake Crossover step too small Switch pivot feet Travel Step through slowly Bring the ball down and it gets caught on defender's body.	Ball to eyes Rip the ball high Diamond position Protect with the inside arm Big step.
V-cut	Set up the defender in one direction, plant and cut to the open spot. On a block to block cut, step low, plant and cut over top of the defender, or step high, plant and cut below the defender.	Round the cut Too vertical allows the defender to bump you off your cut Allow defender to keep hand in passing lane Fail to set-up the defender to gain an advantage.	Plant and push-off your outside foot Use your arm to knock away the defender's arms – swing low to high to avoid a foul Create contact and hold position Low body base of support.
Don Nelson Move	Walk into the defender with one foot between his legs, pivot and seal, sitting on his knee to eliminate his mobility.	No contact – spin in space Fail to maintain contact Too small – do not take up space.	Step in to defender to create contact Find him, feel him, seal him Big shoulders Show a target Shuffle feet to keep position.
Sealing in the post	To receive the ball in the post, create a passing lane: If the defender fronts, seal toward the	Seal to the middle on front which creates a jump ball	Get big Low body base of support

Skill Progression	Demonstrated Ability	Common Flaws	Teaching Points
	baseline to protect the ball and wait until the ball is overhead to go get it; If the defender plays behind, jump to the pass; If the defender plays three-quarter, show a target and maintain the seal.	with a help defender Break the seal too soon, which allows the front defender to recover Push-off Fail to jump to the ball Small target Stand upright Fail to hold seal.	On a front, call for the ball with both hands Use hip to hold off defender Create a big seal and square shoulders to passer Meet the pass Diamond the ball upon reception.
I Cut	If a perimeter player drives at a post player, the post player re-locates. If the drive is to his bottom foot, he circles up the lane line or under the basket to the opposite block; to his top foot, and he circles to the short corner.	Get back on heels Turn back to the ball Hide behind a defender Hands down Not ready for the pass.	Square shoulders to the ball handler Circle to give space Keep hands high and show a target Be prepared to move to the pass Be aggressive.
Reverse Move	Steps your top foot to the middle of the key. As the defender moves to the middle, dribble and drop your bottom foot to the basket, making a reverse pivot on your top foot, sealing the defender. Gather on two feet and finish with a power lay-up.	Jump off one foot No balance on spin Expose the ball Change hands with the dribble Ball low on the pivot – expose to help defenders Pivot too slowly.	Sell the middle move Keep the ball in the same hand until both hands are on the ball Drop the baseline foot quickly – point toe toward the rim Pick up the dribble after the baseline foot is on the ground Keep the ball high off the dribble.
Quick Spin	Use against an aggressive defender. Make a quick front pivot on the baseline foot and step to the basket while dribbling with the baseline hand; use your elbow to nudge and hold the defender in place on the	Dribble too late – travel Too high – bumped off-balance	Go against defender's momentum Do not fight the pushing – use it

124

Skill Progression	Demonstrated Ability	Common Flaws	Teaching Points
	pivot and finish with a reverse lay-up or a jump stop power lay-up.		against him. Attack the defender's front knee
Sweep	Use the inside foot and execute a reverse pivot, sweeping the ball low to clear space for a shot, fake or to drive directly by the defender on the sweep.	Sweep the ball too high – bring the ball through the Box Fail to protect the ball Step backward on the sweep Shuffle feet Use the outside foot and get stuck on the baseline	Keep the ball below the knees or across the hairline Read the defense and make the appropriate move Push-off the pivot foot to avoid shuffling your feet.
High Post (Inside pivot)	In the high post, use an inside pivot to square to the basket; square aggressively and drive off the defender with the initial pivot to create space for a shot or clear space for a crossover step and drive.	Square to the basket in multiple steps Step backward with the pivot Shuffle feet Expose the ball Head down.	180-degree pivot Be aggressive Stay positive with the pivot Protect ball Square into a good shooting position.
Short Corner Moves	Use the sweep moves to create space for a shot or start a drive to the basket.	Get stuck on the baseline Step negative Fail to protect the ball Travel.	Attack a gap Be aggressive with pivot Protect ball Be decisive Use one or two quick fakes of necessary.

Shooting Skill Progression

Skill Progression	Demonstrated Ability	Common Flaws	Teaching Points
One-Hand Form Shooting	Start from the Hard2Guard position with shooting hand under the ball. Keep the off-hand three inches off the ball to shoot with one hand only. Push from the lower body and finish with elbows above your eyes and fingers pointed at the target.	Hand placement Ankle extension Thumb Twisting the body	Sit hips back Weight on the balls of the feet with feet flat Hand under the ball Middle and index fingers centered Fingers spread Shoot from small to tall.
Two-Hand Form Shooting	Start from the Hard2Guard position with shooting hand under the ball and off-hand on the side. Push from the lower body and finish with elbows above your eyes and fingers pointed at the target.	Bring the ball to the weak hand Start shot from middle of the body Set with hand on side of the ball Thumb the ball with the off-hand	Move in a straight line from the shoulder to eye level and the finish Off-hand falls off the ball as the wrist begins to follow through.
Stationary Catch and Shoot	Start with one foot planted forward and call for the ball with your shooting hand (fingers up). Step in with your foot as you receive the pass, rotate the ball into shooting position, lift, release and follow-through.	Off-balance Knees bent too far forward No step-in Step too far and over-rotate Twist to shoot Shoot on the way down.	Show the shooting hand as the target hand Keep hips square to the rim and directed over the feet – no twisting Shoot early in the shot.
Free Throws	Take a deep breath, step to the free throw, get into your shooting stance and do your routine. Finish the routine and come set with fingers pointing toward the rim and the wrist cocked. Take another breath, exhale and shoot.	Rush the shot Too much knee bend Bend knees forward Set position in middle of your body Fingers pointed to the side at the set position Inhale while shooting.	Long, slow deep breath before stepping to the line Do your routine in your shooting position Exhale before shooting Set with hand on top of the ball, fingers pointed to the rim, and wrist cocked.

Skill Progression	Demonstrated Ability	Common Flaws	Teaching Points
Catch and Shoot off a 1-2	Step in with your first step as you receive the pass and take the second step into your shooting position with body squared to the basket. Catch the ball at the depth of your shot, rotate the ball into shooting position, lift, release and follow-through.	Over-rotate when stepping Turn hips Narrow base Stand up as you step forward Shoot on the way down Fall forward on the catch Hitch in the shot Ball too far back over the head.	Step-in with feet in a "heel-toe" position with shooting forward Sit hips back and down on the reception Shoulders over knees and knees over toes Stay crouched as you step in Extend straight-up, so hips extend fully Jump straight up and down Shoot from around the forehead – do not bring the ball too far back.
Straight line shooting on the move to the basket	Move to the basket and anticipate the stop when the ball is in the air. Start the deceleration on the first step of your 1-2-step, not in between steps. Catch the ball at the depth of your shot, rotate the ball into shooting position, lift, release and follow-through.	Balance Narrow base Head forward Knees forward Over-rotate Stop on the second step with weight forward Flat shot Shoot the ball late in the jump on the way down	Anticipate the stop Step in aggressively Stay crouched Lower hips as you approach the ball rather than leaning back to slow down Keep head centered over the body Shoulders over knees and knees over toes Come to a zero point and stop forward momentum before jumping for the shot – without the zero point, you jump forward.
Shooting off a curl cut	Anticipate the stop and step to the catch with the inside foot. Pivot to the basket as the second foot steps into the shot with shooting foot forward Catch the ball at the depth of your shot, rotate the ball into shooting position, lift, release and follow-through.	Drift Narrow base Not squared to the basket Squares too far/over-rotate Stand up too tall	Bend knees as you approach the ball Point toe at the target. Shoot small to tall Shoot out of a telephone booth – up, then out. Stop momentum and stay in one plane on the shot.
Shooting off a down screen	Anticipate the stop and step hard to the catch with the inside foot to reduce the angle of the pivot. Pivot to	Not squared to the basket Drifting away from the basket	Catch on the inside foot and square to the basket Square body with toe to the target

Skill Progression	Demonstrated Ability	Common Flaws	Teaching Points
	the basket as the second foot steps into the shot with shooting foot forward Catch the ball at the depth of your shot, rotate the ball into shooting position, lift, release and follow-through.	Traveling (Reggie Miller footwork) Fade away	Sit hips down and get to a zero point.
Shooting off a flare screen	Set feet on the catch, establish balance and shoot.	Never stop momentum Feet not set Keep moving away from the basket	Sprint off the screen and turn hips quickly to the ball Catch with feet set Step in to the shot.
Straight line shooting off dribble	Dribble straight at the basket and step in to the shot with a 1-2-step.	Shooting hand to the weak side No balance Fall forward	If dribbling with shooting hand, bring the off-hand to the ball If dribbling with the off-hand, sweep the ball quickly across the body to the shooting hand Anticipate the stop with the first step Sit hips back and down and jump straight up.
Shooting off the dribble on a curl	Dribble into the shot and stop with an inside foot 1-2-step.	Wrong footwork Not all the way squared Over-rotate Shooting hand to the weak side of the body	If dribbling with shooting hand, bring the off-hand to the ball If dribbling with the off-hand, sweep the ball quickly to the shooting hand Hips and shoulders inline with the feet
Shooting off an offensive dribble move	Use an offensive move to create separation, get feet set and shoot the off the dribble jump shot.	Off-balance Feet not set Not squared to the basket Fade away Start the shot in the middle of your body	If dribbling with shooting hand, bring the off-hand to the ball If dribbling with the off-hand, sweep the ball quickly to the shooting hand Square hips to the basket Hips back and down for balance.
Shooting off a step-back	Off the dribble, push off your inside foot and jump away from your defender in	Off-balance Not squared to the basket	Step-back in the shape of a "V" Turn hips and square on

Skill Progression	Demonstrated Ability	Common Flaws	Teaching Points
	the shape of a V, land on two feet and shoot.	No spacing Fade away	the hop Land on-balance with shoulders over knees and knees over toes Straight-up on the shot.

Technical Drills

I. Foundation Stage

Extension Lay-up Drills: Start on the wing at the three-point line, free throw line extended in an operational position. Spin the ball and receive on a one-count. Use one dribble; utilize a big first step and extend with the dribble.

- Crossover step (right foot pivot) right hand lay-up: Step to the basket with left foot. Dribble with the right, or outside, hand. Finish with a right-hand lay-up, jumping off the left foot.
- Crossover step (right foot pivot) right hand reverse lay-up: Same as above, except make a reverse lay-up with right hand on the left hand side of the basket.
- Crossover step (left foot pivot) left hand finger roll: Step with the right foot across the body to beat the defender to the middle. Dribble the ball with the left (outside) hand. Finish at the front of the rim with a finger roll.

X-Lay-ups: Make as many lay-ups in 30 seconds (45 seconds, one minute) as possible. Start at the elbow, dribble and shoot a lay-up. Rebound the ball and then touch the baseline before running to the other elbow and returning for a lay-up from that side. Continue in this pattern until time elapses.

Full Court Lay-ups: Players pair up and each pair has one ball. Player 1 sprints up the wing and Player 2 passes to P1. P1 receives the pass and attacks the basket. P2 chases P1, attempting to prevent the lay-up. After shooting, P1 grabs the ball and steps out of bounds to outlet to P2 and become the defensive player. Next group starts when the first group gets to half court.

Pistol Pete Series

- *Ball Slaps:* Slap ball from hand to hand, building strength in fingers.
- *Fingertips:* Use fingertips to pass ball back and forth between hands; work the ball up and down.
- *Around the Head:* Pass ball from hand to hand, making a circle around player's head.
- *Around the Waist:* Pass ball from hand to hand, making circle around the waist.
- *Around the Legs:* Legs together, pass ball from hand to hand around legs.
- *Around each leg:* Begin with legs together. Pass ball from hand to hand, completing two revolutions. Step back with the left leg, and make two revolutions around the right leg. Step left leg forward and make two revolutions around both legs. Step right leg back and make two revolutions around the left leg.
- *Figure Eight:* Pass the ball from hand to hand, between and around legs, making the shape of an eight.
- *Figure Eight and1:* As with the figure eight, pass the ball between your legs from right to left, around your left leg and then back through your legs to your right hand. Instead of passing the ball back through your legs, wrap the ball around your back from your right hand to your left and then continue with the figure eight with the same pattern: one, two, around the back….
- *Dribbling Figure Eight:* Keep the ball low and dribble between and around your legs in the shape of an eight.

Red-Light-Green-Light: On a green light, take off with a speed dribble; on a red light, stop in a protect dribble. If the player fails to stop quickly or properly, he returns to the baseline. Winner is the first player to the other baseline.

Baby Crossover: With ball at ankle level, snap the ball from one hand to the other proceeding down court, the slower the better. Push the ball from side-to-side: hand dribbles on the side of the ball, not on top, pushing from one side of the body to the other with fingers pointed to the floor.

Cone Workout: (1) Place a cone at the top of the key. Start on the baseline and dribble toward the top of the key, circling around the cone and returning to the basket for a lay-up; (2) Place a second cone in the baseline corner; start on the baseline, dribble around the cone at the top of the key, around the cone in the baseline corner and finish with a reverse lay-up; (3) Place a third cone in the opposite baseline corner; start on the baseline, dribble around the first cone, around the second cone, around the third cone and finish with a running hook at the front of the rim.

Cal Passing: Players line up with three players in each group; first player has a ball. Player 1 takes three dribbles, jump stops, pivots to face his line, and makes a chest pass to Player 2. P2 repeats the drill while P1 runs to the end of the line. Use all the passes.

Monkey in the Middle: Player 1 starts on defense. Player 2 and Player 3 start about 15-feet from each other. P1 must get a steal or a pass deflection to get out of the middle. The player who commits the turnover becomes the next person in the middle.

Bull in the Ring: Three players start in the middle as defenders and the others form a giant circle as stationary offensive players. Two defenders trap the ball and the third defender tries to steal the pass. Offensive players have one dribble and cannot pass to the immediate next player. If the offense completes a pass, the middle defender and one of the others trap the receiver. Defense needs a steal to play offense.

Utah Line Drills: Players form five lines on the baseline and start in a Hard2Guard position. On "Go!" the first five players jog to the free throw line, while the second five get in a Hard2Guard position. Each group makes a quick stop at the free throw lines, half court and the baseline and waits for subsequent commands. The commands are: Front Pivot, Reverse Pivot, Space Step, Drive Step, Sweep, Crossover Step, Shot Fake or any combination.

Protect Dribble: Start in a wide stance. Dribble the ball straight down by back foot. Create an arm bar with off hand to protect the ball from defenders. Put chin on your front shoulder to see the court.

Kill Dribble: Begin with dribble about waist level and then "kill" the dribble to ankle level. Pound the ball to raise it to waist level (keep hand on top of the ball) and repeat.

Baseline Shuffle: Start on the baseline with left foot forward and ball in the right hand by the right foot in a protect dribble stance. Shuffle forward three dribbles and then shuffle back to the baseline. As players progress, change to a sprint forward and a shuffle backward. Work both hands.

Baseline Shuffle and Crossover: Add a crossover when their back foot hits the baseline. Sprint forward, shuffle backward, open shoulders to the floor and crossover and then close stance and continue with opposite hand. Dribble with right hand forward and shuffle back. When right foot hits the baseline, drop the left foot so feet are parallel and crossover the ball from right to left; then step forward with the right foot to close stance and dribble with the left hand.

Side-to-Side: With the ball in one hand, dribble from side to side.

Front-to-Back (Push and pull): With one hand, pull the ball back and then push the ball forward, so ball moves from the front to the back.

Behind the Back: While stationary, sit down in a low stance and dribble the ball from hand to hand behind your back (under your butt).

Perfect 10: Start the ball in your weak hand. Make ten front-to-back dribbles, followed by ten side-to-side dribbles. On final dribble, switch hands and perform ten side-to-side dribbles followed by ten front-to-back dribbles. End with ten behind-the-back dribbles. Return to the start on any mistake.

Dribble Tag: Each player has a ball inside the three-point line. Goal is to protect one's own ball and knock everyone else's ball outside the boundary. Make the boundary smaller as players get knocked out. Once knocked out, players stand around the boundary and try to steal someone's ball so they can re-enter play.

Slug Hustle Drill: Form three lines on the baseline and start with back to the court. Coach yells "Defense," and the first players slap the floor, get into a defensive stance and yell, "Ready!" Coach says, "Go," and players zigzag to half court. At half court, each player takes a charge, gets up quickly and sprints to the other baseline where they dive for an imaginary loose ball.

II. Fundamentals Stage

Three in a Row: Start directly in front of the basket. Use proper form and shoot. Make three in a row and step back. On a miss, take one step forward. Work to the free throw line.

3x5-Shooting Drill: Start in the middle of the lane with one leg forward and step in to each shot. Make five in a row with the right leg forward and five in a row with the left leg forward. Move back and repeat. Shoot from three spots.

15-Shooting Drill: Start in the middle of the lane and make five straight jump shots. Step in to each shot. After five straight, take a step back. Make fifteen straight shots: all jump shots with complete lift and extension. Start over on a miss. Shoot for 2:00.

Zone Shots: Player 1 shoots, Player 2 passes and Player 3 rebounds. Use two balls. P1 shoots from the wing while P2 passes from the opposite side; P3 rebounds and outlets to P2. P1 points inside foot to the rim and squares to the passer with hands up and knees bent. P1 receives pass, pivots to the basket and shoots. After shooting, he retraces his shot back to the starting point and waits for the next pass. Make 10 and rotate.

Slide Shooting: One player rebounds and the other shoots. Shooter starts at one elbow and shuffles to the other elbow with hands calling for the ball. Shooter catches the ball and shoots. After finishing his shot, he returns to his stance and slides to the other elbow where he catches and shoots. Make 10 and rotate.

Confidence Shooting: Team stands in a single file line at the block. Use three balls. Take turns shooting until the team makes 15. Rebound your shot and give the ball to the next player. Move to the opposite block, then midway up the free throw line on both sides and then the elbows. Finish with free throws.

5x5-Shooting Drill: Shoot from each baseline, each wing and the middle; make five shots at each spot before moving to the next spot. Make 25 shots total and rotate passer and shooter.

Oiler Shooting Drills: Four players form a line at the top of the key; Player 1 does not have a ball, but the others do. P1 sprints to the baseline, turns and runs back toward the line receiving the pass in the lane. He pivots, shoots and rebounds his shot. P2 passes to P1 and sprints to the baseline following P1. Use same pattern to shoot from different spots.

Oiler Kick-out Shooting Drill: Form a line at the top of the key. One player starts on the wing. P1 passes to the wing (P2) and cuts to the ball side post. P2 passes to P1 and relocates. P1 passes to P2 for the jump shot. P1 cuts to the wing and receives the pass from P3, while P2 rebounds.

Straight-line Shooting: Start at half-court, run to the free throw line, catch and shoot. Use a left-right 1-2-step for one set and a right-left 1-2-step for the next. Make five shots and progress accordingly. If working in pairs, alternate shots: shoot, rebound and pass to your partner before returning to the starting point.

Two-dribble Pull-ups: Start beyond the three-point line and use two dribbles to get to a mid-range jump shot. Stop on-balance and shoot. Rebound and go to the end of the line. Shoot going down the middle and on each wing. Drive to the basket, not to the baseline. Use a right-hand and left-hand dribble.

Circle Drill: Players form a circle around a target/basket. They jog to their right and when the coach says "Shot," players plant the inside foot and square to the target in shooting position with an imaginary ball ready to shoot. On "Go," players run in the other direction, and repeat, squaring on command.

Elbow Shooting Drill: With two players, Player 1 shoots and Player 2 rebounds. P1 catches the ball at the elbow and shoots. P2 rebounds. P1 runs along the half-circle above the free throw line to the other elbow, catches and shoots. Shoot 10 and rotate. Step into the ball with an inside foot 1-2 step.

Super Six Two-ball Drills

- *Together*: bounce balls at the same time.
- *Alternate*: balls move opposite of each other; as one hits the ground, dribble the other.
- *Side-to-side*: keep hand on top of the ball, bounce the balls at the same time and move the balls from side to side.
- *Front-to-back*: keep hand on top of the ball, bounce the balls at the same time and move the balls from front to back; push and pull: hand moves in front of the ball and behind the ball.
- *Crossover*: bounce the balls at the same time and push the balls from side to side, changing hands.
- *X-dribble*: hands cross to make the shape of an "X" on every other dribble.

One-Dribble Crossover: Take one dribble with the right hand and crossover to the left hand. Take one dribble with the left hand and crossover to the right hand. Eliminate any hesitation, especially any hops, on the change of direction. Extend with each dribble. Stay low throughout the drill and keep the ball below the knees throughout the drill.

Foster 1v1 Drill: Offensive player starts on the baseline and the defensive player starts at the free throw line with the ball. Defensive player passes to the offensive player, sprints to half court, turns and picks up the offensive player, attempting to keep him away from the paint. Defensive player must force the offensive player to change directions and not just run right past the defender. Offensive player receives the pass and attacks the basket.

Mikan Drill: Make a right hand lay-up; rebound the ball out of the net and step to the left side of the rim with your right foot. Jump off the right foot and make a left-hand crossover lay-up. Rebound and step with your left foot to the right side and make a right-hand lay-up. Keep the ball above your shoulders and complete without traveling. Square shoulders to the backboard on each shot. Make 20.

Reverse Mikan Drill: Start under the basket facing the court. Step to the left side with your left foot and make a right-hand reverse lay-up. Rebound and step to the right side with your right foot and make a left-hand reverse lay-up. Keep the ball above the shoulder level and complete without traveling. Make 20.

Peth's Post Positioning Drill: Start with an offensive player and a defensive player. Each whistle simulates a pass from the elbow-extended to the baseline, requiring the defense to change his position from ¾ front (or half-front) on the high side to ¾ front (or half-front) on the low side. The offense fights to hold his position while the defense fights to make an X-step in front of the offensive player. Each player plays offense for 60 seconds and switches to defense.

Block2Block Post Move Drill: Work with a partner and start with one ball at each block. Run to the first block, pick up the ball and make a post move. After converting the basket, sprint to the other side and repeat. The partner grabs the rebound and sets the ball on the block. Go for 60 seconds each for each post move. In a three person group, one player plays soft defense.

2v0 Pressure Passing: Two players start 10 to 12-feet apart. P1 starts with the ball and P2 sprints about 20 feet and breaks back toward the ball. P1 waits for P2 to cut to the ball and passes to him. P2 receives the pass and pivots to face up court. P1 sprints ahead and breaks back to the ball. He receives the pass and pivots up floor. Work the entire length of the floor.

2v2 Pressure Passing: Add defense to the *2v0 Pressure Passing Drill*. Offensive players make aggressive V-cuts to get open and protect the ball while waiting for teammate to get open. No dribble. Utilize pass fakes to pass around defenders and pass to your teammate's outside hand.

Gael Passing: Play 2v2. Offense starts with the ball, but cannot dribble. Offense must stay inside the three-point line. Offense attempts to complete passes while defense applies pressure. Any defensive deflection or touch results in a turnover. Play to eleven.

Two Minutes Perfect Defense: Players spread out. Coach acts as an offensive player; players react to his movements. When the coach dribbles to his right, the players slide to their left. When the coach lifts the ball to his shooting position, the players close out. When the coach shoots, the players block out and return to defensive position. When the coach extends the ball out in front, players take a charge, get up quickly and return to their defensive stance while doing rocket feet (pitter-patter). When the coach puts the ball on the floor, players dive for a loose ball, get up quickly into the defensive stance and do rocket feet. Go for two minutes. Start over if any player makes a mistake.

III. Training Stage

Team Corner Curls: Form one line at the left elbow and one in the right corner. First shooter curls from the right corner to the right elbow and receives the pass. He rebounds and the passer and shooter switch lines.

Partner Shooting Drill: P1 passes to P2 and closes out to the shooter. P2 shoots and follows his shot to rebound. P1 contests the shot and relocates, moving continuously and calling for the ball. P2 passes to P1 and contests his shot.

Two-ball Shooting Drill: P1 shoots, P2 passes and P3 rebounds. Use two balls. P1 shoots and cuts from the elbow to the baseline. P2 passes the second ball to P1 ball, while P3 rebounds the first ball and passes to P2. P1 shoots and cuts to the elbow. Use different areas on the court and different passing angles. Shoot 10 shots and rotate.

Three-line Shooting Drills: Players form three lines on the baseline; lines A, B and C. The first person in each line does not have a ball, but the other players do. A1, B1 and C1 sprint beyond the three-point line (the volleyball line) and cut back to the ball. They call for the ball, catch and shoot. They rebound their ball and return to their line. Once A2, B2 and C2 pass the ball, they sprint to the line, cut back, catch and shoot.

Five-Star Shooting Drill: Form five lines: one under the basket (with ball), two off the elbows and two on the baseline. P1 under the basket throws to P2 at the elbow and follows his pass. P2 passes to the opposite baseline (Player 3), who passes to the other baseline (Player 4). P4 passes to P5 at the opposite elbow and P5 shoots. The next player in line rebounds and passes to P1.

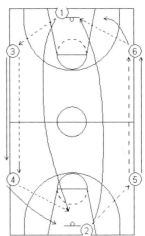

Bronco Fast Break Shooting: Form four lines: one at each basket on each side of the court, a little higher than the free throw line-extended. P1 throws the ball off the glass (P2 does the same thing at the opposite end) and passes to P3, the first person in line. P3 passes to P4, who is at the front of the line at the other end. P3 follows and goes to the end of P4's line. P4 passes to P1 who shoots a jump shot. P4 rebounds and passes to P5 on the other side of the court. P1 fills P5's line (right).

Sooner Fast Break Shooting: Five players form a line at the free throw line facing half court. Player 2 and 3 have balls. Player 1 sprints to half court, cuts towards the sideline at a 45-degree angle, and then cuts towards the basket at a 45-degree angle. P2 passes to P1 and sprints to half court. P1 catches, shoots, rebounds and returns to the end of the line. Shoot within your range. Make 15 shots and switch sides (below left).

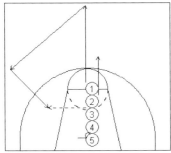

Trojan Transition Shooting: Players form a line at half court (with a full team, use both sides). P1 starts under the basket with a ball; P2 is the first person in line without a ball; and P3 is the second man in line with a ball. P2 sprints toward the basket and receives the pass from P1. P1 passes and runs at the shooter, pressuring the shot without trying to block it or foul the shooter. P1 continues and receives a pass from P3. P2 rebounds and passes to P3 sprinting to the basket. P1 receives the pass and dribbles to the other basket using a speed dribble, makes a hesitation move at the three-point line and makes a lay-up. P1 rebounds and sprints to the end of the line (left).

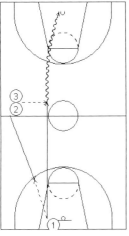

One Dribble Pull-ups: P1 shoots, P2 passes and P3 plays token (three-quarter speed) defense. P2 passes to P1, and P3 closes out to defend the initial move (stop on the dribble). P1 makes a shot fake (ball to eyes), extends away from the defender with one dribble and pulls up for a jump shot. Initially, have the defense close out to force a certain direction; a couple shots to the baseline and a couple to the middle. Eventually, allow the defender to close out without instruction so the offensive player must read the defense. Passer becomes the next defender, defender becomes the next shooter and shooter follows his shot, rebounds and takes the ball to the passing line.

30-Shooting Game: P1 shoots and P2 rebounds. There are five spots on the floor (baseline on each side, 45-degree angle on each side, and the top of the key) and three shots per series: first shot is worth three points; the second shot is worth two; and the third shot is worth one. P1 starts under the basket, sprints to the sideline, cuts towards the pass, receives the ball at the three-point line and shoots. P2 rebounds. After shooting, P1 touches the sideline and cuts to the ball. He catches, shot fakes, takes one dribble and shoots. After shooting, he touches the sideline, cuts toward the ball, catches at the three-point line, shot fakes and drives for a lay-up. After the lay-up, he moves to next spot, touching the sideline near the hash mark and cutting towards the basket. Continue through all five spots for a possible total of 30 points.

Eight-minute Shooting Drill: In three or four-man groups, make 35 shots from each block; 35 shots from each elbow; and then five three-point shots from each of five spots. Player shoots, rebounds his own shot and passes to the next man in line. Drill lasts eight minutes.

Seven Free Throw Shooting Game: Form line along free throw lane. Each player starts with seven points. Players can only lose points: once a point is lost, they cannot gain it back. The first shot is worth one point: if missed, the shooter goes to the end of the line with six points. If made, shooter remains at seven and the next shot is worth two points. If the next shooter misses, he loses two points and P3 shoots a one point shot. If P2 makes the shot, then P3's shot is worth three points. Last player left with points wins.

Olympic Shooting Drill: P1 shoots until he misses and P2 rebounds. Shots in the paint are worth one point; 10-foot bank shots are two points; free throw line jumpers are two points; three-pointers are three points. Shooter keeps moving and catches in shooting position. On a missed shot, shooter rebounds and the rebounder shoots. Teams shoot for two minutes. If coach sees a player catch not in proper shooting stance, team is eliminated. First place team avoids running; second place runs sprints for a minute; third place for two minutes; disqualified teams and any others run for five minutes.

Homer's Seven Spot Series Shooting Drill: Place seven chairs around the perimeter in your shooting range: on the baselines, the 45-degree angles, the elbows and the top of the key. Start under the basket and pass the ball to a partner/coach. Curl around the first chair, catch the pass, shoot, rebound, pass to the coach again and move to the next chair. Work through all seven chairs and then back to the starting point. On the second time through, pump fake, explode to the basket and finish with a lay-up. Work once through the seven chairs with a left-handed dribble and once with a right-handed dribble.

Full Court Pull-ups Shooting Drill: Dribble the length of the floor and pull up for jump shots at various angles within the shooter's range. Vary each shot, adding hesitations, fakes, step-backs, etc to make the shots more game-like. Dribble with both hands.

Second Six Two-ball Drills

- *One-high/One-low Drill*: Dribble one ball ankle-high while dribbling the other ball waist-high. The balls bounce in different patterns, not a simultaneously or alternating. The two balls and two hands act independently of each other, with 2-3 small dribbles for every big dribble.
- *Alternate High-Low Drill*: While dribbling one ball high (waist) and one ball low (ankles), alternate on every third dribble. Start with the right hand dribbling low and the left hand dribbling high, and after three dribbles use the kill dribble to switch with the right hand high and the left hand low.
- *Dribble Jugging Drill*: Start with a ball in each hand resting at waist level. As you dribble the ball with your right hand, pass the ball from your left hand to your right hand and catch the

dribbled ball with your left hand. Repeat so that the ball travels in an elongated circle. Increase speed.
- *Scissors Pass Drill*: Start with a ball in both hands. Dribble the ball from right to left through your legs while passing the other ball from left hand to right hand across your midsection. Receive the first ball with the left hand and repeat.
- *Power Dribble*: Bounce the balls simultaneously to get a rhythm. Step forward with your left foot and dribble the ball in your left hand through your legs (from behind) and back to your left hand while dribbling with your right hand. On your next step with the right foot, dribble the ball in your right hand through your legs (from behind) and back to your right hand while dribbling with your left hand. The balls bounce simultaneously.
- *Reverse Power Dribble*: Bounce the balls simultaneously to get a rhythm. Step backward with your left foot and dribble the ball in your right hand through your legs (from behind) and back to your right hand while dribbling with your left hand. On your next step with your right foot, dribble with your left hand through your legs (from behind) and back to your left hand while dribbling with your right hand. The balls bounce simultaneously.

Scissors Dribble: While walking forward, dribble the ball through your legs without any extraneous dribbles. Dribble from front to back like a through-the-legs dribble. Start with the ball in the right hand and as the left foot steps forward, dribble the ball through-the-legs (under the left leg) to the left hand. Step ahead with the right foot and dribble the ball through-the-legs to the right hand.

Between-the-legs/Around the back: Dribble through the legs and then immediately around the back while taking one step forward for each dribble. The double move trains control on the second dribble, which makes moves more effective. Concentrate on reception of the dribble: do not allow the ball to creep up the wrist. Eliminate hesitation between dribbles.

Miller's Move: Start with the ball in the right hand and make a sideways dribble pushing the ball to the middle of the body. Receive the ball with the right hand and dribble the ball through the legs to the right receiving the ball outside the body on the right side with the right hand. Dribble the ball behind the back to the left hand and repeat.

Dribble Gauntlet: Begin with one offensive player on the baseline and four defensive players facing the offensive player. Divide the court into four zones: each defender plays one zone (baseline to free throw line, free throw line to half court, half court to free throw line and free throw line to baseline). Use one-half of the court's width, so the sideline and the midline mark the out of bounds. The offensive goal is to dribble through the gauntlet; the defense's goal is to stop the offensive player. If the defense steals the ball, offense sprints to the baseline and starts again. To create a competition, time the players and add penalty seconds for every turnover. After the first player finishes, he becomes the last defender, and every defender steps forward until they reach the offensive line.

Touch-and-Turn Post Drill: P1 does backboard (rim) touches. Explode on each jump and land on balance. Passer at the top of the key yells "Turn!" after 6-10 jumps. As the passer yells, he passes to P1, who turns, locates the ball, catches and finishes a lay-up. After scoring, he outlets to the passer and does backboard touches again.

High Post Series: Flash from the block to the high post to receive the pass. Use an inside reverse pivot:
- Drop step to the basket lay-up.
- Drop step to the basket, jump stop, power lay-up.
- Sweep, jab step middle, crossover move, lay-up.

- Sweep middle, dribble, spin to the outside, lay-up.
- Sweep, jab step middle, crossover move, dribble twice, spin to the middle, baby hook.

Jersey Post Drill: P1 starts with the ball at the right guard spot and dribbles at P2 on the right wing. P2 receives the dribble hand-off from P1, dribbles middle and passes to P3 as he flares from the left guard spot to the left wing. As P3 receives the pass, P4, on the left block, steps into the paint and executes a Don Nelson Move: step into the defender and reverse pivot to seal the defender. P3 passes to P4 who makes a move and scores. Players follow their pass to the end of the line and P4 rebounds and moves to the top (right).

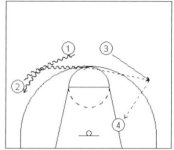

1v1 Post Play: Split team into even groups at two baskets: one offensive player, one defensive player and the others surround the three-point line as passers. Offense fights for position and attempts to score; defense attempts to prevent the basket; and passers try to pass to the offensive player. If the defender rebounds, he outlets and becomes the offensive player. If the offensive player rebounds, he tries to score. Play to one point; winner stays on offense, next player enters on defense and the loser goes to the end of the rotation. Play to seven.

2v2 Live: Play to three baskets. Fouls count as a basket. Next team passes from each wing. A bad or intercepted pass is the offensive player's fault. Offense can set screens, go to the high post or the short corner, post on the block, etc in order to catch the ball and score. Offensive rebound is live; on a defensive rebound or steal outlet to the wing and then the ball is live. Coach calls fouls.

IV: Competition Stage

Interval Curls: Start in the corner and curl toward the elbow. Catch and shoot. Jog back to the baseline after the shot. Sprint into each shot. Make 3 shots and switch shooters.

Right Wing America's Play Shooting Drill: Start on the right block. Turn and set a cross screen in the middle of the key. Sprint to the top of the key, catch the pass from the right wing and shoot. Make four (right).

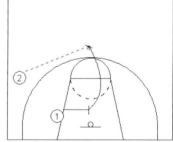

Left Wing America's Play Shooting Drill: Start on the left block. Turn and set a cross screen in the middle of the key. Sprint to the top of the key, catch the pass from the left wing and shoot. Make four.

16 Shooting Drill: Shoot from four spots (the baseline on either side and the wing/guard position on either side). Move quickly from spot to spot. Never shoot at the baseline twice in a row. Shoot 16 shots (5 times around the arc). Set a goal.

I-Shooting Drill: Form a passing line at the free throw line extended beyond the three-point line and a shooting line under the basket. The Shooter starts on the block. The passer attacks the paint from the baseline angle (shooter's bottom foot); the shooter creates space by floating directly up the free throw line. The passer jump stops and passes the ball to the shooter at the elbow. If the passer penetrates middle (shooter's top foot), the shooter opens to the ball and drifts to the short corner.

Sparks Shooting Drill: Form a line at three-quarter court on the right-hand side with one player at the guard spot on the left-hand side. P1 dribbles at a cone that is five feet before half court, makes an open court move and penetrates to the middle of the floor with a left hand dribble. In the middle of the floor, P1 makes a push pass to P2 at the guard spot. P2 receives the ball and shot fakes. P1 steps inside the three-point line to set-up a flair screen, and then uses the screen (chair set-up just inside the three-point line on the lane-line extended) to get open on the right wing. P2 makes an overhead skip pass to P1 who catches and shoots. P2 rebounds and P1 sprints to replace P2. P3 attacks as soon as P1 shoots. After P2 rebounds, he speed dribbles to the other basket, makes an open court move at the three-point line and finishes with a lay-up (right).

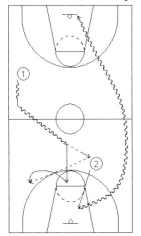

Husky 35 Shooting Drill: Form three lines at half-court with two balls in the middle line. The first person in the middle line passes to the first person in one of the wing lines, and he passes across to the other wing, similar to a three-man weave. The second wing receives the pass and shoots; the team is awarded three points for a made three-pointer and two points for a made two-pointer. If the shot is a miss, and one of the three players gets the rebound in the air, they score the put back and the team is awarded one point. If the ball hits the ground, the team starts again at zero. The second group starts after the first group shoots. Goal is to get thirty-five points in two-minutes (change the time for appropriate levels).

Pirates Shooting Drill: One player shoots and one player rebounds/passes. Shoot for three minutes. Shooter shoots five consecutive mid-range jumpers worth one point as teammate rebounds and passes. Catch on the move: no standing. Rotate every five shots. After one minute, shoot mid-range pull-up jumpers off one dribble worth two points. During minute three, shoot 3-point shots worth three points. Shooter keeps score and passer ensures they rotate after five shots. Players compete against teammates or against a goal.

Sweden Full Court Shooting Drill: Form three-man teams with one teammate starting on each baseline with a ball and one at half court. P1 at half court sprints toward the three-point line, receives the pass, shoots and retrieves the ball, while P2 passes to P1 and then sprints to the other end. First team to 18 baskets wins.

Rip-Through Pull-up Shooting Drill: P1 starts on the baseline and P2 starts with a live dribble between half court and the top of the key. As the dribble enters into the offensive scoring zone, P1 makes an L-Cut to receive the pass at the free throw lane-extended, beyond the three-point line. P1 receives the ball and makes a reverse pivot on his outside foot, sweeping the ball below his knees and attacking to the baseline. Extend away from the imaginary defender with one dribble and shoot a pull-up jump shot, or a step-back jump shot. P2 passes the ball and sprints to the weak side to rebound and then enters the baseline line, while the shooter follows his shot and takes the ball to the passing line.

Open Court Move Shooting Drill: Start at half court and combine open court offensive moves with pull-up jump shots. Work from each side and directly down the middle. Set up a chair as a defensive player and have the offensive player attack the chair, make a change of direction move, extend with the next dribble and hit the pull-up. Use a hesitation dribble, hard crossover, in-n-out, through-the-legs and behind-the-back, as well as double moves. Follow the shot and return to half court.

Logger Drill: Place eight chairs throughout the court from free throw line to free throw line. Make six free throw line pull-up jumpers to complete the drill. Dribble from end to end and make an open court move (hard crossover, hesitation, in-and-out, around-the-back, through-the-legs) at a minimum of three chairs.

20:00 Shooting Drill: Start with the Mikan Drill. Make 20. Go to "Around the World." Make 2 shots from each block, each second hash, each elbow and then a free throw. If you miss and the rebound hits the ground, start over. Then, start at one elbow and make a lay-up and then hit the other elbow and make a lay-up. Make 20 lay-ups. Make 5 elbow jumpers in a row. Shoot three-pointers for the remainder of the time and rebound own miss.

Perfect Square Ball Handling Drill: Start in one baseline corner. Dribble to half-court with the outside hand and make three in-and-out moves. At half court, jump stop and dribble through-the-legs. With the ball in your inside hand, dribble along the half-court line to mid-court and make a pull-back crossover dribble. Dribble with the outside hand to the sideline and make a spin dribble. With the ball in the inside hand, dribble at the elbow, make a hesitation-crossover at the three-point line and finish with a lay-up.

1v2-2v1: One player starts on offense and two players start on defense. The offensive player attempts to advance the ball up court and jump stop in the key for a shot; the defense traps and prevents the offensive player from advancing the ball. On a change of possession (made basket, rebound, steal, violation), the two defenders move to offense and attack 2v1 against the original ball handler.

Berkeley Pass and Finish: PG starts at half-court with the ball and is played by a defensive player. One player begins in the key as a second defensive player and the other players form lines in either baseline corner. The PG's objective is to beat the top defender and draw the second defender. Once the defender commits, the PG chooses one of the offensive players from the corner and passes. The receiver attempts a lay-up, while the other player plays defense.

3v2: Start with three offensive players at half court and two defenders protecting each basket. Other players fill lines at each basket. The three offensive players attack in a 3v2 fast break. If the offense scores, they get the ball out of the net, outlet the ball and attack the other basket. If the defense creates a turnover or rebounds a miss, the two defenders outlet to the middle man (point guard) and attack the other basket. New players enter on defense, and the middleman remains the same. As long as the offense scores, they stay on offense; defenders must get a stop to play offense; otherwise, they go to the end of the line.

Box Passing: Two teams set up in a box formation. The PG has the ball and calls out the name of a teammate. That person cuts, or uses his stationary teammates as a screen, to get himself open. After completing the pass, the original PG fills the vacated spot, and the pass receiver calls out a name. The receiver must stay where he receives the ball; he does not go back to the top. On a turnover, the defense starts at the top with the ball and the team in a box formation. Winning team is the first to complete 10 consecutive passes.

Block Passing: Similar to "Box Passing," except the goal is to create a passing angle allowing a player to receive the ball on the block in post up position. Players move and cut to get open. If the defense plays on the high side, then the offense works the ball to the corner, as there is no dribbling. If the defense plays low, then the pass from the top is open. Team must complete three block touches in one possession to win.

McHale Drill: Tip the ball against the backboard continuously with the left hand while the right hand grabs the rim (or net). Do 10 and then switch to the right hand side. Tip the ball with the right hand while left hand grabs the rim. Repeat on the left hand side for a total of 30 tips.

Tap-Outlet-Finish Post Drill: P1 does backboard touches with a ball. When P2 calls, "Ball!" P1 pivots and fires a quick overhead pass to P2. After passing, P1 sprints to the other block, v-cuts back to the ball, receives a pass and finishes with a power move. He rebounds and resumes backboard touches.

Touch-Slice-Score Post Drill: Four player drill: two passers and two post players. Post Player 1 begins with the ball in his hands doing backboard touches while Post Player 2 waits to play soft defense. When Passer 1 yells, "Turn!" PP1 outlets the ball and follows the pass. PP1 touches the ball in P1's hand, then sprints to the basket. PP2 sets a screen near the lane-line, allowing PP1 to slice to the opposite block. After PP2 sets the screen, he follows to play soft defense. PP1 receives the pass from Passer 2 and finishes with a post move. PP2 grabs the ball out of the net and begins his backboard touches and repeats the same drill.

Cardinal Post Warm-up Drill: Begin with Mikan Drill: Make 20. Sprint to the sideline and back. Catch the pass from the coach and finish with running hooks. Make 10 from each side. Next, do pop-ups: repeat jumps as high as possible. Coach throws the ball and player gets the ball and finishes with a put-back. Make five. Next, run a mini-suicide. Run to the free throw line and finish with a right-hand lay-up. Run to the three-point line and finish with left-hand lay-up; run to half-court and finish with a right-hand lay-up.

UCLA Rebounding Drill: Three players per basket; one shooter, one offense and one defense. The shooter shoots perimeter shots from wing to wing, while the offensive rebounder starts anywhere outside the key. Defensive player starts in proper defensive position relative to the shooter and the offensive player. The defensive player must get three consecutive successful rebounds. A successful rebound is a defensive rebound passed to the shooter. The offensive player can defend the pass, foul the defensive player and generally make it tough for the defensive player to make the outlet pass.

Bruin Rebounding Drill: Three offensive players start on the perimeter against three defensive players. Coach starts from various positions, and defense must defend accordingly. The remaining players form three lines around the three-point line. To get credit for a defensive rebound, the defense must outlet the ball to the first player in one of the three lines. Score one point for defensive rebounds and play to seven. Team must get an offensive rebound to move to defense, and a team remains on defense until they relinquish an offensive rebound. New team enters on offense.

Noble Defense Drill: Start with a line at the three-point line, free throw line extended at each basket. First player starts on defense. Each player stays on defense until they face all the other players. Each possession ends either with a basket or with the defense getting the ball by rebound or steal. After the defense gets the ball, he sprints to the next person and checks the ball, while the offensive player runs to the end of the line at the other end of the court. Winner is the player with the most defensive stops.

Chapter 5: Psychological Skills

Coaches say basketball is at least 50% mental; yet, no coach spends 50% of his practice time on psychological skills or training. Psychological Skills Training is an important and underrated facet of skill and team development, and one area where a team or player can gain a competitive advantage.

Sports psychology is a broad category encompassing many aspects of performance, learning and coaching. Several skills and tools may assist coaches and players in the talent development process, such as:

- Visualization/Imagery
- Relaxation Strategies
- Arousal/Anxiety
- Concentration/Attention
- Learning Orientation
- Motivation
- Mental Toughness
- Self-image/Self-esteem

Mental Toughness

The concept of mental toughness is widely used, but rarely defined. Coaches know it when they see it, but cannot articulate it and rarely know how to develop it. Vince Lombardi said mental toughness is "a perfectly disciplined will that refuses to give in. It's a state of mind – you could call it character in action." Sports psychologist H.A. Dorfman prefers to call it "mental discipline." Dr. Alan Goldberg suggests its "defining traits are focus, calmness under pressure and the ability to let go of mistakes," (Anderson). Mental toughness encapsulates many things, but whatever it means, coaches want players to possess it.

Mental toughness combines the characteristics of the ideal player: competitive, disciplined, calm, focused, resilient, confident, driven, intense and tough. A player with mental toughness:

- Embraces challenges rather than shirking from them.
- Believes wholeheartedly in his ability to accomplish the task.
- Concentrates on the immediate task.
- Controls the "controllable" and does not allow the uncontrollable to interfere with his concentration: John Wooden said, "Don't let what you cannot do interfere with what you can."
- Plays with a consistency of effort and intensity.
- Relaxes under pressure.
- Is unafraid of failure.
- Understands the difference between pain and injury.

We see mental toughness when:
- A player steps to the free throw line and makes two free throws to win the game in a hostile environment.
- A player plays through pain to help his team.
- A player plays the whole game in a tightly contested overtime game.
- A player misses a shot to win a game, but takes and makes the same game-winning shot at the next opportunity.

- A player handles the adversity of a loss like a champion.
- A player blocks out the distractions and focuses on the task.
- A player accepts responsibility for a mistake rather than trying to pass the blame.
- A player performs to his peak ability regardless of score, opposition, environment or officials.

To develop mental toughness, players must be able to let go of mistakes. Holding onto mistakes hinders a player's confidence and concentration. Great competitors do not dwell on past performances – good or bad – but prepare for the present task. They use past success to fuel their confidence, while learning from past mistakes and letting them go. Mentally tough players accept responsibility and acknowledge their mistakes. Players who refuse to take responsibility for their actions or make excuses lack mental toughness.

Players must take ownership of their performance and preparation. They must understand that they control the result – positive or negative. Success or failure does not happen to an individual; the individual makes it happen through his approach, his outlook, his effort, his concentration and his competitiveness.

Coaches and athletes must think in the positive, not the negative. When a player steps to the free throw line, a coach often yells, "Don't miss short." This imprints the negative image in the player's mind. The mind does not differentiate the positive from the negative, and the result is often a miss off the front of the rim. Instead, coach and think in positive terms. I teach players to develop a cue word to quiet their mind and imprint a positive image. Rather than thinking, "don't miss short," develop a cue word like "Finish," or "Swish" that reflects the desired result.

Mental toughness involves resiliency, overcoming a mistake and handling pressure. Coping techniques and psychological skills training help players to develop mental toughness. Goldberg suggests using relaxation techniques. Relaxation techniques enable a player to play tough by staying calm. Deep breathing coupled with visualization relaxes the body while preparing for the skill execution. Goldberg also suggests using cues which teammates or the bench can use to focus players on the task. These cues, just a simple word (like my free throw example), are effective when there is no time for a conversation.

Though a somewhat vague term, mental toughness is a very real attribute that coaches desire. Developing mental toughness is a process. Just as one cannot wake up one morning and declare himself a great shooter, he cannot decide to be mentally tough. Mental toughness is a characteristic which develops through experience, especially when an understanding coach or parent guides the experience. In some ways, it is the sum of sports psychology expressed through competition – a mentally tough player combines the psychological attributes which lead to success: a player who seeks challenges, learns from mistakes and wants the ball in the tough situations.

Competitiveness
Compete derives from the Latin "com," which means together and "petere," which means seek. Compete, in its root form, means "to seek together." The English definition is "to be in rivalry."

In the English version, competition is a battle to beat an opponent; in the Latin version, competition is a battle to seek one's best. Rather than battling an external opponent, the opposition helps a player reach his best performance: the better the opposition's play, the greater his opportunity to play at his highest level. In the Latin version, competition is internal. At the end of great matches where both players play at a high level, like the 2008 Gentlemen's Wimbledon Final between Rafael

Nadal and Roger Federer, it is cliché for the announcers to say that it is a shame for someone to lose. If viewed through the Latin definition, neither loses: the competitive arena brought out each player's best. The result is secondary.

When we imagine competitiveness, we picture the will to win. However, everyone wants to win. How does that desire separate one from another? Nobody puts on a uniform intending to lose. Therefore, the will to win insufficiently describes a competitive player.

Instead, with an eye to its Latin roots, competitiveness means to embrace a challenge. Where most see obstacles, a competitor sees opportunity. A competitor has a positive outlook. Playing Tiger Woods or Nadal is an almost unwinable proposition. However, a competitor sees an opportunity to bring forth his best performance. Rather than dodging the challenge, he embraces the opportunity. The competition excites him. If Nadal faces Federer and each plays his best tennis, they bring out each other's best and elevate each other's performance. While many hope a great opponent has an off-day, a competitor wants to play a great player at his best to elevate his own play.

In Dr. Denis Waitley's *The Psychology of Winning*, he writes about Earl Nightingale's experience at the Great Barrier Reef. Nightingale notices that on the side of the reef protected from the sea, the coral is pale and lifeless, while the side exposed to the tide and the waves is filled with life and bright colors. He asks his guide for an explanation and the guide answers:

> "The coral on the lagoon side dies rapidly with no challenge for growth or survival, while the coral facing the surge and power of the open sea, thrives and multiplies because it is challenged and tested every day. And so it is with every living organism."

Competitors thrive because they embrace challenges and tests while others wilt because they seek the safer harbors. Competitors want the ball at game's end, while others happily allow someone else to take the shot because they fear the consequences. Competitors do not fear the missed shot or the loss, but are motivated by the challenge which tests their physical and mental skills and elevates their performance. By seeking these situations, the competitor is prepared to perform, which creates a greater likelihood for success, which in turn builds confidence so he continues to seek more challenging experiences.

Woods and Nadal are great competitors because they prepare to win and never allow the opposition or course to affect their performance. They may have a bad day or lose a match, but they enter the stadium or walk to the tee with a championship mentality. Lesser competitors allow the opponent to dictate their focus and effort; they do just enough to win because they view competition as a result, not a performance.

Great competitors understand that they are their own eternal opponent. While playing physical opponents, their struggle is internal. Their goal is to improve and play to their maximum ability every time they play.

Concentration

Dr. Goldberg says, "Concentration is the ability to focus on what's important and let go of everything else… identify the most important thing to think about at any given time." Players have hundreds of distractions. If a player's concentration shifts to these distractions, his focus leaves the task.

Players who lack mental toughness shift their focus. When they tire, their mind wanders and their fatigue leads to mental mistakes. The most important play is the current play. If a player misses a shot and allows it to affect his defense, he lacks mental toughness. Once a play finishes, one cannot change the outcome. Focusing on the past hinders one's current performance. Many times, players miss a shot or commit a turnover and in their frustration foul the opponent. After the turnover or missed shot, they must shift their attention to defense; fouling often signals mental weakness, as the player's frustration or fatigue overwhelms him and he loses concentration.

When a player focuses on something outside his control, like an official's call, a missed shot or a fan's heckling, three things happen:
1. His stress increases.
2. He gets tight and nervous.
3. His confidence drops.

This happens when players play the "what if…" game. What if I miss? What if we lose? What if the team blames me? Rather than diverting attention to "what ifs…" concentrate on the immediate task. "You cannot play tough if your focus is somewhere else," says Dr. Goldberg. Playing "what if" cannot solve a problem; thinking about the negative consequences of a missed shot cannot help the player make it; worrying about a coach's possible reaction will not help the player make the play. A competitive player ignores these distractions and maintains his focus, embracing the challenge rather than contemplating the negative result. By embracing the situation, he stays in the moment and maintains his concentration. He focuses on the immediate task and things within his control: his effort, his performance, his attitude, his response.

The mind directs all actions; those we do not think about (breathing, walking) are ingrained in our muscle memory. Our bodies understand how to work, and our central nervous system sends information to our muscles without conscious thinking. During a game, players are immersed in the action and there is no separation between body and mind; players do not think, but play on instinct, habit and automatic actions. "When all a person's relevant skills are needed to cope with the challenge of a situation, that person's attention is completely absorbed by the activity. There is no excess psychic energy left over to process any information but what the activity offers…people become so involved in what they are doing that the activity becomes spontaneous, almost automatic; they stop being aware of themselves as separate from the actions they are performing," (Csikszentmihalyi). In pressure situations, players think too much. Rather than relax, they think about the negative result, which alters their performance and reduces their success.

Coaches and parents tell players to concentrate as they prepare to shoot a free throw. However, you cannot actively concentrate. "The great Zen master D.T. Suzuki described this non-thinking state: 'As soon as we reflect, deliberate, and conceptualize, the original unconscious is lost and thought interferes,'" (Douillard). During the course of the game, the player is in the flow; however, at the line, he loses the flow. "Tony Gwynn said, 'When you're in it [the Zone], you don't hear the crowd, you don't think about the situation, you don't think about nothin'. It's something way beyond confidence. I mean, I'm usually fairly confident, but this is like – I don't even know what the word would be.'"

During games, imagery can be useful. "The mind cannot center on two things at once. As one set of sensations or images moves into the center stage of your mind, the others fade into the background," (Mikes). When shooting a free throw, the shooter must fine center on the center of the rim; if the player worries about a past miss or focuses on using more legs, he shoots with mis-directed attention. Proper visual centering is essential for a great free throw shooter; any shooter who shoots with his attention distracted will shoot less than optimally.

Confidence

"A diamond is just a chunk of coal that performed well under pressure." – Anonymous

Confidence is the belief in one's own abilities. In a team setting, confidence involves trust: coaches must trust players, players must trust the coach and the players must trust each other. If an element is missing, the team lacks confidence, and the doubt manifests itself as selfish play, uneven substitution patterns and more. As an individual, confidence simply means that one feels prepared to complete the task.

Confidence differs between situations. One feels confident shooting a free throw with a 20-point lead, but does he shoot with the same confidence with three seconds remaining in a tied game? Why not? The free throw does not change; it is the same shot. Why does our belief in our ability waver between situations?

The difference between shooting with a 20-point lead and in a tied game involves competitiveness and concentration. These three concepts – confidence, competitiveness and concentration – are closely related. The competitor's confidence remains strong because he embraces the situation. Michael Jordan said: "I never looked at the consequences of missing a big shot. Why? Because when you think about the consequences, you always think of a negative result." By embracing the situation and ignoring the consequences, he concentrates on the task rather than allowing his mind to wander. The competitiveness and concentration create confidence and the player believes in his ability. When he succeeds, his confidence builds, as he knows more concretely that he is prepared to perform in tough situations.

Bill Parcells said:

"Confidence is only born of one thing: demonstrated ability. It is not born of anything else. You cannot dream up confidence. You cannot fabricate it. You cannot wish it. You have to accomplish it…I think that genuine confidence is what you really seek…That only comes from demonstrated ability."

How does one perform confidently in a new situation? For instance, how does a player step to the free throw line in a tied game and remain confident if he has never shot such an important free throw?

Preparation builds confidence. NFL Hall of Fame kicker Morten Andersen insists that pressure occurs only when the task is more difficult than your skill. Preparation dispels pressure because the player understands the task is within his skill level. When the player steps to the free throw line, the question is not whether he can make a free throw – as he has made thousands of free throws – but whether he can make a free throw at that exact moment. Players use routines to remain calm and build confidence. Subconsciously, the routine reminds a player of the thousands of free throws he has made. The sense of the familiar alleviates the pressure. Pressure is not real; it is something you put on yourself. Pressure builds when the player thinks about the negative consequence.

If the player makes the free throws, his confidence builds. If he misses, he must learn from the experience and forget it; allowing the missed shot to linger creates more uncertainty and doubt the next time. Many players avoid the situation in the future, hiding from the ball. However, a competitor seeks the same situation and learns from his previous mistake; if his mind wandered when he missed, he develops a technique to quiet his mind and allow his body to perform. He does not view the previous miss as a failure, but as a learning experience. This difference separates the high achievers from the low achievers, the mentally tough from the rest of the pack.

Confident players are optimistic and possess a positive self-perception. They understand that they create their success or failure. When they fail, they do not blame a lack of ability, but a lack of effort, concentration or preparation. Missing a shot or losing a game is not evidence of a lack of talent, so changing the result is within the player's control. Players who lack confidence credit their success to luck or the opponent's failure, so the success has no impact on their future expectancy of success. When they fail, they blame their lack of ability and see the loss or failure as evidence that they are not good enough.

Desire motivates confident players, while fear motivates unconfident players. As Dr. Waitley writes in *The Psychology of Winning*, "fear restricts, tightens, panics, forces and ultimately scuttles plans and defeats goals," while desire "attracts, reaches, opens, directs and encourages plans and achieves goals." The difference is evident in players, as many go to the free throw line motivated by fear ("I hope I don't miss," or "I hope I don't airball") rather than desire ("I hope I make this shot").

The confident player's positive outlook creates an expectancy of success. By thinking and believing that success is possible, success occurs. Meanwhile, the unconfident player expects the worst, which usually happens.

The impact of confidence cannot be overstated, as some players believe in their potential for success and make it happen, while others believe in their potential for failure and realize it. True confidence develops from demonstrated ability. However, one can begin to develop confidence through preparation and a positive outlook. As they say in show business, "Fake it 'til you make it." You cannot fake confidence, but if you believe strongly in your ability – even if there is no previous experience to justify the belief – the positive self-perception and optimism create the effects of confidence, which give the player a greater opportunity to realize success and build confidence through the demonstrated success.

Self-Image/Self-esteem

A low self-concept usually results from being told directly or indirectly how bad we are at a task or how ineffective we are in developing relationships with our peers. An athlete's self-image is the way the athlete views or feels about himself and is based on his perception of his abilities. Coaches, parents and other players influence his perceptions.

Motivation

Motivation is the direction and intensity of effort. Motivated players want to learn and improve. When players become unmotivated, a coach must step back and address the players' needs. Why is the player unmotivated? Players have lives outside the court, and something away from the court – like a family illness, an upcoming test or a problem with a boyfriend – could affect the player on the court. In these instances, motivate players by using the court as an oasis away from whatever bothers them. If they devote their full energy to the practice or the game, they forget about their real life burdens for the two hours. Also, as the role of the coach expands into many levels – including father figure – talk to the player away from the court to understand his or her situation. After all, sometimes children make a minor problem into a life altering ordeal and a little perspective lightens their heart and re-motivates them. But, sometimes the problem is serious and the coach simply has to understand and give the player some space during practice.

The problem is not always away from the court. Sometimes, the problem is on the court, either with a teammate or the coach or possibly the player's mindset. By stepping back and evaluating the situation, the coach may see how a comment or a reaction might have affected the player, and the coach can address the situation. Some coaches do not like to admit a mistake, but most players do not expect a perfect coach. A coach who admits a mistake and communicates with the player can enhance his motivation.

In Abraham Maslow's Motivation Theory, individuals have a hierarchy of needs, and one must meet the lower needs before he concentrates on higher level needs. Below is an example of Maslow's hierarchy applied to basketball:

Physiological Needs: Players need appropriate rest, hydration and nourishment. How many kids arrive at practice hungry, either because they cannot afford proper nutrition, do not understand nutritional needs or are too lazy to eat properly? How many growing boys skip breakfast and eat two meals a day? How many players suffer from dehydration because they wait until they are dehydrated before they drink water or a sports drink? How many get insufficient rest at night or between workouts? These physiological needs must be met before the player concentrates on higher needs.

Safety Needs: A safe environment for basketball practice is a floor free of hazards and an environment where a player does not feel threatened or intimidated by coaches or other players. Coaches also must work to prevent injury, whether exhaustion, dehydration or an acute injury and take players' safety needs seriously. Coaches must be aware of their tone of voice, sarcasm and body language. Players from different backgrounds react differently. An innocuous joke to one may deeply offend or hurt another.

Social Needs: When players join a team, their motivation is to be active and social. They want to belong and feel like they contribute. Many kids cite lack of playing time as a reason they quit sports. Of course, not playing gets boring, but the player also feels a loss of connectedness. Players want to belong and feel they are an important part of the group. Several of my high school teammates grew disenchanted with our team because they never played; however, our team manager loved the team, coach and practice though he never played. When the players did not play, they felt less important because a player's role is to play. The team manager had a well-defined role which made him feel important and he enjoyed the experience more than some players, even though the coach cut him from the team. Not playing hurts and gets frustrating, but the disassociation causes a larger psychological impact. If players are not going to play, the coach must find another way to make the players feel important and feel like contributing members of the team.

Esteem Needs: Players build self-esteem and confidence through learning and mastering new skills. In the learning process, coaches need a positive, encouraging presence, so players understand mistakes are part of the learning process. When players are scared to make a mistake or when coaches overreact to mistakes, players' self-esteem and confidence are adversely affected.

Self-Actualization: In Maslow's terms, self-actualization, the highest level in his hierarchy, is a need to make the most of one's abilities and to strive to be his best. Maslow believed self-actualization was reaching one's potential. In a basketball sense, this model is to help players maximize their potential as basketball players. However, one must meet his other needs before seeking to fulfill his potential.

Attribution Theory

The way a person attributes his success or failure factors into his motivation and work ethic. The Attribution Theory uses three categories: Stability (is the factor permanent or unstable); Locus of Causality (is the factor internal or external); and Locus of Control (is the factor within his control). Motivation increases if the athlete believes the factors are stable, internal and in one's control (Gould).

For example, a player can explain a successful shot by saying, "I made the shot because I am a good shooter," (Stable) or "I made the shot because I was lucky" (Unstable).

He could say, "I made the shot because I work hard every day shooting 500 shots after school," (Internal) or "I made the shot because it was an easy shot" (External).

Or, he could say, "I made the shot because I used proper shooting mechanics and shot inside my shooting range," (In one's control) or "I made the shot because the defense played poorly" (Out of one's control).

If the player believes he made the shot because he was lucky, it was an easy shot or the opponent played bad defense, making the shot does not improve his future expectancy of success. Because he attributes his success to factors outside his control, the factors can easily change. This success does not improve his motivation or his confidence. When he is unsuccessful, he is not inspired to work harder, but instead gives up because the failure means he lacks sufficient talent.

As a coach learns about his players' personality, and the way they attribute their success and failure, the coach can motivate a player by focusing the player on stable, internal and in one's control comments. Direct comments toward these concepts, so players develop confidence and maintain motivation. When a player says that he made a shot because he was lucky, correct him and focus on his effort or his shooting ability. The best players believe that success is within their control and depends on internal factors. Therefore, help players develop these beliefs through comments and feedback.

Intrinsic vs. Extrinsic Motivation

Intrinsic motivation is motivation which comes from within, while extrinsic motivation comes from an external source. Younger players tend to have greater extrinsic motivation (winning a trophy means a lot to a young player), while older players tend to have greater intrinsic motivation (the trophy is just a plastic figurine, but it represents the sense of accomplishment which the player values).

Extrinsic rewards can be informational or controlling. A controlling reward depends on a successful experience: the coach tells the team that he'll buy them ice cream if they win the game. An informational reward enhances intrinsic motivation because it informs and is not performance dependent: a parent buys a child an ice cream after the game because he played hard. The reward does not depend on performance and the player did not play simply to get a reward. Instead, the reward tells the player that he played well, regardless of the game's score or his statistics. The problem, of course, occurs if a player relies on a reward or feels as if he played poorly if he does not get a reward after a subsequent game.

When players only play hard if they get a reward, they are extrinsically motivated. This happens with bench players. An extrinsically motivated player who does not get playing time may stop practicing hard. The answer is not punishment, or even playing time. In such a situation, a coach must address the player's motivation and find a way to motivate the player even if he does not play.

For this reason, asking players to set goals (below) and getting to know players personally help a coach to understand the players' motivations. Being on the team and being a good teammate motivates some players; in this case, talking to the player about playing hard at practice to help the team and his teammates improve might motivate the player to practice harder. For some, reaching the next level is their goal and a coach can talk to them about practicing hard to improve their skills and prepare for their opportunity. If a player just wants to win, the coach can talk about the importance of practice in the overall scheme and illustrate a practice player's importance to prepare the starters to play against tough opponents. If the coach knows the player's goals, he can use the goals to create a scenario which changes the player's extrinsic motivation from focusing on playing time to a more personal motivation.

Arousal vs. Anxiety

In <u>Motivated Minds</u>, Deborah Stipek introduces the "Just Right" challenge. A "Just Right" challenge is one which is one level above a child's current level of performance. This concept is similar to Mihaly Csikszentmihalyi's requirements for flow, a situation which involves a person completely in an activity.

A lack of challenge equals boredom; however, if the demand is too high, the player feels anxiety. Anxiety "is a negative emotional state characterized by nervousness, worry, and apprehension," (Gould). The challenge needs to be sufficient to arouse the player, but not too difficult to cause anxiety. This is the "Just Right" challenge. Nobody enjoys a blowout, whether your team wins or loses. Most people prefer playing a closely matched opponent. This creates just enough nervousness to get excited, but not enough to feel anxious or apathetic, if the opponent is too good.

A coach has little control over his schedule in most situations. However, he does control his practice environment. During this time, create "Just Right" challenges. Create different objectives for different players, as players often possess different experience and skill levels. Talk with players about their goals and accomplishing their personal goals within a team environment. For a really good player, set tougher goals and explain to the player that he expects more from him, while setting easier goals for the majority of the team to match their skill level. When playing an inferior opponent, challenge your most talented player to fill a different role; rather than scoring, ask him to facilitate and make his teammates better. This creates a new goal which stretches his current ability. Creating the appropriate challenges for individual players distinguishes great coaches.

Goal Setting

When I coached a professional women's team, I had two young players who sat the bench during the previous season. The previous coach stripped them of their confidence and the other team members did not view them as equals. I had 10 players on the team and told them that I use an 8-person rotation. However, I told them what to do to earn playing time. I gave them goals and when they reached the goals, I gave them the playing time that they had earned. Even though both players remained role players and never played more than eight minutes in a game, they said it was by far the best season in their entire career.

Why do players practice? What motivates them? Coaches assume players want more playing time. Maybe they want to improve their skills. But, if we do not ask them, do we really know? If nobody asks, do they even know? How can a coach help a player reach his potential if the coach does not know the player's goals? When I ask, few players know. Some know their goals deep down, but they have never verbalized them. By verbalizing their goals, they make them real. They are accountable. They go from wishes and hopes to a concrete goal. After establishing the goal, create a path to reach the goal. Without a goal, why train or practice every day? "Training without goals and a deadline is just exercising" (Anonymous). Setting and sharing goals enhances communication between coach and player.

As players develop, setting goals enhances the learning process, facilitates communication and increases motivation and effort. When a coach and player talk about the player's season goals, they understand the other which builds a relationship and enhances communication. When working with players to set goals, follow the S.M.A.R.T. guidelines: Specific, Measurable, Attainable, Realistic and Time.

Goals maintain motivation during a poor season. When I coached a high school team which struggled with its won-loss record, we played hard game after game and practice after practice because our goals did not involve the game's outcome. From the start of pre-season practice, we concentrated on controlling our own performance, win or lose, rather than focusing on the result. Originally, I set this focus because we won our first game by 70 points. But, after we lost our leading scorer for the season and played better teams, the same goal maintained concentration and effort through our losses. If the goal from the start of the season had been winning, what would we have done when we lost game after game?

> **Be S.M.A.R.T.**
>
> **Specific:** Write down a specific goal. Rather than "To be a better basketball player," or even "To be a better point guard," strive to have a 2:1 assist to turnover ratio or to hit 40% from the three-point line.
>
> **Measurable:** Keep track of improvement. "To get better" is not measurable. Set goals that are easy to measure because they keep you on target.
>
> **Attainable:** "The goal must be reachable which means you must be willing to pay the price to get there."
>
> **Realistic:** An unrealistic goal will lead to less motivation, concentration and effort. Motivate yourself to achieve the stated goal, so begin with a realistic goal to build confidence through achievement. Rather than trying to shoot 1000 shots a day, start with 100.
>
> **Time:** Set a time frame in which you want to turn your dream into reality, i.e. by the start of next season.

Visualization

Visualization – like other skills – must be practiced to be effective. Visualization is similar to a real experience except it occurs in the mind (Gould). People mistakenly believe visualization is either unimportant or easy to do; however, "Jerome Singer, the Yale psychologist who has studied daydreaming and mental imagery…has shown that daydreaming is a skill that many children never learn to use. Yet daydreaming not only helps create emotional order…but it also allows children (and adults) to rehearse imaginary situations so that the best strategy for confronting them may be adopted," (Csikszentmihalyi). Visualization is not a tool everyone has at their disposal, but a coach can train visualization at practice.

Visualization conditions perfect practice and prepares the body to perform optimally because "you use neural pathways similar to those you use in actual performance of the movement," (Gould). In essence, the mental imagery works as physical practice because the mind does not differentiate between the two.

Visualization relaxes the body and mind; the athlete is free to concentrate without mind interference. "Perhaps a better way to describe the player who is 'unconscious' is by saying that his mind is so concentrated, so focused, that it is still. It becomes one with what the body is doing, and the unconscious or automatic functions are working without interference from thoughts," (Gallwey).

Some general principles for visualization include:
1. Make imagery as realistic and detailed as possible; use all the senses.
2. Practice imagery regularly.
3. Use mental imagery while in a relaxed setting or frame of mind; the use of a relaxation technique – such as deep and calm breathing – prior to the imagery is beneficial.
4. Conduct the imagery in real time.

5. Imagine the execution of the skill and the result.
6. Practice Perfection.

To practice visualization with your team, find a quiet place where the players can relax and guide the players through their initial exercise. Challenge the players to use all their senses. Imagine making a game-winning free throw. Imagine stepping to the line. What do you hear? What do you feel? What do you smell? A more vivid experience is more rewarding. Tell players to go through their routine and make the shot. What happens? How do they feel? What do they hear? What do they see? After players learn to relax and create their own visualization experience, encourage them to practice on their own.

Visualization is an important tool for skill development, especially in 1v0 drills. When they are confident, encourage players to use visualization during practice, especially in offensive drills without a defender or defensive drills without an offensive player. When players imagine game situations and visualize the defender, they prepare more successfully for game competition with the same practice time and effort as other players. 1v0 drills have limited effect because they fail to incorporate decision-making. Visualization can hasten the player's development against live defenders because he has a frame of reference, which creates a quicker decision-making process.

In a simple lay-up drill, the average player mindlessly runs at the basket and finishes lay-up after lay-up, while the successful player imagines a defender and makes a game move. On one repetition, he hesitates before attacking the basket; then, maybe he makes a crossover and finishes at the basket; maybe on the third repetition, he finishes with a reverse lay-up. The details are unimportant; the thinking process gives this player an advantage, as he prepares mentally for different situations and shots.

When players are comfortable using visualization, they can use it during games, when stepping to the free throw line or when sitting on the bench preparing to play. These instances prime the body for the moment; the visualization is mental preparation for the physical action, which builds confidence and sharpens focus.

Relaxation Strategies

In addition to visualization, relaxation breathing is an essential skill to develop. When tense, use deep breaths to control your breathing and calm your body. Say, "I am inhaling, I am exhaling," as you breathe to quiet your mind, focus on your breathing and stay in the moment. Inhale deeply through your nose and exhale slowly through your mouth. When players are huffing and puffing, their body senses danger. When the player controls his breathing, he calms his nerves. "In the lower lobes of the lungs are an abundance of parasympathetic nervous system receptors. When activated with nasal breathing, they calm the mind and rejuvenate the body," (Douilliard). This nasal breathing calms the body.

After controlling your breathing, use visualization to relax under pressure. Close your eyes and imagine the situation. I use visualization before games, so players visualize their performance. A confident player with a positive outlook visualizes his role in a victory. To maximize the player's visualization, create a calm, comfortable environment. Next, use the deep breathing exercises to relax. Ask the players to visualize the game in as much detail as possible. Remind them to visualize positive results: making shots, stopping the opponent, winning the game. Ask them to use all their senses: What noises do they hear? What do they smell? More vivid visualization has a greater impact.

While these Psychological Skills will not help a player with poor shooting mechanics or an untalented team, they may help a player with good mechanics or a good team who struggles during games or under pressure. However, like any other skill, players must practice visualization and relaxation breathing.

Learning Goal vs. Outcome Goal

Stanford University professor Carol Dweck classifies people as Growth Mindset or Fixed Mindset. People with a Growth Mindset possess a "Learning Orientation." They view learning as a process and believe they can develop their talents over time. A setback does not indicate a lack of talent, but a need to work harder. People with a Fixed Mindset have an "Outcome Orientation" and believe that talent is fixed or innate. A setback indicates a lack of talent, and the person often gives up, rather than working harder.

When I was young, I won a math contest and my insular environment considered me a bit of a math genius. I had never done any extra studying or work to achieve this designation, so I believed in my gift and developed a Fixed Mindset. When I reached higher levels of math, and struggled, I sought an easier path, dropped out of the advanced or A.P. math curriculum and never took a college math class. When I reached more advanced levels and struggled, I was not motivated to work harder, but instead found my identity as a "math talent" threatened.

Individuals develop a Learning Orientation or Outcome Orientation early in life and their parent's and teacher's comments often affect their orientation. Toddlers pick up messages from their parents. When parents judge and punish mistakes, children fear mistakes and avoid risk. When parents make suggestions or teach a child after a mistake, the child sees a mistake as an opportunity for learning and growth.

> "Students for whom outcome is paramount want to look smart even if it means not learning a thing in the process. For them, each task is a challenge to their self-image, and each setback becomes a personal threat. So they pursue only activities at which they're sure to shine – and avoid the sorts of experiences necessary to grow and flourish in any endeavor. Students with learning goals, on the other hand, take necessary risks and don't worry about failure because each mistake becomes a chance to learn," (Dweck).

Growth Mindset people believe their effort determines their success, not their inherent gifts or traits. Maximizing their potential is within their own control and determined by their effort and opportunity. Nobody reaches any level of success without hard work, so coaches and parents must encourage a Growth Mindset through comments targeted at the player's effort and improvement, not just the outcome or result.

When I first train a player, I ask them not to worry about makes and misses. I encourage mistakes – a common refrain is: "If you're not making mistakes, you're not getting better." I direct my comments toward creating a Learning Orientation because growth and improvement supersede success in that setting. Unfortunately, coach and parent expectations often pressure players into an Outcome Orientation, as comments pertain to made baskets or turnovers, not signs of improvement. In the face of these comments, maintaining a Learning Orientation is difficult, though it is important for a player's future development.

> "Research has revealed that in a motivational climate of mastery or task goal [learning] orientation, there are more adaptive motivational patterns, such as positive attitudes, increased effort and effective learning strategies. In contrast, a motivational climate of outcome orientation has been linked with less adaptive motivational patterns, such as low persistence, low effort and attribution of failures to (low) ability" (Gould).

Csikszentmihalyi concludes that "what characterizes people who use their skills to the utmost is that they enjoy the hardships and the challenges of their task. It is not that they are more likely to encounter pleasant experiences but that they persevere when they meet difficulties that would daunt others and occasionally succeed in turning experiences that others find meaningless or threatening into highly enjoyable ones."

These studies suggest that expert performers develop the proper motivational strategies for success because they cope with failures, whether a loss, a poor performance or a challenging question, and learn from mistakes without losing confidence. Through motivation to develop new skills and core values of hard work, expert performers excel through their work ethic, never giving up on a task or problem until they master it. They view learning skills and improving as a challenge, not an admission of failure. They work hard to pursue greatness and go outside their comfort zone to improve. These motivational strategies help the athlete maintain confidence when others lose it and persist where others quit. While those who lean toward outcome goals are afraid to fail, expert performers strive to get better and are unafraid of challenges and commitment.

Chapter 6:
Practice Planning

"Failing to plan is planning to fail." – UCLA Head Coach John Wooden

Introduction

Coaches often overlook the importance of planning practice. Its importance cannot be overstated. As former UCLA Head Coach John Wooden said, "It is quite probable that the success or failure of most coaches is in direct proportion to their ability to devise practice drills to meet their particular needs." Wooden scheduled time each day so he could plan the day's practice.

A practice plan:

- Keeps the coach organized;
- Helps the coach maximize practice time, space and resources;
- Keeps the practice on-task;
- Forces the coach to prioritize; and
- Empowers the assistant coaches and managers.

In addition to planning individual practices, create a master plan for the season, which covers the goals and objectives and a path to each. Divide the plan into parts to periodize the season. Periodization, a concept popularized by Tudor Bompa, breaks the year into different phases to maximize the training benefits. Typically, the year divides into three phases: preparatory (pre-season), competitive (in-season) and transition (off-season).

For a youth coach working in a short 8-week recreation league, the different phases do not apply and the coach makes a general season plan. However, during the Competition Stage where teams and players train year-round, periodization prevents physical and psychological burnout and maximizes the training benefits.

When planning the season, create a general plan based on general themes. For instance, if coaching an under-8 team with four practices before our first game, I may concentrate on general tactical skills and the rules through the four practices. Before each practice, I write my individual practice plan based on this theme. As I plan the next practice, I make the general theme into a specific plan, choosing the drills and the amount of time to spend on each section of practice. My general theme gives me an overview of what I want to accomplish, but as the season progresses, I adjust and adapt to the situation and create the more specific plan for each practice.

In the Competition Stage, periodization helps a coach manage a year-round schedule. By creating a full year plan, the coach schedules periods of active rest and monitors the accumulation of training. By looking at the full season, the coach starts with the play-offs and works backwards to peak for the play-offs. Without a plan, some teams peak in the first month of the season and burn out by the play-offs. The coach uses the plan to coordinate the players' resistance training, practices and game schedule. If the team plays on Wednesdays and Fridays, he might make Monday a tough practice with lots of scrimmaging and then back off and do more skill work and game preparation on Tuesday and Thursday. However, without planning, he may treat every practice as an individual practice, rather than one of many practices aimed at developing the players over time to achieve the desired results, typically play-off victories.

Like Wooden, I use an index card to plan individual practices and take notes during the practice on the back. When I plan subsequent practices, I refer to my notes to remember which drill worked well and which players played together. I save the index cards and review them when planning the next season.

Before planning a season or a practice, the coach must decide his philosophy. He must know what he wants to emphasize and which drills he plans to use every day. Former Washington State University Head Coach Dick Bennett said: "It's not what you practice; it's what you emphasize." St. Louis University Head Coach Rick Majerus works on three things in every practice: transition defense, free throws and individual development. He emphasizes these three things because he works on them every day. University of South Carolina Head Football Coach Steve Spurrier says that there are "everyday drills" that you do every single practice. These are typically warm-up drills or fundamental drills which players can do quickly and without much explanation, leaving time for the coach to teach the skills rather than teaching new drills every day.

What three things do you emphasize?

Be specific. Defense, offense and rebounding cover everything, but do not narrow the emphasis. What three things do you value above all else? How do these things fit your personnel? Do you build from your strengths or fix your weaknesses? Like Majerus, I focus on transition defense. I believe that if you force a team to score against your defense in a 5v5 situation, you greatly increase your opportunity for success. I also focus on individual improvement; with older players, I focus on post/perimeter breakdowns. With younger players, I focus on general skill development to develop global players with the necessary skills to move to the next level. My third focus changes depending on my personnel. With younger players, I focus on movement skills because I see so many players plateau as they get older because they lack proper movement skills. I use the Dynamic Warm-up to focus on acceleration, running form and lateral movement. With older players, I focus on 3v3 play to maximize game-like repetitions.

What are your "everyday drills" and what do they train?

Develop core activities focusing on the fundamentals which require constant repetition. This approach:

- Emphasizes fundamentals throughout the season;
- Eliminates wasted time and energy from teaching new drills and trying to organize players;
- Frees the coach to give feedback related to skill execution, not drill execution;
- Allows players to concentrate on learning the skill, not the drill;
- Enables players to train multiple skills in a limited amount of time.

Excellence is established through deliberate actions, performed consistently and carefully, made into habits, compounded together, added up over time. You can never be too good at the fundamentals. Development is the first priority for the youth player.

Planning a practice differs depending on situation. A coach must evaluate:

- Number of players
- Number of coaches

- Duration of practice
- Part of season (pre-season, pre-league, league, play-offs)
- Number of baskets
- Age of players
- Practices per week
- Games per week
- Players' experience and skill level

Managing Time

A plan organizes the coach and creates a better use of the available time and resources. With a practice plan, assistant coaches anticipate the drills and teaching sessions and prepare the court immediately. Managers know their role before practice starts. This planning saves time and empowers the assistant coaches and managers because they understand their role and feel included in the process, rather than learning about the next drill or teaching point at the same time as the players. To manage time efficiently during practice, incorporate these things into the practice plan:

- Match-ups for drills and scrimmages
- Free Throws
- Water Breaks
- Conditioning
- Equipment
- Back-up Drills

Plan back-up drills because sometimes you run low on time and need a quicker drill or sometimes a drill fails to get the desired response. Rather than get frustrated or resort to running, change the drill or change the practice tempo. If there is no energy or enthusiasm during a defensive drill, have a back-up drill in mind, maybe a more active or more competitive drill.

Practice Expectations

Establish expectations from the first practice and remain consistent throughout the season. Players meet expectations. If you allow players to walk to the huddle on the first day, you will yell at them all season to run to subsequent huddles. Habits form quickly in accordance to the coach's expectations. Set high standards and the players will respond, as long as you remain consistent.

Practice Concepts

Keep training sessions to an hour for younger children and progress gradually; a varsity practice should be no longer than two hours. With younger athletes, vary the activities and keep them short. Complete a training exercise at the peak of intensity, enjoyment and competition rather than play to the point of boredom and fatigue. Get beginners playing a game, though not necessarily the real game, quickly and continue playing as much as possible. Young players want challenges; they want to develop skills, to test themselves, to demonstrate competence. Challenge young athletes accordingly and focus on skills they can master. We do not want practice to be something young players dread ("I *have* to go to practice").

Use the practice plan to engage players, limit instruction and keep players active. Eliminate standing around. Utilize equipment. If two baskets are available, why have 11 players watching one player shoot on one basket? Use the practice plan to manage time and run an efficient practice, but remain flexible.

Have a reason for every drill. Know why you do what you do. With young players, fundamentals are the "everyday drills." Fundamental skill development is most important for players to advance to more competitive levels, and the most successful teams consistently execute fundamentals.

Use the practice plan to prepare players for the practice. Share the basic outline with players before practice and use a daily or weekly theme to motivate players. For instance, in the week before a big game against a bigger team, use toughness or rebounding as a theme and emphasize it through every drill and scrimmage.

The following is a general practice format. However, with the younger age group (8-11 especially), the warm-up and the small-sided games should comprise the majority of practice time. In the later years of youth basketball, spend more time on technique, skill work and combination drills.

Practice Format
- **Dynamic Warm-up**: Activate the central nervous system, which prepares the body for high level work. A warm-up builds in intensity. Static-stretching is counterproductive as a warm-up because the purpose is to improve muscle coordination, elasticity and contractibility and breathing efficiency for the activity. Use the warm-up to do:
    o Large amplitude movements;
    o Balance exercises;
    o Flexibility: range of motion with control; hold stretches for one to two seconds;
    o Coordination: total body movements; general movement skill preparation before the sport-specific skill;
    o Core work;
    o Sport-Specific Warm-up: Include sport-specific drills at a lower intensity, like lay-ups or ball handling drills.
- **Fundamentals:** The "everyday drills," likely some footwork, passing, shooting and defense.
- **Skill and technique work:** Teaching or introduction of new skills and/or drills.
- **Combination Drills:** Integration of skills into a game-like environment, like the Shell Drill for defensive movement
- **Small-sided games:** True integration of closed skills into an open environment and the best teaching tool for players once they establish a base of basic movement and basketball skills, like lay-ups, passing and receiving, ball handling and individual defensive footwork.

Teach, Train, Compete

Divide each practice into "Teaching" sessions, "Training" sessions and "Competition" sessions. The time devoted to each varies depending on the age and time of the season. Use the teaching sessions to instruct and break down skills. Teaching sessions are heavy on instruction, feedback and information. However, not every part of practice can involve intense instruction because players will lose interest. Use training sessions to practice skills which you have taught previously. In training sessions, use cue words to give feedback, but avoid the lengthy explanations or instructions. Keep the drills or games moving rather than stopping the action to instruct. Use competitive sessions to teach players how to compete, how to win and lose, how to deal with adversity and how to play as a team while training autonomous skills. Use some cue words with players, but give players more room to compete without interference. Allow them to concentrate on the action, not the coach's instructions or an area of improvement. After the competition session concludes, use a brief instruction session to teach based on the action.

In the above format, the warm-up and fundamental sections include "everyday drills" which train previously learned skills. These are training sessions, though one might make some drills or exercises competitive, especially with younger players, as fun challenges replace precise execution.

The skill and technique work require instruction. Use this period to teach new skills. With younger players, teach a new fundamental skill, while with older players, teach a new aspect of a skill. When players reach the u-18 level, they have been taught or exposed to most skills. However, they can continue to improve.

The combination drills could be competitive or training sessions. Ideally, these drills incorporate the skill learned in the technique work. Skills depend on the opponent – practicing a skill without a defender fails to train the entire skill and makes transfer less successful. Players must practice the decision-making aspect of a skill, not just the technical execution. For instance, if working on how to make a proper cut, play a "Keep Away" game where players cut to get open. Finally, the small-sided games are competition-oriented.

While this is the easiest way to incorporate teaching, training and competition sessions, one can change the order or the emphasis based on needs. However, use the practice plan to highlight the different emphasis of each segment so assistants know when to stop and instruct and when to allow players to play and save their comments for after the drill or game.

Why Practices Fail

Practices fail to improve player's skills because there is the absence of a specific goal, immediate feedback and/or player concentration. When I was a college assistant, we did shooting drills during every practice. We had some good shooters and some bad shooters and everyone remained the same, except one player. He worked out every day. He videotaped himself and studied the tapes. He had a specific goal (improve his shooting mechanics); he had immediate feedback (me and videotape); and he concentrated on the objective (tracked every shot and kept a journal).

Our team practice drills lacked these elements. Group shooting drills were not designed to help a specific player and there was not enough time to give each player specific feedback. Often, the coaches huddled during a shooting drill, eliminating feedback. Players lacked sufficient concentration to make daily improvements on their shooting techniques.

For a drill to have its intended effect, the goal must be clear and specific. Without a goal, shooting drills maintain, they do not improve. Players must concentrate on the task. If players' minds wander, they lack the attention necessary to concentrate on the objective; without the concentration, players work on auto-pilot, maintaining the same mechanics. The coach must provide feedback so players feel the difference between a correct repetition and an incorrect repetition; players must learn the difference so they can self-correct and provide their own feedback.

Practice makes permanent. Shooting drills done without a specific task, immediate feedback or player concentration ingrain the current shooting habits. To alter or change performance, players must train at a conscious level to override the automatic skills.

Sample Practice Plans

Stage 1

The Stage 1 practice plan is one-hour because most u-10 teams in my area practice for one-hour once or twice a week. Each team and situation is different, and the art of coaching is using the example and altering it to fit one's own situation and personnel. An initial practice is certainly different than a mid or late season practice, so adjust accordingly, as this is an early season-type practice.

00:00-00:10 Dynamic Warm-up
- ¼ Speed Build-up (jog and back pedal)
- Quick Skip
- Body Weight Squat
- ½ Speed Build-up
- High Skip
- Squat Jump
- ¾ Speed Build-up
- Side Skip
- Ankle Hop
- Sprint w/Falling Start

00:10-00:15 Tennis Ball Drop
00:15-00:20 Pistol Pete Series and Dribble Tag
00:20-00:30 Teaching Session: Lay-ups
- Lay-up Progression
- Extension Lay-ups

00:30-00:40 Volleyball Passing
00:40-01:00 2v2 King of the Hill

Stage 2

The Stage 2 practice plan is one-and-a-half hours because most 12-and-under teams in my area practice twice a week for 90 minutes. While practice plans differ early in the season as opposed to late in the season, this is likely an early to middle of the season plan, depending on one's feelings about the on-ball screen. If a coach does not have a ladder, use a line on the ground and innovate.

00:00-00:15 Dynamic Warm-up
- ¼ Speed Build-up
- Quick Skip
- Monkey Shuffle
- Bodyweight Squat
- ½ Speed Build-up
- 10 Push-ups
- Power Skip
- Carioca
- Mountain Climber
- ¾ Speed Build-up
- 10 Push-ups

- Side Skip
- Ankle Hop
- Burpee
- Ice Skater
- Sprint w/Falling Start
- 2 x :30 Bridge
- Ladder Drills
    - One foot in
    - Two feet in
    - Shuffle
    - 180 Hops
    - Slalom

00:15-00:25 2v2 Rugby
00:25-00:35 Ball Handling and Finishing
00:35-00:50 Form Shooting
00:50-01:05 Teaching Session: On-ball Screen
01:05-01:30 3v3 Games with on-ball screens

Stage 3

Most teams in this age group practice for 90 minutes because of gym constraints. However, the younger players (junior high school) likely practice two to three times per week, while the older players (high school) practice or play five times per week. This is the gradual progression, increasing the volume and intensity of training when kids are prepared developmentally.

00:00-00:15 Stations (Two players per station; 1:00 per station)
1) Mikan Drill (switch at :30)
2) Mirror Drill (:15 on, :15 off, switch leader)
3) X-Lay-ups (switch at :30)
4) T-Drill (alternate)
5) Pistol Pete Warm-up
6) Walking Lunge w/balance
7) Squat Jumps

00:15-00:25 Shooting Progression: Elbow Shooting, Straight line Shooting and One-dribble Pull-ups
00:25-00:35 Army Drill
00:35-00:50 Shell Drill into 4v4 Cut Throat: work on defensive rotations on cuts and dribble penetration
00:50-01:00 1v1 Foster Drill
01:00-01:10 3v3 Cut Throat: baskets with an assist count double
01:10-01:15 Free Throw Shooting
01:15-01:25 5v5 Full Court Scrimmage
01:25-01:30 Partner Stretch

Stage 4
00:00-00:15 Dynamic Warm-up
- ¼ Speed Build-up (jog and back pedal)
- Quick Skip
- Carioca
- ½ Speed Build-up
- High Skip
- Straight-leg March
- Knee Hug
- ¾ Speed Build-up
- Alternate leg Bounds
- Lunge Matrix
- Full Speed Sprint
- Ladder Drills

00:15-00:25 Guards: Full Court Offensive Moves w/finish
        Posts: Mikan Drill, Tap-Outlet-Finish
00:25-00:35 Shooting Progression: Three-in-a-row, Straight-line Shooting, Interval Curls
00:35-00:45 Army Drill
00:45-00:55 Guards: 1v1 w/a skip pass
        Posts: 2v2 Live
00:55-01:00 Free Throw Shooting Drill
01:00-01:10 3v3 Cut Throat- no dribble
01:10-01:30 Game preparation: walk through opponent's offense/defense/OB plays; go over any offense/defense/OB play which troubled us in previous game
01:30-01:45 Scrimmage 5v5 Full Court
01:45-01:55 Situation Games: best of 5
01:55-02:00 Partner Stretch

Year-Round Periodization

    Practice planning is an arduous task, as a coach attempts to cover, completely and concisely, dozens of tactical and technical skills, while conditioning the athletes and preparing for games. Planning a season is more difficult and requires imagination, creativity and vision. Coaches anticipate their team's needs based largely on experiences with a former team. Cooperation between coaches at different levels and better guidance from the top ensures continuity in athlete development and helps coaches create realistic expectations for their new players. With this cooperation, players develop progressively, in a steady, age-appropriate manner and maximize their potential.

    The following plans move from general to specific and offer an emphasis and an example, not the absolute way. A coach determines the best method for his team; this is a guide to enhance basketball development.

SEASONAL EMPHASIS

During each season, train all skills. However, the following guide offers a seasonal emphasis. The first skill listed receives the greatest emphasis, followed by the second skill.

Post-Season (March-May): Active Rest/Athletic Skills (Speed Training/Mass Building)

Off-Season (June-August): Tactical Skills (Unstructured Games)/Technical Skills

Pre-Season (September-November): Athletic Skills (Power, Quickness, Conditioning)/Technical Skills

Season (November-March): Tactical Skills

STAGE EMPHASIS

In each stage, train all skills; however, each stage has a major and minor emphasis for development.

Stage 1: **Foundation**
Athletic Skills (General Movement Skills/Acceleration)
Tactical Skills (General Play/rules)

Stage 2: **Fundamentals**
Technical Skills (Basic Skill Fundamentals, especially Shooting)
Athletic Skills (Lateral Movement)

Stage 3: **Training**
Technical Skills (Individual offense)
Tactical Skills (Movement without the ball)

Stage 4: **Competition**
Tactical Skills (Team and position specific skills)
Athletic Skills (Power)

STAGE & SEASON BREAKDOWN

Stage 1: **Foundation**

Post-Season: Play another Sport

Off-Season: Play another Sport

Pre-Season: Play another Sport

Season: 45% Tactical, 40% Athletic and 15% Technical

Stage 2: Fundamentals

Post-Season: Play another Sport

Off-Season: 40% Tactical (pick-up games), 30% Technical and 30% Athletic

Pre-Season: Play another Sport

Season: 40% Technical, 30% Tactical and 30% Athletic

Stage 3: Training

Post-Season: Active Rest followed by 40% Athletic, 40% Technical and 20% Tactical

Off-Season: 40% Technical, 30% Tactical and 30% Athletic

Pre-Season: 40% Technical, 40% Athletic and 20% Tactical

Season: 45% Tactical, 35% Technical and 20% Athletic

Stage 4: Competition

Post-Season: Active Rest followed by 40% Athletic, 40% Tactical and 20% Technical

Off-Season: 45% Tactical, 40% Athletic and 15% Technical

Pre-Season: 40% Athletic, 35% Technical and 25% Tactical

Season: 55% Tactical, 30% Athletic and 15% Technical

Chapter 7:
Coaching Effectiveness

The first six chapters describe the "what" of coaching: a player development outline through four distinct stages and three major skill groups. However, it does not say "how" to coach. The following two chapters explain different aspects of effective coaching, tackling how to coach.

An effective coach creates a positive learning environment for players; makes all players feel important; sets high expectations; creates a winning team culture through attention to details and development of the correct habits, not an overemphasis on the game's outcome; encourages mistakes as part of the learning process; motivates players through positive reinforcement; develops the global player; devises a system to exploit his team's strengths; teaches sportsmanship; develops competitiveness; helps players set goals; identifies the root cause of an error; teaches to his players' different learning styles; individualizes drills to challenge each player at their skill level; gives as little or as much feedback as is necessary and appropriate; and makes the season a positive, fun experience for every player.

The Role of a Coach

According to Webster's, a coach is "an instructor or trainer of athletes." However, a modern day coach fills many more roles from father figure to mentor to motivator. We judge coaches by their won-loss record and game-time adjustments because we see these moments, but coaching comprises much more than one's ability to adjust to a 2-3-zone or call a timeout at the right moment.

Coaching is a hundred different things which depend on the situation, the players' ages, the players' skill levels, the league, and more. A coach fills many roles beyond simply instructing the players or leading the team during competition. In reality, a coach is an:

- **Advisor/Mentor**: Players have many life choices in and out of basketball and often seek the counsel of their coach. A coach might advise a player through the college selection process or simply serve as a reference on a job application.
- **Chauffeur**: Driving players home from practice or to and from games often becomes part of the job, though this presents a liability risk and should be avoided if at all possible.
- **Counselor**: When players need advice, and want to talk to someone they trust, sometimes they talk to their coach. I have had players talk to me about their parent's fighting, a teacher hitting on them and more. Every player-coach relationship is different, but players often trust a coach more than a teacher and approach their coach when they need adult advice, but do not feel comfortable talking to their parents.
- **Instructor/Demonstrator**: A coach teaches the sport and demonstrates the proper execution of skills. If the coach cannot demonstrate the skills, he needs to use an advanced player or video so players see the correct demonstration, especially for visual learners.
- **Friend**: Coaches and players develop friendships. This obviously changes depending on the player's age, but personal relationships develop between coaches and players, and many players return to their high schools or colleges just to talk to their former coach.
- **Motivator**: Even the most internally motivated players need additional motivation at some point. Good coaches understand which players need more motivation, and who needs less, and adjust accordingly.

- **Organizer**: Coaches often organize transportation, food, game times, officials, practice times and locations and more for the team. Without a coach's organizational skills, many teams and clubs would cease to exist.
- **Supporter**: Players often need a champion, someone who they can count on for support, especially if their home life is less than ideal. Oftentimes, especially for kids who latch onto sports as the one positive thing in their lives, their coach is their number one supporter, and the support helps the players navigate life. In the average secondary school, teachers dish out 18 criticisms for every compliment. When those children go home, their parents deliver 12 criticisms for every word of praise. According to research at Stanford University and the University of Washington, the magic ratio for improving performance is five positives for every criticism. With the classroom and home ratios, players need a lot of support from peers and coaches (Thompson).

Few of these roles apply to the traditional role of a coach as the on-court instructor, motivator and manager. However, coaching is a multi-faceted position which entails a great deal of responsibility because youth coaches work with players during the formative stages of their lives, and in many cases, coaches spend as much time with a player during the season as do his parents. While a coach cannot replace a mother or father in the child's life, coaches play a large role in a child's development, especially if the coach works with a player for a series of years, not just one season.

On the court, a coach educates athletes – he prepares them physically, psychologically and socially. Knowing the athletes and drawing out their full athletic capabilities is success. Coaching is a people job. Coaches must know their athletes and understand their motivations. Coaches must relate to, develop and set expectations for their players, and must have a commitment to the individuals and the team.

Communication

Communication between a player and coach may be the most critical component of an effective coach. If a player hears his coach, but does not listen, he is apt to make a mistake. If the coach cannot express himself clearly, players misunderstand or ignore instructions. Few things frustrate a player more than a coach who contradicts himself or fails to explain himself clearly. Few things frustrate coaches more than players who do not respond. A communication breakdown creates conflict and affects team chemistry. A coach must understand the importance of communication and the tools to ensure players understand, and he must listen to players' point of view.

Effective communication is the cornerstone to successful coaching. Communication includes:
- **Sending and Receiving**: Listening and comprehension are as important as speaking clearly.
- **Verbal and Nonverbal**: Gestures, body language and presence are forms of nonverbal communication. Nonverbal and verbal communication must communicate similar messages, as any incongruity negatively impacts the reception of the message. Often players respond to the nonverbal message, not the verbal message, so coaches must ensure their messages align. As much as 70% of communication is nonverbal.
- **Content and Emotion**: Criticism and critiquing are a part of coaching. However, any criticism or critiquing must involve the skill, not the person or team. Separate the content from a coach's feelings about the receiver. Critique the action, not the individual.

- **Direct or Indirect**: A coach can communicate directly with a player or use others, like a captain, to help convey a message. Direct communication is best in almost every situation. However, with older players and a responsible captain, a coach can convey his message indirectly through the captain. Also, when a player is particularly sensitive to instructions or criticism, the coach may address the entire group and communicate indirectly with the player through the group instruction.

Communicating with athletes is not pontificating or offering a sermon. Instead, use clear, concise and precise communication. More is not always better, as an athlete can only comprehend a certain amount of information. Often, especially with younger players, coaches overwhelm players with instruction. The instruction may be valid and correct, but the volume makes it inappropriate. Effective learning occurs if the athlete is able to use the instructions. Bombarding the athlete with too much information can compromise learning. When teaching a concept or skill, or correcting a player's technique, focus on one or two aspects. Quality of communication is more important than quantity. Coaching is not about proving how much the coach knows, but the effect the instruction has on the players.

Communication takes several forms, verbal and nonverbal. The most effective communication is when a coach matches his presentation with the athletes' learning styles. There are several common approaches on the court:

- **Verbal Explanation**: The coach explains the concept or instructions verbally. These explanations must be concise and meaningful to the athlete, not too conceptual or theoretical. Specificity is important.
- **Cues**: A coach often uses single words or short phrases that correspond to a desired response which the athlete quickly comprehends. For instance, a coach might say, "Finish," if a player is short-arming or missing short. The quick reminder triggers the right response because the athlete and coach share a frame of reference.
- **Demonstrations**: Show the players the execution of the skill. Demonstrations must be accurate and specific. If you cannot demonstrate a skill or move correctly, use an advanced player. When I go to my boxing class, the instructor demonstrates one combination, but then corrects us because he thinks he demonstrated something else. When demonstrations do not match the verbal explanation, they confuse players. Cue words direct the athletes' attention during a demonstration.
- **Questioning**: Students and athletes retain more information when they discover the information rather than being told the answers (Kidman). Rather than tell a player his mistake, ask a directed question. If the player misses, ask: "What did you feel?" The questioning forces the athlete to think about the feel of the shot, so he develops the awareness to provide his or her own feedback. Alternately, the coach might ask: "Where did the ball go?" and follow-up with "Why?" Rather than tell the player that he missed short because he did not extend his lower body forcefully, the coach directs the athlete to the answer. If the athlete struggles, the coach leads him to the answer. This instruction often confuses players unaccustomed to a coach asking for the players' opinions and works better with more mature players.

I attended a coaching clinic, and a coach asked the presenter how to handle a player who makes the same mistake over and over even though the coach "tells him and tells him" what to do. The clinician focused on the player's motivation, which may or may not be an issue. However, what if the player is not an auditory learner? The coach said that he told the player repeatedly, but he never mentioned demonstrating the error or the correct execution. He never mentioned asking a question to judge the player's comprehension. He assumed that because he offered the explanation, the player understood it, and because the player did not execute correctly, he simply did not want to play or he was a bad player.

Players make mistakes for three reasons:
1. They don't understand.
2. They aren't good enough yet to do what is asked of them or at least not good enough yet to execute consistently.
3. They don't care.

    This coach believed his players fit into the third category and sought assistance on addressing this issue. However, while this is an issue, especially in situations where a parent pushes a child and the child is not as enthused as the parent, my experience suggests that most mistakes occur because of the first or second categories. Most kids do care and they do want to improve.

    When I worked basketball camps, every camp had a defensive station where players stood in their defensive stances. Coaches yelled at players to "get lower." However, few coaches ever demonstrated a low stance or used a specific description other than "butt down." I never heard a coach tell a group that a low stance means "the top of the thighs are parallel to the ground." However, nearly every coach questioned the group's effort level. The coaches assumed players gave a half-hearted effort because it was not the "fun" station. They never stepped back to evaluate their instructions and the lack of specificity. For a player who stands upright, any bend in his knee feels like a low position, even if it falls far short of the coach's desired position. However, if the player lacks a specific guideline, he goes with his feeling and does not understand the coach's grumpiness. Before blaming a player's lack of desire, examine the instructions and explain the same concept in a different way to see if it makes more sense to the player or group. Remember Swen Nater's book about John Wooden: <u>You Haven't Taught until They Have Learned</u>.

    If players do understand, and still make mistakes, they might be in the Cognitive Stage of learning, which is characterized by inconsistent performance and mistakes. These mistakes are not wrong, per se, but a part of the learning process. They are necessary for improvement, and growing frustrated with these mistakes will hamper a player's learning and may turn the problem into the third category because the player loses interest and feels like a failure. If players understand and have the ability, the problem may be their motivation, desire or mindset.

Feedback

    Coaches recognize and correct errors more often than they notice the correct or positive plays. In a positive environment, mistakes are stepping stones to development. Athletes learn from mistakes. When a player feels valued, he is more open to criticism or coaching. When the player feels he cannot do anything right or when he feels as though the coach punishes or judges every mistake, his receptiveness diminishes.

    Feedback is the information a coach relays to a player after he performs a skill. Coaches may use verbal explanations, cue words, demonstrations, video or other means to facilitate the player's learning. Players who receive feedback tend to acquire greater quality skill technique.

Coaching is about effect. Telling someone the correct way is not necessarily coaching. The best coaches make the game simple. They focus on helping players perform, rather than blaming players for mistakes. The best coaches search for answers and solutions and find ways to communicate to each player so the individual hears and implements the instructions or feedback.

When giving a player feedback:

- *Tell him what is right, not what is wrong.* Tell a player what to do, rather than what not to do. I often hear coaches yell, "Don't make that pass!" after a turnover, but rarely hear an explanation focused on the correct pass. Pointing out mistakes embarrasses the player, especially during the middle of a game. Instead, instruct him to make a bounce pass the next time or to fake a pass to make a pass. Educate, do not embarrass.
- *Ask permission.* Rather than start with critiques, ask the player if he wants help. Some kids are not ready to make the effort to improve, and sometimes a kid is just not in the mood. However, most of the time, a player is more receptive to the instruction if the coach asks if he can show something to the player because the instruction is on the player's terms, not the coach's.
- *Ask questions.* Give the player a chance to explain his mistake so you fully understand. Did the player make the bad pass because he did not see the help defender or because he thought that his teammate was cutting? The response to the mistake differs because these are two different mistakes: one arises from a miscommunication or a misreading of his teammate's cues and the other is a symptom of tunnel vision which could derive from a lack of skill, lack of experience or lack of anticipation.
- *Repeat yourself when necessary.* Repetition is a primary teaching tool, and it is better to repeat an instruction than to assume the player understood.
- *Limit the instruction.* Emphasize one point; do not overwhelm the athlete.
- *Back up to the beginning of the mistake.* When the player makes the bad pass, was he dribbling with his head down before he passed? Did he throw to a voice? What started the sequence of events which led to the mistake?
- *Make sure assistants use the same terminology.*
- *Establish eye contact.* Wait until the player is ready to listen before instructing. Instructing to the back of his head leads to a breakdown in communication and eventual frustration.
- *Use mistakes to teach, not to blame or ridicule.* Correct the action; do not make the correction personal. For instance, the player may have made a bad move, but he is not a bad player.
- *Use the Sandwich Method.* Sandwich a criticism between two positive comments. Avoid "but" as the transition: "Good job pushing the ball up court, but…" When a coach uses the sandwich method too often, and especially when he uses the "but" transition, players ignore praise and wait for the "but" every time they receive a compliment or praise, even if none is forthcoming.

Leadership

Coaching is leadership. To a great degree, the coach dictates the player's experience, as the coach sets the tone, leads the activity, determines roles and playing time, sets and enforces rules, and organizes the team's time. When players leave a sport, many of the reasons they give for their departure relate directly to the coach, his style and his decisions.

A coach's role changes throughout the development process. Eight-year-olds have different needs and expectations than 17-year-olds and need a different type of coach. However, even though the coach's role changes throughout the development process, and some skills and personalities are better suited for one stage or another, some aspects of coaching leadership remain consistent.

From a leadership standpoint, an effective head coach develops a vision for the team, establishes a strategy for achieving that plan and inspires everyone to carry it out successfully. A leader:

- Accepts personal responsibility;
- Develops athletes and people;
- Helps each athlete according to his individual needs;
- Focuses on objectives, goals and solutions, not problems;
- Understands that discipline requires attention, fairness, confrontation and consistency;
- Teaches, rather than expecting performance;
- Motivates, supervises and helps.

A leader's personality and outlook affect his approach and leadership style. In the *Harvard Business School*, Professor Scott Snook writes:

What you believe about human nature influences your leadership style. "If you believe people are fundamentally good—good meaning that they're trying to do their best, they're self-motivated, they want to perform—then your fundamental leadership style will be one way. It will be empowering them, getting obstacles out of the way, and setting high goals while maintaining standards.

If you believe people are fundamentally bad—if you believe people are constantly looking to get over and get by and won't do anything unless they're watched—then you'll tend to lead with a very transactional management style that's built primarily around rewards and punishments. Tight supervision, a controlling type of leadership style characterized by a great deal of social distance between leaders and led."

Our society is based largely on rewards and punishment because most people do not trust others. However, life is a series of self-fulfilling prophecies. A coach's expectations influence his treatment of individual players, which affects their performance and learning. If a coach believes his players try hard, are self-motivated and want to perform, he creates an environment which motivates and inspires this effort. When players feel their coach believes in them, they play hard and perform. A coach's praise for their hard work increases their motivation. When a player knows the coach trusts him and will not yank him out of the game for a mistake, he plays more confidently and the confidence inspires more effort and success.

When a coach believes players are lazy and constantly trying to get over on the coach, the coach quickly makes players run sprints in practice or substitutes a player from the game for a mistake. Players feel the coach does not trust them and their confidence wanes. As players' confidence suffers, so too does motivation. An unmotivated, unconfident player is less likely to play hard, which reinforces the coach's belief that the player is lazy and leads to more punishment. Eventually, the team's morale suffers, winning becomes more difficult and losing leads to added frustration.

Empowerment

An empowerment coach:

- Asks players questions to facilitate learning;
- Forces players to discover solutions;
- Includes players in the learning process;
- Gives players some control of their environment;
- Encourages decision-making;
- Listens to the players;
- Treats players as individuals.

The empowerment style motivates players to learn. Players retain and understand the important tactics and skills. They learn the whole game, not segmented parts. The empowerment style complements Decision Training (below) because the coach guides the players rather than dictating the environment. The coach's role is not to transfer his knowledge to the players, but to assist the players with their self-discovery, so they learn not only the skill technique, but also transfer the technique to different situations. An empowerment coach concentrates on mastery goals, not outcome goals. He sees his role as developing the individual player and team, not just winning games. Often this approach takes time, so teams fare better at the end of the season than at the beginning.

On the other end of the coaching spectrum is a prescriptive or autocratic coach. A prescriptive coach:

- Controls the players' behavior;
- Coaches all players in the same way, like an assembly line;
- Develops robotic players who have a limited understanding;
- Emphasizes memorization;
- Takes over and discourages individual thinking.

A prescriptive coach is common with the *Peak by Friday* mentality because the coach sees his role as to produce a winner, not to develop a team and individual players. Coaches feel pressure to win immediately, so they take the shortest route, which is a Behavioral Style (below), and tell athletes exactly what to do and how to do it. They discourage deviation from the plan because they do not trust the players.

Last season, I watched a very talented high school team. The team was clearly the area's best, with five or six future NCAA Division I players. However, they never seemed to play well and failed to win the championship. Their coach was a prescriptive coach and players were noticeably tentative. The coach yelled and screamed and quickly yanked players out of the game for minor transgressions.

While this behavior is commonplace, and some successful coaches use this approach, imagine playing for this type of coach. As the ball swings to you, do you shoot? What if he takes you out if you miss? What if he takes you out for not shooting? Now, imagine playing for a coach who trusts his players and believes his players are self-motivated and trying to do their best. This coach is less likely to take out a player for a simple mistake. In which situation are you more confident?

Coaches use a prescriptive style because they believe in the position's power and do not want to show weakness. The opposite is true. Many prescriptive coaches do things one way because that is all they know; they do not ask for players' advice or encourage questions because they are insecure. An empowerment coach confidently engages his players. He knows coaching is not about holding a position of power, but an opportunity to nurture and guide players and their development.

An empowerment style is an effective means to increase players' basketball IQ, motivation, learning and development. Rather than supplying the answers, coaches ask questions. This approach takes time to develop as a coaching style and to implement, but the players learn more. "Solving problems through coach questioning enables athletes to explore, discover, create and generally experiment with a variety of moving and tactical processes," (Kidman and Hanrahan).

Initially, players may not respond to an empowerment style. I have to assure new players that I am not asking trick questions. Instead, I question players to gain perspective and to force the player to think rather than give him the solution. If a math teacher tells the student the answer every time he makes a mistake, but never asks the student about his thinking process or shows the student how to solve the problem correctly, how is the student supposed to solve the next problem? Memorization only works with the exact same problem. If the student answers six when the teacher asks, "What is 2x4?" and the teacher says that the answer is eight and moves to the next question, how does the child learn? He learns that 2x4 = 8, but will he know the answer to 3x4? Maybe the student does not understand the symbol "x" or maybe he has not differentiated between the concept of multiplication and addition. If the teacher never discovers the reason for the error, how can he help the student? If the student never thinks about his error, how does he learn? It is much easier to give the student the correct answer, but what does that accomplish?

Coaches should explain their style to players to prepare them for the questions and assure the players that the questions are to facilitate their learning. An empowerment style increases the athlete's kinesthetic awareness, as players who feel what they are doing have a better chance of replicating the proper mechanics or correcting a bad habit than those who are told the problem.

Instructional Style

If you look at a range of instructional styles or methodologies, analytical is on one end and global on the other. An analytical coach says, "Put your foot there, put your hand there, etc." A global coach says, "He has the ball, stop him from scoring." The global coach allows the player to do it and lets him sort out the most effective way. Effective coaching moves up and down this spectrum.

In college, I had two types of professors: the first stood at the podium and lectured, sometimes using slides on an overhead projecture to "diversify" his lecture and attempt to meet our different learning styles; the second walked through the aisles, asked questions, encouraged questions, created a dialogue and engaged the students. Naturally, I learned more from the second type who involved students in the learning process. With the first type, the professor stood there, and I tried to collect his knowledge; with the second, the professor used his expertise to help us discover new thoughts or ideas and think through these questions and thoughts; we took ownership of the knowledge created.

Teaching involves more than filling the player with strategy; instead, an expert performer thinks for himself. Coaching is, in some ways, like preparing a student for the SAT's. An individual cannot memorize every single vocabulary word that might appear on the test; instead, an instructor gives the test-taker tools to use to figure out the answer even if he has never seen or heard the word.

Teaching young players to play basketball is often difficult and telling them exactly what to do seems so much easier. Success does not happen overnight; teaching youth players to play basketball is an on-going process. While telling players what to do might make for a better performance in the next game, teaching players how to play the game prepares the players for a lifetime of basketball fun and success.

University of Calgary professor Joan Vickers differentiates between Behavioral Training and Decision Training in her research into the optimal coaching methods. Beavioral Training is the more traditional approach to skill building and leads to short-term success, so coaches use this method as it fits with the *Peak by Friday* mentality.

Behavioral training features blocked practice drills where the following characteristics exist: the same skills are practiced to perfection; high levels of feedback are given constantly; instruction is delivered using simple to complex progression; and where there is limited simulation of what really happens in games (Vickers).

Decision Training is a more advanced form of coaching which is often more difficult for coaches and players, and therefore the learning process is slower than with the Behavioral Training. While a BT coach sees immediate success with his methods, a DT coach may not see similar progress. In the *Peak by Friday* environment, coaches abandon DT and move to the BT methods. However, those who stick with DT methods see better long term results.

What is being advocated today is the use of random and/or variable practice drills, delayed and/or reduced feedback as skill develops, the use of whole instruction, questioning, video feedback and video modeling. Collectively, these new methods completely change the practice environment where the athlete learns to deal with the realities of the game and where they become more self-sufficient (Vickers).

A DT practice combines technical and tactical drills wherever possible and uses small-sided games to simulate the true game environment. Because they train in a more game-like environment, they perform more consistently in games, while those trained in a BT environment show less consistency and skills mastered in practice do not necessarily transfer to games, especially in new or unusual situations.

As an example, many coaches use a standard, rigid press break. Teams practice the press break 5v0 and memorize the cuts. They scrimmage for a couple minutes against one type of press. Some coaches have different press breaks for every type of press imaginable, while others prepare for the most popular press and use the same press break if a team counters with something new.

During this practice time, players learn one skill: how to follow directions. The coach rarely explains why a player cuts to a certain spot or passes to a certain player, and coaches rarely deal with alternatives because they feel more secure with absolutes. Unfortunately, basketball is not a game of absolutes. Things change.

When I teach a press break, I teach spacing against a trap, and I teach the inbounder to loop. If we are unsure whether it is a man, zone or run-and-jump, the inbounder loops around the player with the ball, leaving 10-15-feet of space. If the inbounder's player traps the ball handler, we adjust into our diamond spacing. If the inbounder's defender follows the inbounder, we clear and allow the point guard to handle the ball 1v1 without bringing help defenders into his way.

With these concepts, we can play against any press, anywhere on the floor. We do not need a separate press break to face a 2-2-1, 1-2-2, 2-1-2, 1-3-1 or a half court trap. Players understand the proper spacing and we practice attacking presses 5v5 or 5v6. We do not do 5v0 drills because nobody knows where to cut without first reading the defense. A 5v0 drill is artificial. As much as possible, we practice the game situation. If we struggle passing out of the trap, maybe we reduce the drill to a 2v2 passing drill where we focus on passing against pressure. Again, even though we reduce the players, so it is not the game, the drill trains game-like skills in a game-like manner.

Creating a Culture

When I worked basketball camps, I motivated players by talking about a "Championship Mentality" rather than listing different rules. While other coaches told the players would not to do, I told my teams that to be a champion required doing everything with a championship mentality, whether running from station to station, sitting attentively when a coach lectured or picking up their trays after they finished eating. Aristotle said, "We are what we repeatedly do. Excellence, then, is not an act, but a habit." I said that if we wanted to win the camp championship, we had to make winning a habit and approach every session and every aspect of the week with a Championship Mentality. While we jogged to stations or sat attentively and listened to speakers, other coaches dealt with behavioral problems. "No walking! No talking! No dribbling!" Rather than inspire, these rules and admonishments created an adversarial relationship between player and coach as the coach tried to retain his power and the player tried to subvert it.

> To be capable of making Waves, you need an organizing principle more inspirational and compelling than rules…Thinking and communicating in the language of *should* - values-based language - by its very nature inspires…The language of values inspires us because values are aspirational in nature. They propel us to higher ground…Values do double-duty; they inspire us to do *more than* while simultaneously preventing us from doing *less than* (Seidman).

Most coaches start the season with a list of things not to do. While coaches make these rules as clear as possible, players test their boundaries. Rules generally create a confrontational relationship. When a coach creates a rule, he tells a player he cannot do something. Players – and people in general – do not like to be told what they can and cannot do without any part in the decision. So, players find ways around the rules. Soon, 15 rules become 20 as coaches make rules to eliminate ambiguities caused by other rules.

Rather than react to situations and implement new and more specific rules every time something happens, I prefer to create a positive environment where players take responsibility for themselves. I set expectations for behavior – be ready to go when practice starts, be respectful of teammates and coaches, play hard and no excuses – and reinforce the expectations.

When I coached J.V. girls' volleyball, one of the players forgot her uniform for a game. Without me knowing, she borrowed a varsity player's uniform. I found out after the game as she quickly changed. I told her that if I had known, I would not have played her.

Her response was classic. "That's not fair. You never told us that we couldn't play if we did not bring our uniform." A 16-year-old girl thought it was unfair not to play if she forgot her uniform. After the comment, I decided to make some new rules, like telling them they had to bring their shoes. This is the problem with rules: is common sense a rule? If it isn't explicitly stated, can it be punished?

> "Rules fail because you cannot write a rule to contain every possible behavior in the vast spectrum of human conduct. There will always be gray areas, and therefore, given the right circumstances, opportunities or outside pressures, some people might be motivated to circumvent them. When they do, our typical response is to just make more rules. Rules, then, become part of the problem," (Seidman)

Creating a positive culture takes work. Rather than write rules, the coach sets standards and expectations which he expects the players to meet. Often, the coach allows the players to determine their own team rules – then the players know the rules with no ambiguity and cannot argue with the rule's fairness when they break it, because they wrote it. Often, a motivated group writes more stringent rules and penalties than would a coach.

A positive culture is one where the team emphasizes its goals – and the things they must do to achieve them – and this guides the team's behavior. If the team wants to win a championship, the goal requires certain behaviors – Practice in Proportion to your Aspirations. A team cannot say that it wants to be a champion and then show up late for practice. A positive team culture focuses on the actions and behaviors that the team wants to do to achieve its goals, rather than those a coach wants to stop. Players address teammates openly and honestly and set the expectations for the year, and the players know that if they fail to live up to the expectations, they let down their peers more than the coach, which is far more powerful.

Rather than write a laundry list of "Don'ts" and "Cannots," create a team culture using a minimum of rules, but setting high expectations. My two rules are:

1. As long as players behave as adults and accept responsibility as adults, I treat them like adults; once players prove they cannot handle the responsibility, I treat them as their behavior dictates. As an example, for a college team, rather than give a steadfast curfew, I might remind the players of the responsibility to their team and the importance of being at one's best for tomorrow's game. When I was a freshman in high school, at an all-boy's high school, our cross country coach set a curfew. During the afternoon, I and some teammates met some co-eds and decided to sneak out after curfew. He caught us and I'll never forget his statement: "We are not here to fraternize with girls." We had no idea what fraternize meant, but we were just going to the pool. He never spoke about the team or the race. He used rules and intimidation (he threatened to have me expelled). I never liked him and never felt like I was on a team. If he used a more positive approach, bringing the team together around a positive culture of teamwork and competition, I would have been less inclined to sneak out after curfew because I would have felt a responsibility to my teammates. I felt no responsibility to his rule or his intimidating tactics and I never ran after that season, though I was one of the top runners, because I disliked the coach and his attempts to intimidate.

2. The 24-Hour Rule: After games, I will not discuss playing time issues with a parent or player for 24 hours, allowing both parties to step away from the action and calm down before initiating a conversation that otherwise may escalate into an argument. After 24 hours, I think it is fair to have an adult conversation with player or parent to address his concerns; however, the parent/player must also be prepared to hear an honest answer, which may deflate one's ego.

These are my two rules. Beyond these rules, I follow the sage advice of John Wooden and treat players fairly, not equally, adjusting to each player's needs, desires, concerns, personalities and individual circumstances. Each player is different. Eliminating steadfast, equal treatment across the board can be problematic, and it requires a relationship with each player to maintain a cohesive unit. It is not perfect, but no system is, and it takes work, but everything worthwhile requires effort.

When I coached women in Europe, I had a young, emotional center who lived on her own in a new town, had jumped from the 2nd division to the elite league and was playing a new position in a new style of play with new teammates. I was "easier" on her than the other players because she was new, young and emotional. She was easily frustrated because life off the court failed to meet her expectations, so she was constantly in a bad mood when practice started, and she simply was not as good as she thought, which added to her frustration. On the flip side, when the team leader, an experienced 26-year-old forward with nine seasons of professional experience showed similar frustration, I acted quickly. These two players could not be held to the same standards. It would be unfair to treat them equally.

According to one workplace survey, people want three things:
1. *Equity*: to be respected and to be treated fairly;
2. *Achievement*: to be proud of one's job;
3. *Camaraderie*: to have good, productive relationships (Seidman).

Are basketball players any different? Players want to feel like the coach respects and cares about them; they want to feel like they are part of the team; and they want to feel like they are improving and play a role in the team's success. If a coach makes sure a player feels all these things, playing time, shot attempts, wins and losses and other common excuses for players' displeasure disappear.

Chapter 8: Learning

One of a coach's primary duties, especially during the all-important Fundamental and Training Stages, is to teach the game's basic skills, fundamentals and tactics. For a player to learn the skills and strategies of a sport requires motivation, concentration, processing of information, memory, making decisions and using feedback. Kids learn best when:

- They really want to learn something.
- They know that a significant other cares about their development.
- The have a very clear model of the learning task.
- They feel that the task is challenging but attainable.
- They have many opportunities to practice in a positive environment.
- They clearly understand the relationship between the practice and the real activity.
- They get feedback about the quality of their performance.
- They are not threatened by immediate or constant failure.
- Significant others, especially peers, recognize their efforts, improvement and successes.
- They quickly apply what they have learned in what they see as real situations.

To teach effectively, coaches must understand the way players learn and use different techniques and strategies to meet their learning needs. Coaches must understand the different learning styles, the three phases of skill execution and the difference between a closed and open skill to enhance their coaching.

I. Learning Styles

Individuals possess four primary means to process information:

- Vision
- Auditory
- Kinesthesia
- Thinking

Visual learners learn by watching a demonstration. An auditory learner learns best through the use of language. Kinesthetic learners learn by doing. A thinker analyzes the movement and asks questions to gain a better understanding; these athletes often process information slowly and in multiple ways. Most people have a dominant style, but everyone uses all four styles to some degree. If coaches understand the different learning styles and identify their players' individual learning styles, they can enhance the players' learning by adjusting or varying their teaching style.

Most athletes, in my experience, are visual or kinesthetic learners. However, most coaches use an auditory coaching style, teaching through verbal instructions. While verbal instructions represent one approach, coaches must vary their instructions to meet the needs of all players.

Visual Learners

- Receive information through their eyes.
- Learn by watching a demonstration, video or model.

Rather than tell a player, a coach must show the visual learner. Demonstrations must be clear and precise, as a visual learner uses the demonstration as his principle means of instruction. With young players, especially beginners, players may not know what to look for in a demonstration. The coach must cue the players to the specific focus of a drill or instruction. Often, a coach uses a demonstration and expects a young player to copy the demonstration. However, the player's focus may differ from the coach's. The coach may demonstrate a low crossover, but the player focused solely on changing hands with the dribble, not the height. To improve instruction, a coach must direct the player's attention through cues.

Visual demonstrations and feedback are essential to the learning process, which is why many teams and coaches use videotape. "Movements are learned through visual and feeling images," (Gallwey). Video allows the player to watch himself without judgment; the truth is captured on tape. By seeing himself on the tape, the athlete sees things he never realized. Oftentimes, for instance, players insist they are "low" until they watch themselves on tape and see they stand almost completely upright. Video creates an awareness that no amount of yelling or instructing produces.

Auditory Learners

- Learn through sounds, rhythms and verbal instructions.
- Need specific, clear and concise verbal explanations.

Coaches should provide opportunities for athletes to talk through plays, movements, skill cues, and game strategies with other team members and/or coaches. An auditory learner may see a demonstration, but not understand its relevance. Specific language is best with an auditory learner; vague language leaves room for interpretation. If the coach wants the crossover dribble below the knees, he needs to explain verbally that he wants the dribble and the reception of the dribble below knee height; simply telling a player to have a low crossover leaves room for interpretation, and the unclear expectation can lead to frustration between coach and player when their interpretations do not coincide.

Kinesthetic Learners

- Learn by doing.
- Process information through movement.
- Must feel the action, drill or skill.

After a demonstration and explanation, kinesthetic learners need to walk through the move or drill to understand. Players often fidget and move while the coach instructs; they are not misbehaving. Instead, they attempt to perceive the information through their particular learning style. When a coach explains shooting mechanics, for instance, a kinesthetic learner mimics the action to learn, not to distract.

> "If you asked a group of teaching professionals to write down all the important elements of hitting a forehand, most would find it easy to distinguish at last fifty, and they may have several categories for each element. Imagine the difficulty for the tennis player dealing with this complexity…On the other hand, understanding the swing, and remembering its feel, is like remembering a single picture. The mind is capable of that

and can recognize when one element in one picture is slightly different from another," (Gallwey).

As kinesthetic learners initiate the skill or drill, ensure perfect execution, as the kinesthetic learner creates his frame of reference through his movements, rather than the demonstration. With a visual learner who makes an initial mistake, a coach recalls the demonstration and illustrates the difference between the demonstration and his execution. However, the kinesthetic learner creates his own frame of reference through the feeling of his movements; if his frame of reference is incorrect, correcting the mistake is more difficult because a correction feels different than his frame of reference, and different equals incorrect.

Since kinesthetic learners learn by doing, use these players in demonstrations. Kinesthetic learners are often labeled ADD because typical school instruction fails to meet their learning needs, so they fidget and try to make sense of concepts through moving in their confined space. When learning on the basketball court, these players tend to mimic a coach's demonstration or role play his instructions. Rather than hearing an instruction and immediately understanding, the kinesthetic learner must do the action. The kinesthetic learner stands in the back of the group and acts out the action as it is described or demonstrated. Often, coaches censure this activity because it is a distraction; however, for these players to learn, it is a necessary course of action. Therefore, using a kinesthetic learner to demonstrate solves both problems: (1) the player acts out the instructions and (2) the coach negates the distraction in the back of the group.

The Thinker

- Asks "what if…" questions.
- Solves movement problems creatively.
- Needs time to think, analyze and process information.

When coaching a thinker, ask questions and give the player time to think, analyze and process information. Coaches need patience with thinkers. Thinkers ask the "what if…" questions that tend to bother a coach when he has limited time and numerous goals to accomplish. From an adult perspective, the questions often seem silly and some take offense, as if the player is trying to trick the coach or question his authority. However, in most cases, this is how the thinker learns; he is making sense of the skill or situation. He is methodical and makes sense of the information in a variety of ways, including asking questions. On the court, these players usually take more time to figure out the drill or the skill. Rather than growing frustrated because the coach believes the player did not listen to the instructions, the coach should be aware of any thinkers on his team and adjust accordingly, giving the player more time to make sense of the instructions. Like with a visual learner, a thinker can benefit from videotape, especially if given the opportunity to see the mistake and discover his own solution.

Conclusion

In a game, a kinesthetic learner does not have time to act out the play before running it and a thinker does not have time to ask his "what if…" questions. Therefore, coaches need to simplify their instructions during timeouts. They also need to practice timeout situations. In practice situations, coaches typically use a verbal explanation and a player demonstration; however, in a game, they draw instructions on a dry erase board. While this makes perfect sense to an adult, some players cannot adjust quickly. Therefore, practice timeout situations to prepare players to learn outside their primary learning style.

Through understanding a player's learning style, a coach can teach more effectively and meet the player's instructional needs. With experience, identifying different learning styles becomes easier, as players give signs of their dominant style. Kinesthetic learners need to walk through the drill a couple times before they understand; thinkers ask a lot of questions; visual learners need a demonstration and fail to make sense of language; and auditory learners listen and understand. Sometimes, by mistake, a coach says one thing and demonstrates another. For instance, he instructs players to dribble with their left hand, but he demonstrates a right-hand dribble by habit. The auditory learner is more likely to dribble with his left hand, while the visual learner dribbles with his right hand. Therefore, to enhance learning, be clear and precise with language and demonstrations because not every player learns in the same way.

II. Three Phases of Skill Execution

When learning a skill, we go through three distinct phases: Cognitive, Associative and Autonomous. These sequential phases illustrate the process of acquiring a skill.

- Cognitive Phase – Identify and develop the skill's component parts; form a mental picture of the skill.
- Associative Phase – Link the component parts into a smooth action; practice the skill and use feedback to perfect the skill.
- Autonomous Phase – Develop and refine the learned skill so it is automatic; involves little or no conscious thought or attention while performing the skill.

Each player learns at a different rate, so these phases are not age dependent. A novice player starts in the Cognitive Phase and progresses depending on his concentration level, his effort, his coach's feedback and more. However, as a player learns a skill, he proceeds through each phase.

Cognitive Phase

In the Cognitive Phase, athletes:

- Struggle to make sense of language and translate it into action.
- Think rather than act.
- Cannot differentiate between the feel of the correct execution and the incorrect execution.
- Lack body awareness.
- Need the coach to be the primary source of feedback.

During this phase, skill execution is:

- Inconsistent
- Awkward
- Slow
- Requiring great effort
- Unnatural

This phase is like building a computer, putting the parts together and preparing the computer for operation. Players require considerable feedback, so the coach guides the players' learning. The emphasis is perfect repetitions, not speed or volume. Flaws developed during this phase magnify as the player grows.

The first step in learning a skill is for the athlete to observe and comprehend the skill. This phase is cognitive in that athletes mentally process the skill. When helping a player develop the perfect skill execution, a coach must manage criticism. If the player feels that nothing he does is good enough, he suffers from de-motivation. Rather than criticizing or examining the negative aspects or the mistakes, mention the positive aspects. When teaching a player to shoot, for instance, mention the proper stance and build from the positives. Many times coaches harp on the negatives; the goal is to build the skill. Building through the positives is more effective than critiquing every mistake.

It is easy to overwhelm the athlete with too much information or to do too many new things at one time. Practice one new skill at a time. When learning to hit a baseball, use a tee to limit the required motor abilities. If a new player steps into a batter's box against a live pitcher, he must learn the form of the swing, to keep his eye on the ball, to track the ball from the pitcher's hand and to decide whether the pitch is a strike. For a new batter, especially a young athlete, this is sensory overload, and the athlete is almost sure to fail, which leads to frustration. However, on a tee, the athlete controls his learning, as he places the ball where he wants it and swings when ready. He is not learning to hit a thrown ball, but learning to swing, which is the first part of hitting. When his comfort level increases and he understands the swing, he moves to the next level and concentrates on the swing's power and works toward facing a live pitcher.

The athlete also must understand the learning process. Learning is a series of mistakes. When a young player learns a new skill, he compares himself to his peers and their development. If his peers learn quicker, he judges himself poorly, and his negative thoughts hinder his development. Timothy Gallwey suggests in <u>The Inner Game of Tennis</u> that "the first skill to learn is the art of letting go the human inclination to judge ourselves and our performance as either good or bad…Be clear about this: letting go of judgments does not mean ignoring errors. It simply means seeing events as they are and not adding anything to them." The athlete hitting on a tee must not see missing the target as failure, but instead recognize the mistake (which requires instruction as in the Cognitive Stage, the athlete needs accurate feedback) and learn from the attempt. If he focuses on the negative result, he is likely to make the same mistake, as he fails to learn from his prior attempt and is not aware of his error.

Athletes learn at different rates and some acquire skills earlier than others. One challenge facing coaches is to design drills, instruction and practices for players of varying ability and different learning stages.

Associative Phase

In the Associative Phase, skill execution is:

- More consistent.
- Not yet automatic.
- Requiring full concentration.
- More fluid.

This phase is like programming the computer, writing the code and preparing the computer to generate immediate responses. Players begin to feel and be aware of their own mistakes and start to self-correct. Consistency improves and players feel the difference between the correct and incorrect skill execution.

A coach's role is to enhance the player's self-feedback. Use questions as an instructional approach so players do not rely solely on the coach for answers. If a player misses a shot, for instance, rather than pointing out the mistake, ask the player what he felt. As players improve in their self-analysis, the skill execution improves as the player makes his own corrections.

"As the athlete enters this stage, many of the basic fundamentals and mechanics of the skill have been learned. The mistakes are fewer, less serious and, more importantly, the athlete is capable of recognizing many of his errors and is aware of how to take the proper steps to correct them. The goal now is to refine the skill," (Mannie). The coach's role shifts; now, as opposed to constant feedback, the coach is less vocal, but more specific with his instructions. "It is paramount that the coach continues to provide the athlete with useful, specific information and constructive feedback throughout this stage," (Mannie).

After establishing consistency, add quality repetitions so the player can make minor adjustments and master the technique. The coach guides this process, rather than dictating it. When a player takes charge of his own learning, as opposed to following orders, he is more motivated. Guide the process through the appropriate mix of instruction, motivation and questions depending on the individual and situation.

Autonomous Phase

In the Autonomous Phase, skill execution:

- Requires little to no thinking.
- Is automatic.
- Is consistent.
- Is habitual.

The Autonomous Phase is the finished computer, when answers appear immediately or programs run effectively. The athlete understands his errors and corrects his mistakes. The final phase is reached after much practice, quality repetitions and experience. The skill is habitual or automatic, requiring little to no thinking to execute, so the athlete can devote his attention elsewhere. When shooting, the player focuses visually on the target without questioning where his elbow is or how his hand is aligned. He is fully aware and understands his mistake based on the feel, not the result.

The Autonomous Phase is reached when learning is almost complete, though complete mastery takes years. Refining the skill requires minor tweaks to parts of the skill. For instance, refining a player's shooting technique may mean creating a quicker release. The technique does not change; however, the player eliminates extraneous motion to refine the skill. During this phase, the speed of execution is paramount.

In this phase, the coach asks questions as opposed to answering them. Continuous feedback is not as effective as intermittent feedback. Guide the athlete's learning and pull the answers from within, through the athlete's heightened awareness. "The only way to truly know if the athlete has accrued this higher level of learning [autonomous stage] is to quiz him rather than lecture him," (Mannie).

During repetitions to refine its execution, the coach ensures maximum effort and critiques the details. In the learning process, instruction grows more specific; initially, most instruction and effort centers on the big, general issues of the skill's execution. In the Autonomous Phase, the details become important, like the dipping of the ball between the catch and the release. In some cases, with a player who developed poor mechanics and shoots with major flaws, this means starting over again to re-learn the skill's proper execution because small refinements are insufficient.

III. Un-Learning or Re-Teaching

Correcting a mistake or changing a bad habit is a different learning process than learning a new action. If drawing a picture, one approaches a blank canvas differently than drawing over an unfinished work. When drawing over another work, the artist decides whether to erase the previous work as thoroughly as possible or incorporate the previous work into a new design.

A flaw is a defect in the mental and physical blueprint of the skill. A mistake is just a momentary lapse. If an athlete has a flaw, he cannot change the flaw without recognizing it. He is not a blank canvas, but one with markings, and he has to see the markings to erase and replace them. "The essence of physical learning is developing distinctions, becoming aware of the differences between two actions and recognizing the consequences of each," (Shoemaker). Changing a flaw requires differentiating between the flaw and the desired action; the body should choose the more efficient means, once it understands the difference.

"The first step is to do an error analysis. If the player's skills and techniques show no consistent pattern and the errors are fairly random, then re-teach the skill sequence. However, if the error shows a pattern or consistency, i.e. it is a 'learned, ingrained, resistant error,' and we are dealing with an 'unlearning' task," (Baxter). Re-teaching the skill sequence occurs early in the learning process, in the Cognitive and maybe the Associative phases. Unlearning occurs with an autonomous skill.

When unlearning, the athlete must be aware of his previous habit before he unlearns the habit and moves forward. "When people become more aware of key areas of their swing, their shots become more consistent…increased awareness allows the body's natural instincts to come into play, and these instincts make the swing more powerful and efficient," (Shoemaker).

Dr. Paul Baxter, an Australian sports psychologist, developed a method for unlearning incorrect form/mechanics and teaching the proper way. His method is called the Old Way/New Way Method:

1. Point out the error.
2. Explain why it is wrong.
3. Ask player to show how he or she normally holds the ball.
4. Improve the player's awareness of what he or she normally does that is wrong. This step is crucial for the rest of the procedure to work.
5. Show the player the correct position for holding the ball.
6. Show and explain the differences between their way and the correct way.
7. Systematically and repeatedly rehearse these differences, having the player do it their way first, then do it the correct way, comparing these two and then describing the difference.
8. When the player seems to have the two ways sorted out in his mind, then and only then proceed with systematic practice of the correct way.
9. Instruct the player in the correct procedure for follow-up and self-correction for this specific skill problem.

As Shoemaker says, "The key to learning is to be aware of differences." Using awareness is similar to Gallwey's natural learning process. As opposed to building a new skill on top of an old skill, the New Way/Old Way method involves the key component of the natural learning process: awareness. When we learned to walk, we found the most efficient way to move forward. As balance improved, crawling was less efficient than walking, so we walked. The child is not changing or replacing an old method, but finding the most efficient course. "A child doesn't have to break the habit of crawling, because he doesn't think he has a habit. He simply leaves it as he finds walking an easier way to get around," (Gallwey).

When shooting, children learn with a variety of different mechanics to find a way to get the ball 10-feet in the air, and, with the popularity of the three-point line, 19-feet to the basket. Few children learn properly or shoot shots close to the basket to build proper mechanics.

As athletes gain strength, they find it easier to get the ball to the basket. At that point, they should find a more efficient shooting technique. In terms of Gallwey's natural learning process, it is not unlearning, but forgetting and starting anew. However, to forget, one must be aware; to gain awareness, illustrate the old method and the new desired, more efficient method.

Along with awareness, the athlete must reserve judgment; he should feel the differences and not evaluate the results. Initially, any new movement feels awkward and less successful. The athlete returns to the Cognitive Phase, which is effortful, slow and awkward. However, "a child learns by trial and error, by awareness of action and result…The child doesn't cloud his or her awareness by judging the results, the child simply observes the results, and very soon develops a feel for walking that lasts throughout life," (Shoemaker). An athlete should approach a new skill in the same manner, observing the results and developing a natural feel for the more efficient way to shoot the ball.

The essential elements for coaches working with players who are developing new skills or refining old skills is understanding the stages involved in learning and the different rivers of advice. Gallwey describes two distinct rivers: "Throughout the ages there have always been two streams of advice for people who wanted to improve a skill. I call one of the river of 'formulas' and the other the river of 'feel'…The river of formulas produces a formidable flow of technical instructions arising from the detailed analysis of any skill…The second river of advice has been about mastering the human dimension of existence – the domain of thinking and feeling," (Gallwey).

A coach who paddles in one river misses the experience of the other, while one who paddles in both shares the best experiences of each and uses the best methods. A close-minded coach starts in one river, grows comfortable and stays, afraid to venture into the unknown. An open-minded coach tries each river before deciding where to return and how much to take from each. Through awareness of the two rivers, a coach is more likely to explore both methods and look inwards to enhance his coaching. Without awareness, many coaches rely on what they did as players, limiting their coaching to their immediate experience.

The best skill development coaches (not necessarily wins and losses) possess the technical wherewithal and understand the manner in which their athletes learn and develop. Without one or the other, the coach will never develop his players to the fullest.

IV. Open vs. Closed Skills

There are two types of skills: open and closed:

- Open Skills: movement goal is unknown and the environment constantly changes.
- Closed Skills: movement is preprogrammed and occurs in a stable, predictable environment.

Learning a skill is a process, not an event. It occurs over a period of time, not in a single moment. For complex skills, like shooting a basketball, there is a progression of learning; one does not become a great shooter in one session or even one season. A player first learns the skill as a closed skill. However, shooting in a game is an open skill. Shooting a free throw remains a closed skill, as it is self-paced, habitual and not affected by the environment.

The challenge is teaching and training open skills in a closed environment. That is, a drill creates a closed environment, as the environment is stable and predictable. A basketball game is an open environment, which means players must train open skills. However, playing games does not provide the time to master the technique of the skills, nor the repetitions to automate the skills.

Therefore, in a sense, these skills evolve into two skills: first, the actual technique (closed skill) and then the game execution of the technique, which is the true expression of basketball skills (open skill). When we speak of the technique of shooting, this is the closed skill. However, the open skill involves the ability to choose and perform the right technique successfully with a minimum of effort: the player must interpret information from his environment (Is he open? Does a teammate have a better shot? Is the defender too close? Is the shot in my range? Is the shot a good shot considering time and score?) and execute the movement (elbow in, hand under the ball, triple extension, follow-through). Developing the technique (closed) uses Behavioral Training, while developing the skill (open) requires Decision Training.

With all the basketball skills, whether ball handling, footwork, shooting or defense, athletes learn the technique and then incorporate it into game play. Therefore, players need time to learn the technique in a closed, controlled environment, as well as numerous repetitions in an unpredictable, open environment to train the perceptual aspects of the skill.

The open vs. closed training emphasis differs during the different phases.

- **Foundation Stage**: open skill training to build enthusiasm for playing
- **Fundamental and Training Stages**: closed skill training to master technique
- **Competition Stage**: open skill training to use the techniques in a changing environment

The emphasis, drills and instruction create a bell curve: at the earliest ages, the instruction and isolated technique work is minimal. Young athletes lack the cognitive and perceiving abilities to retain and transfer closed training to an open game environment, so use open skill training to introduce the game and build enthusiasm. As players move to the Associative Phase, technical mastery gains importance, and more time and emphasis are spent mastering technique. As players master the technique and move to the Autonomous Phase, players transition the improved technique and closed skills to an open, unpredictable environment and use their knowledge and skills to play successfully in competitive games.

V. How to use the learning phases, stages and styles?

Information is useful only in context. So, how does a coach use the information presented?

- Identify your learning style as people tend to instruct in their dominant style.
- Be aware of your athletes' learning styles.
- Be cognizant of the athletes' phase of learning and their corresponding needs.
- Be aware of an individual's stage of learning for different skills.

> **When learning a new drill:**
>
> Do you listen to instructions?
>
> Do you have to see the drill written down or on video?
>
> Do you need to walk through the drill before teaching it?
>
> Do you ask multiple questions and analyze it?
>
> If you answer a definite yes, that is your dominant learning style, which likely makes it your dominant teaching style.

Coaches should also have an awareness of the different learning stages and understand that players in the Cognitive Phase need more time and should encourage their thinking as a process of development, as opposed to exhibiting frustration because the player cannot perform at game speed. The primary purpose of youth sports is to aid physical development and the attainment of motor skills. However, somewhere along the line, our achievement-based society lost track of the purpose.

The learning process cannot and should not be rushed. Each athlete has a different speed of learning and a coach's challenge is to incorporate each into an effective practice which challenges everyone and nobody falls too far behind. Each athlete must go through the different learning stages to develop fully.

> "When we plant a rose seed in the earth, we notice that it is small, but we do not criticize it as 'rootless and stemless.' We treat it as a seed, giving it the water and nourishment required of a seed. When it first shoots up out of the earth, we don't condemn it as immature and underdeveloped; nor do we criticize the buds for not being open when they appear. We stand in wonder at the process taking place and give the plant the care it needs at each stage of its development. The rose is a rose from the time it is a seed to the time it dies. Within it, at all times, it contains its whole potential. It seems to be constantly in the process of change; yet at each stage, at each moment, it is perfectly all right as it is," (Gallwey, Tennis).

Instead of judging oneself, appreciate the stage of development and do what is necessary to further one's learning and awareness to improve and develop. Competition is inward; one's goal should be to reach one's own potential, not to be better than another person. Developing a skill, like learning in the classroom, is an internal battle, and the self-discovery process is essential to the learning. A coach should guide the learning and direct the player to the best methods, but in the end, the athlete must go through the learning process in order to develop and retain the needed skills.

Traditional coaching ignores learning strategies and the classical definition of educate, focusing on filling the player with information. Players are inundated with instruction and never fully develop their sport or motor skills because they lack the freedom to explore and discover on their own.

Appendix I:
Injury Prevention

Today's athletic development system applies a great deal of performance pressure to young athletes, which fuels a year-round competitive environment. While *The Cross Over Movement* argues against early specialization and year-round competition, change takes time and effort. In the meantime, players need rest and regeneration to perform optimally in this environment. Rest means between practices and between seasons and sleep each night.

Sleep Deprivation

According to Peter Walters, Assistant Professor of Kinesiology at Wheaton College, athletes must get enough sleep. Walters identifies three areas that can be affected by a lack of sleep:

(1) **Cardiovascular performance**. Accumulative sleep deprivation has been shown to reduce cardiovascular performance by 11%. So how much sleep do you have to miss before this begins to happen? Studies have shown that 30-36 hours of sleep deprivation can result in a loss of performance. If an athlete needs eight hours of sleep yet only gets six, he will accumulate enough sleep debt in 15 days to significantly reduce his cardiovascular performance.

(2) **Information Processing**. During sleep our brain has a chance to sort, prioritize and file all the information we have taken in during the day. Mental functioning decreases nearly twice as rapidly as physical performance.

(3) **Emotional stability**. Even minimal levels of sleep loss result in an increased perception of effort. Your athlete will feel more fatigued, his/her mood will have dropped and clearly they will not be in the type of mental state needed for a top performance.

Recovery, Regeneration, and Rest

In basketball, hard work is the answer. If our team looks tired at game's end, we run more at the next practice. However, what if this approach is wrong? What if less running, not more running is the answer?

Former Georgia Tech Assistant Coach Kevin Cantwell told a story about current Utah Jazz guard Matt Harpring. For years, I have heard about Harpring's relentless work ethic and incredible strength. Cantwell said they could not get him to stop working out. He was always in the gym and always lifting heavy.

Then, right before Christmas, he hurt his ankle. The staff thought he would miss several games. The next game was a week later at Miami. On the way to Miami, Harpring told Cantwell he wanted to play. Former Georgia Tech Head Coach Bobby Cremins said no way because he could not walk without a limp. Harpring insisted. The staff relented, provided they did not see any sign of the injury during warm-ups. They did not know how he was playing on the ankle; it was bad.

Harpring had one of his best games. He sky'd over the rim for rebounds and finished with nine boards and double-digit points. They had never seen him jump so high. He had not worked out since he hurt his ankle. It was probably the only time he played with fresh legs in his career. But, he did not listen to the staff and returned to his usual routine.

Kids play year-round. At some point, fatigue builds. Every day, players tear down their bodies and barely give them sufficient recovery time and nutrition to perform again the next day.

Recovery involves multiple dimensions. An over-trained, under-recovered athlete has to deal with physical, psychological, social, and environmental factors. Physical recovery includes training and nutritional changes. Psychological recovery demands a renewed feeling of relaxation, energy, and motivation. Social recovery revolves around the quality of relationships with others, as well as social activities that re-connect the athlete to normal relaxing activities of every day living. Environmental recovery may even mean a change of location, at least long enough so that other strategies have a chance to work…An effective recovery can be a combination of passive, active, and proactive measures… Moderate exercise, says current research, is better than total rest for most athletes. Finally, a proactive strategy means that you can anticipate recovery and regeneration needs and plan for them. Develop a periodized schedule of training, competition, and regeneration for each week, month, and year (Verstegen).

Rest is not a four-letter word, and every athlete should incorporate some measure of rest, recovery and/or regeneration into their daily, weekly and annual programs. On a daily basis, an athlete should use a foam roll as regeneration before and/or after workouts. On a weekly basis, an athlete should incorporate light days; schedule a light workout the day after a game and concentrate on light running to get the blood flowing and some form shooting drills. On an annual basis, an athlete should plan a rest period after the high school season to regenerate and refresh before off-season workouts to prepare for the following season. These rest periods are essential to maximize training and prevent athlete burnout.

Balance and Ankle Injuries

Ankle injuries are the most common acute injury for basketball players. While many players wear preventative braces or tape their ankles, evaluating and improving one's balance may be the secret to reducing ankle injuries.

University of Wisconsin reporting in the *Clinical Journal of Sports Medicine*, found that subjects who demonstrated poor balance had nearly seven times as many ankle sprains as subjects who demonstrated good balance (Verstegen).

To evaluate your balance, and assess your risk of ankle injury, use the following tests:

Star Excursion Balance Test

- Cut athletic tape into four 6 to 8-foot strips.
- Lay two strips on the floor in the shape of a "+".
- Place the remaining two strips on the floor intersecting the "+" at 45° angles (form an "x").

Now, to test an athlete, have the athlete:

- Stand on one leg at the center of the "star."
- Reach with the opposite leg in a particular direction as far as possible, touching the tape with either the forefoot or toes (mark this point for future measurement.)
- Return to the starting position after each reaching trial.
- Repeat a test if unable to maintain balance on the stance leg during the reaching motion or if the reaching leg is used to provide support during the test.
- Perform tests in all eight motions to allow for side-to-side comparisons.

Researchers from Rocky Mountain University of Health Professions in Provo, Utah found that high school basketball players with asymmetrical reach distances (as little as 4 centimeters) had a greater risk of experiencing a lower extremity injury" (Brummitt).

Balance Strength Test

- Close your eyes.
- Stand on one leg and raise your other knee to hip level.
- Balance for 10 seconds.

An inability to balance for 10 seconds makes a player 2 ½ times more likely to suffer an ankle sprain than those who can do it, according to researchers at the University of Connecticut, who say the test reveals poor proprioception (balancing strength).

> "Proprioception is controlled by sight, the brain and nerve endings in joints," says Tom Trojian, MD, the UConn team physician. Closing your eyes eliminates visual cues for a truer indication of ankle performance. (*Men's Health*, Jan/Feb 2007).

To improve your balance, do the following exercises. In a study of more than 700 basketball and soccer players, those who performed these exercises had 38% fewer ankle sprains than those who did not (*Men's Health*, Jan/Feb 2007). Perform each move for 30 seconds on each leg, three to five times a week.

Single-Leg Balance

Hard: Stand on one leg for 30 seconds.

Harder: Try it with your eyes closed.

Single-Leg Dribble

Hard: Dribble a basketball while balancing on one leg.

Harder: On one leg, throw chest passes to a partner.

Unstable Balance

Hard: Stand on a balance board.

Harder: Rotate your hips from side to side while standing on the balance board.

Single-Leg Unstable

Hard: Stand on one leg on a balance board.

Harder: Do it with your eyes closed.

Unstable Dribble

Hard: Stand on one leg on a balance board and dribble a basketball.

Harder: Using the same set-up, pass the ball to a partner.

Ankle Rehabilitation

In my experience, few players sufficiently rehabilitate ankle sprains, so the injuries plague players long after the pain dissipates. When asked about ankle rehabilitation exercises, Art Horne, Associate Head Athletic Trainer at Northeastern University said:

> General activities include balance and proprioception drills, multi-planar theraband strengthening, light plyometrics and jump landing mechanics as rehabilitation progresses. Initially, specific activities include towel assisted heel cord stretching with knee bent and straight to maintain heel cord length, elevated ankle pumps in which the athlete dorsiflexes and plantarflexes the ankle in an elevated position to maintain ROM and help decrease initial swelling (Horne).

Physical Therapist Jeff Olivio added:

> Both Open and Closed chain exercises are a must. Open would include theraband isolation muscle strengthening exercises in all planes. Closed chain would include single-leg balance on wobble board, trampoline, foam cushion etc. You need to challenge your joint proprioceptors through balance training. You must also begin plyometric training gradually. Hops to more advanced jumps. The key to rehab is making sure your rehab entails training in all three planes: Sagital (forward/backward), Coronal (side-to-side) and Transverse (rotational) planes (Olivio).

Knee Injuries

ACL injuries plague women's basketball. Nobody knows definitively the reason why women tear their ACL's two to eight times more often than men. In fact, there likely is not one single reason, but multiple factors. Peter Harmer, a professor of exercise science at Willamette University in Oregon, surveyed sports medicine literature to determine the characteristics and factors associated with injuries among young basketball players. He concluded that:

> Girls are more likely to be injured than boys, especially with knee and ankle injuries. Among girls, knee injuries are more likely to be severe than in boys. Neuromuscular training can reduce the incidence of knee injuries among female players. Acute injuries are more common than chronic injuries (Harmer).

According to the American Academy of Orthopedic Surgeons, only 30 percent of injuries involve contact. Non-contact ACL injuries occur during the eccentric contraction used to decelerate or reduce force; in basketball, this means landing from a jump, stopping or cutting. When one lands, stops or cuts, the force must be absorbed. When done properly, the ankle, knee and hip flex and the force dissipates over a large area. If one of the joints does not flex properly, the force moves to another joint – usually the knee.

One possible factor for girls' higher incident rate of ACL injuries is a lower ratio of hamstring to quad strength: girls tend to be quad dominant and do not engage their hamstrings – their hips – when landing from a jump. Girls land in a more stiff-legged, upright posture, which creates more force at the knee joint. Players who land stiff-legged stomp into the ground; to land properly, land softly with as little noise as possible. The landing starts on the balls of the feet and the player sits into the landing. Rather than sticking the landing on his toes, he lands and flexes his ankle to absorb the force as he shifts his weight back. As the athlete lands, he sits his hips back creating knee and hip flexion in a quarter-squat position.

The ACL is unloaded with proper landing mechanics when the athlete loads the glutes upon landing. When you look at the role of the ACL in the knee, its primary role is to prevent the tibia (shin bone) of the lower leg from sliding forward during movement. When we look deeper into the biomechanics of the human body, we see that the hamstrings originate at the lower pelvis and end on the back of the bones on the lower leg. When they fire (shorten) in conjunction with the glutes upon deceleration of the body, they pull the lower leg back into the knee joint and unload the ACL.

Studies show that the force upon landing on the joints is three to five times greater for females compared to males because they land with a more upright posture and tend to be quad dominant, meaning they activate the glutes and the hamstrings less. A quad dominant athlete transfers weight forward which puts pressure on the knee and stresses the ACL, which must prevent the tibia from sliding forward. When the force becomes too great, the ACL tears and the athlete misses 6-10 months in rehabilitation (Hauschildt).

To teach proper landing mechanics, start with a box jump. Have the player jump onto a small (12-inch) box and land softly, sitting into his landing. Step off the box and repeat the jump. As players progress with proper technique and strength, step off the box and land – this is the first step to a depth jump. Once he can absorb the force, work on a true depth jump: step off the box and jump immediately upon landing. The emphasis is to rebound as quickly and as high as possible, minimizing ground contact. Next, step off the box and add a sprint, back pedal or lateral shuffle to simulate game-like movements. Finally, have the player step off the box and respond to a coach's cue with his movement. This is a long term progression.

According to Michael A. Clark of the National Academy of Sports Medicine (NASM):

> When you jump, if your ankle is tight or your hips and abs are weak, your knee may cave in slightly [right], priming the joint for injury on landing. You can see this happen at the exact moment you land.

An NASM study shows that if your knee caves in, knee stress increases. Inward movement lengthens the amortization phase (the time from landing to take-off), so it has a dampening effect on your vertical jump. To judge a player's susceptibility to a knee injury, use an overhead squat test. The April 2008 issue of *Men's Health* calls the overhead squat "the ultimate strength test."

Overhead Squat (right)

Have players hold a basketball straight overhead and squat:

- Point toes straight ahead
- Sit hips back
- Bend the knees to lower toward the floor.

There are three common mistakes:

- *The player's upper body leans too far forward.* This usually means tight calves which impede the ankles from bending. The torso moves forward to maintain the base of support. To remedy the problem, use a foam roll on the calves and stretch the calves before and after playing [Picture 1 & 2].
- When *the player's knees cave in*, the outer thighs are weak and "one's risk of injury to the ACL may triple, according to researchers at the Cincinnati Sports Medicine Research and Education Foundation." I use a lateral tube walk with players to help combat the weakness [Picture 3].
- When *the player's feet turn out*, the outer calves are tight, which creates ankle stiffness; if the ankles cannot flex fully, the force goes somewhere, usually the knee. Again, use the foam roll on the calves to attack trigger points and stretch before and after playing [Picture 4].

Additionally, Clark suggests three exercises to strengthen the knees:

Single-Leg Balance Reach (like the *Star Excursion Balance Test*): Stand on one leg. With the other leg, reach out to the side, front and back.

Multi-planar Tube Walk: Loop resistance tubing just above the knees. Stand with knees slightly bent and hands on hips [left]. Side-step to the right and to the left [right]. Then walk forward and backward taking steps at 45-degree angles. Side step to half court and return to the baseline.

Multi-planar Hops: Stand on one foot and hop forward to the other foot. Then hop backward to the other foot. Hop laterally and back. Do 12 to 15 repetitions on each foot.

Another basic exercise to incorporate:

Lunge to Balance: Step out with the right foot and lower the body so each knee is at a 90-degree angle [left]. On the next step, drive the left knee up and balance on your right foot [right]. Hold for a count of two and then step forward with the left foot into a lunge.

Hip Flexibility

A *Sports Performance Journal* article suggests that "the hips are the most important part of your body to strengthen with regard to knee pain," while an article in the March 2008 issue of *Men's Health* says:

> More than 90 percent of runners who complain of leg pain lack hip flexibility, say Canadian researchers. That's because if your hips don't work well, neither will your knees and ankles.

The body works as a kinetic chain and often the cause of pain is not the site of the injury or abnormality. Knee pain often results from an ankle or hip problem; however, players treat the injury at the spot of pain, which does not fix the problem long term. The article suggests two stretches to improve hip flexibility:

- Lie flat on your back with your feet planted 2 to 3 inches apart on a wall and your knees bent about 90-degrees. Relax your upper body and focus on a point on the ceiling. Bring your knees together slowly and then move them apart so that your feet roll out to the sides and your soles come off the wall. Keep your feet pointed straight up. That's one repetition. Do three sets of 10.
- Now position your feet 2 to 3 inches wider than your hips and repeat the move, but aim for two sets of 20.

Trigger Points

Basketball players frequently develop trigger points because of the constant, repetitive movements. Trigger points are "small contraction knots" in the muscles (Davies). These trigger points keep the muscle both tight and weak, and they restrict the muscle's ability to work through a full range of motion. Trigger points almost always refer pain: that is, the person does not feel pain at the trigger point, but elsewhere (Davies). As an example, a trigger point in the gastrocnemius (calf muscle) refers pain to the arch of the foot.

A trigger point is painful when pressure is applied directly to it, especially if it is close to the surface. It feels like a knot under the skin; often, the fascia (a thin, translucent membrane that envelops and separates muscles) covering a trigger point "gets tight and inflexible and becomes part of the problem," (Davies). These trigger points feel solid, almost like bone.

Massage is the best treatment. The Trigger Point Therapy Workbook, by Clair Davies, teaches people to self-massage or massage another to release the pressure. However, another form of self-myofascial release is to use a foam roll.

Foam roll exercises apply deep pressure which releases the trigger points. These exercises relax the muscle and allow it to stretch to its normal length (Clark). Otherwise, the trigger points inhibit optimum movement by shortening the length of the muscle. This shortening typically results in lengthening in its reciprocal muscle, which leads to weakness. For instance, "if the muscles on the front of your hips are tight, the butt muscles will be weakened and less likely to function effectively," (Clark). The reciprocal inhibition impacts the performance of the entire kinetic chain, as another muscle must do more than its fair share to compensate for the weakened butt muscles. In running, for instance, the hamstrings do more, which overworks the hamstrings, fatiguing the muscle and potentially leading to an injury. When a player injures his hamstring, we examine the hamstring muscle or tell the player to stretch his hamstrings before he plays. However, hamstring injuries often result from tight hips (Shilstone). Rather than stretch his hamstrings, the player needs to attack the beginning link in the injury cycle: the tightness, or trigger points, in his hips.

Initially, players lack the awareness to feel trigger points as they self-massage or foam roll, unless the trigger points are severe and near the surface. However, if they apply enough pressure, they should feel the points as they foam roll and they can concentrate on those areas. Once the player finds a trigger point, concentrate on the area for 20 – 30 seconds. In general, the four areas for a basketball player to foam roll on a consistent basis are (clockwise from top left): (1) calves; (2) hamstrings; (3) inner thigh; and (4) IT Band.

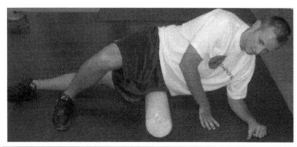

Appendix II:
The Dynamic Warm-up

When training athletes, the primary goal is injury prevention/reduction; second is performance enhancement. Many programs do a static stretch as a team because tradition dictates stretching before playing a sport. However, science suggests otherwise. According to a Japanese study published in the *Journal of Strength and Conditioning*, "Research found that static stretching has no positive effect on muscular performance," (*Men's Health*, December 2005).

A dynamic warm-up prepares the athlete for training and trains fundamental movement skills. Static stretching – the traditional reach and hold stretch – is insufficient to prepare an athlete for quick, powerful movements associated with sports. "Because convincing scientific evidence supporting the injury-reducing and performance enhancing potential of static stretching is presently lacking, it may be desirable for children to perform dynamic exercise during the warm-up period and static during the cool down period," (Faigenbaum, et al.).

"Warming up reduces the viscosity of a muscle, its resistance to its own movement. It improves performance and prevents injury in vigorous activities by two essential means:

1. A rehearsal of the skill before competition commences fixes in the athlete's neuromuscular coordinating system the exact nature of the impending task. It also heightens the kinesthetic sense.
2. The rise in body temperature facilitates the biomechanical reactions supplying energy for muscular contractions. Elevated body temperature also shortens the periods of muscular relaxation and aids in reducing stiffness.

As a result of these two processes, there is an improvement in accuracy, strength and speed of movement, and an increase in tissue elasticity which lessens the liability to injury (Lee).

Injuries often occur because the body is ill-prepared for the intensity of the movement; either the warm-up fails to elevate the muscle temperature and loosen the muscle or the movement exceeds the athlete's normal range of motion; train the full range of motion in warm-ups – not just jogging – to ensure sports preparedness.

A Dynamic Warm-up can include some or all of the following exercises, depending on the goal and time allotment. However, as the primary warm-up for practice or competition, use several different exercises that hit different muscle groups in different directions (not just straight ahead).

Basic Warm-up (down/back)

- Quarter-Speed/Backpedal
- Toe Walk/Heel Walk
- Monkey Shuffle: Shuffle with arm swing; hands cross in front of body and extend above shoulders
- Crossover Step: like half carioca; when moving R-L, your right foot steps across and in front of your left foot, then your left foot steps out; then your right foot steps across again
- Half-Speed/Backpedal
- Skip/Backward Skip
- Lunge: knee stays over your foot; knees form 90-degre angles

- Step-over: lift leg and open hips, like stepping over a small hurdle
- Three-quarter Speed/Back pedal
- Carioca: when moving R-L, your right foot steps across and in front of your left foot, then your left foot steps out; then your right foot steps behind your left foot and your left foot steps again
- Frankenstein Walk: straight leg march; with hands extended in front of your shoulders, kick your foot to your hands
- Heel Kicks: kick heel to butt by bringing knee up in front of the body
- Full Speed/Backpedal
- 45-degree bound: exaggerated running
- Hand Walk: Start in push-up position; walk feet to hands; walk out hands; repeat
- Full Speed/Backpedal

Additional Exercises

- Ankling: keep feet dorsiflexed; run with feet stepping over the opposite ankle
- Squat: sit hips back and down; knees stay over the toes and not in front; put arms out in front to improve balance; weight on balls of the feet, but feet stay flat on the ground
- Side-to-Side Jumps: on two feet, jump over a cone, hurdle or a line on the floor
- Jump Rope Exercises
- Lateral Skip: Skip going laterally; gain ground by pushing off on the trail leg
- Straight Leg Running: kick legs out in front
- Exaggerated Stride Skip: kick heel to butt and extend leg
- Side Lunge: step to the side and keep trail leg straight while getting nose over your knee and toes on the lead side
- Drop Squat (right): start in an athletic stance, move your left leg behind and to the right of your right leg; squat
- Frog: Start in push-up position (below); punch knees to chest; feet land outside hands (below right); push legs back to the start
- Mountain Climber: like the Frog, but alternate legs (below)

References

- Alejo, Bob. "Why Do We Power Clean and what are the Alternatives?" *BobAlejo.com*.
- American Academy of Pediatrics. "Intensive Training and Sport Specialization in Young Athletes." *Pediatrics*, Vol. 106, No. 1, July 2000.
- American Psychological Association. "When Psychologists Teach Coaches how to Coach, Young Athletes Feel Better and Play Longer." *Psychology Matters*, May 29, 2003.
- Anderson, R.J. "Teaching Toughness," *Coaching Management*: 14.6, August 2006.
- Baechle, Thomas and Earle, Roger. (2000). Essentials of Strength and Conditioning. Champaign, IL: Human Kinetics. (pp. 17-20, 83-88).
- Balyi, Dr. Istvan. "Sport system building and long term athlete development in Canada-The Situation and the Solutions." *Coaches Report*, vol. 8, summer 2001.
- Balyi, Dr. Istvan and Hamilton, Ann. "Long-Term Athlete Development: Trainability in Childhood and Adolescence Windows of Opportunity, Optimal Trainability." May, 2003.
- Baxter, Dr. Paul. (n.d.). *Technique Correction, Skill Development, Mental Skills Training Through Old Way/New Way*. Personal Best Systems (personalbest.com.au). Retrieved from http://home.gil.com.au/~systems/bowls.htm, on May 28, 2004.
- Bloom, Benjamin. (1985). Developing Talent in Young People. New York: Ballantine Books.
- Bompa, Tudor O. (2000). Total Training for Young Champions. Champaign, IL: Human Kinetics.
- Bompa, Tudor O. "Primer on Periodization." *USOC Olympic Coach*, Vol. 16, No. 2, Summer 2004.
- Boyle, Michael. (2004). Functional Training for Sports. Champaign, IL: Human Kinetics.
- Bradley, Bill. (2000). Values of the Game. New York: Broadway.
- Brumitt, Jason. "Assessing Athletic Balance with the Star Excursion Balance Test," *NSCA Performance Training Journal*. Vol. 7 issue 3.
- Clark, Michael and Allen Russell. "Self-Myofascial Release Techniques." *Performbetter.com*.
- Clark, Michael. (2006). Optimum Performance Training: Basketball. New York: Regan Books.
- Coakley, Jay. (2001). Sport in Society. San Francisco: McGraw Hill.

- Collins, Jim. (2001). Good to Great – Why Some Companies Make the Leap and Others Don't.
- Chek, Paul. (2000). Movement that Matters. Encinitas, CA: C.H.E.K. Institute.
- Crowley, Kristy. "Energy Specific Training for the Game of Basketball." *The Sports Journal*; Volume 8, Number 2. Spring 2005.
- Csikszentmihalyi, Mihaly. (1990). Flow: The Psychology of Optimal Experience. Chicago: Harper Perennial.
- Csikszentmihalyi, Mihaly, Kevin Rathunde and Samuel Whalen. (1993). Talented Teenagers: The Roots of Success & Failure. New York: Cambridge University Press.
- Damon, William. (1995). Greater Expectations. New York: Free Press Paperbacks.
- Davies, Clair. (2004). The Trigger Point Therapy Workbook, Second Edition. Oakland, CA: New Harbinger Publications.
- Dintiman, George; Ward, Bob; and Tellez, Tom. (1988). Sports Speed. Champaign, IL: Human Kinetics.
- Dixon, Kim. "Overuse sports injuries widespread in kids." *Reuters Health*. February 15, 2007.
- Dorfman, H.A. (2003). Coaching the Mental Game. Lanham, Maryland: Taylor Trade Publishing.
- Dorrance, Anson. (1996). Training Soccer Champions. Cary, North Carolina: JTC Sports, Inc.
- Douillard, John. (1994). Body, Mind, and Sport. New York: Three Rivers Press.
- Dweck, Carol. (2006). Mindset. New York: Random House.
- Elliott, Bruce. "Sport Science Research: Implications for the Tennis Coach." Coaches Information Service, (http://coachesinfo.com).
- Ericsson, K. Anders. (1996). The Road to Excellence. Mahwah New Jersey: Lawrence Erlbaum Associates, Publishers.
- Faigenbaum, Avery. "Dynamic vs. Static Stretching." *Men's Health*, December 2005.
- Gallwey, Timothy. (1977). The Inner Game of Tennis. New York: Random House.
- Gallwey, Timothy. (1988). The Inner Game of Golf, *revised*. New York: Random House.
- Gambetta, Vern. (2002). Gambetta Method. Sarasota, Fl: Gambetta Sports Training Systems, Inc.
- Garber, Greg. "Mindset of the Kicker," ESPN.com: November 15, 2006.

- Gibson, Clive, Mike Pratt, Kevin Roberts and Ed Weymes. (2000). <u>Peak Performance: Inspirational Business Lessons from the World's Top Sports Organizations</u>. New York: Texere.

- Grasso, Brian J. (2005). <u>Training Young Athletes-The Grasso Method</u>. Developing Athletics Inc.

- Gould, Daniel and Robert S. Weinberg. (2003). <u>Foundations of Sport & Exercise Psychology</u>. Champaign, IL: Human Kinetics.

- Harris, A. and Ewing, M.E. (1992). *Defining the Concept of Fun: A Developmental View of Youth Tennis Players*. Presented at the Association for the Advancement of Applied Sport Psychology, Colorado Springs, CO.

- Harmer, Peter. *Sports Performance Journal*. February 16, 2006.

- Hauschildt, Mitch. *NSCA's Performance Training Journal*, Vol. 1, Issue 1.

- Horne, Art. Personal interview via email: April 2007.

- Janda, V, Bullock-Saxton, JE, and Bullock, MI. (1994). "The influence of ankle sprain injury on muscle activation during hip extension." *International Journal of Sports Medicine*. 1994 Aug, 15(6):330-4.

- Kahney, Leander. (2008). <u>Inside Steve's Brain</u>. New York: Penguin Group.

- Karnon, Mike. "Organization and Management of the Maccabi Tel Aviv Basketball Club." *FIBA Assist Magazine*, Vol. 15, 2005.

- Kidman, L. & Hanrahan, S. (2004). <u>The Coaching Process: A practical guide to improving your effectiveness</u>. (2nd ed.) Palmerston North, New Zealand: Dunmore Press.

- Kidman, Lynn. (2001). <u>Developing Decision Makers: An empowerment approach to coaching</u>. New Zealand: Innovative Print Communications.

- Krakovsky, Marina. "The Effort Effect." *Stanford Magazine*: March/April 2007.

- Kriegel, Mark. (2007). <u>Pistol: The Life of Pete Maravich</u>. New York: Free Press.

- Launder, Alan G. (2001). <u>Play Practice</u>. Champaign, IL: Human Kinetics.

- Lee, Bruce. (1975). <u>Tao of Jeet Kune Do</u>. Valencia, CA: Ohara Publications.

- Lee, Timothy; Swinnen, Stephan; Serrien, Deborah. (n.d.) *Cognitive Effort and Learning*.

- MacKay, Mike. Interview via email, 2006.

- Mannie, Ken. (1999). Skill Development: An Open and Closed Case. *NaturalStrength.com*. Retrieved on May 28, 2004.

- McCormick, Brian (2008). *Hard2Guard: Skill Development for Perimeter Players*. San Diego: Lulu Press.
- McCormick, Brian (2008). *Brian McCormick's Hard2Guard Newsletters, Volume 1*. San Diego: Lulu Press.
- McCormick, Brian. "Ankle Injuries." *Hard2Guard Player Development Newsletter, Vol. 1, No. 24*: June 12, 2007.
- Meir, Rudi. "Conditioning the Visual System: A Practical Perspective on Visual Conditioning in Rugby Football." *Strength and Conditioning Journal*. August 2005.
- *Men's Health*, Jan/Feb 2007 "Gauge Your Sprain Risk."
- *Men's Health*, Jan/Feb 2007 "Pillars of Strength."
- *Men's Health, April 2008*. "Overhead Squat."
- Michels, Rinus. (2001). *Teambuilding the Road to Success*. Spring City, PA: Reedswain Publishing.
- Oliver, Dean. (2004). *Basketball on Paper*. Washington, D.C.: Brassey's Inc.
- Olivio, Jeff. Personal interview via email: April, 2007.
- Owens, Lynn M. and Dr. Craig Stewart. "Understanding Athletes' Learning Styles." Coaches Information Services, (http://coachesinfo.com).
- PageWise. (2002). *Psychomotor development and learning*. Retrieved May 28, 2004 from http://utut.essortment.com/psychomotordeve_pqs.htm.
- Phelps, Scott. "Training Youth." *Speed Quest Newsletter*, September 2006.
- Pica, Rae. (n.d.). Fundamentals First. Retrieved May 28, 2004 from http://www.movingandlearning.com/Resources/Articles1.htm
- Santana, Juan Carlos. "Jump higher for basketball season." *Performbetter.com*
- Saskatchewan Education. (1994). *Instructional Physical Education 20 and 30*. Retrieved from http://www.sasked.gov.sk.ca/docs/physed/physed2030/msdevelop.html on June 24, 2004.
- Sergio, Carlos. "The Spanish Basketball Federation Youth Program." *FIBA Assist Magazine*. Winter, 2003.
- Shi, N. and Ewing, M.E. (1993). *Definitions of Fun for Youth Soccer Players*. Paper presented at the North American Society for the Psychology of Sport and Physical Activity Conference, Brainerd, MN.
- Shilstone, Mackie. Interview via phone, November 2006.

- Shoemaker, Fred. (1996). *Extraordinary Golf*. New York: The Berkeley Publishing Group.
- Sliverthorne, Sean. "HBS Cases: On Managing with Bob Knight and Coach K." *Harvard Business School*, August 14, 2006.
- Smith, Abbie. "Break your Speed Limits." *Men's Health*, June 2008.
- Smith, P.J. and O'Keefe, Siobhan. (1999). "Fundamental motor skill development." *The Irish Scientist* [Electronic version]. Retrieved on May 28, 2004.
- Staph, Joseph. "15 Thoughts on Basketball Movement." *The Stack Magazine*. November 2005.
- Stewart, Dr. Craig and Owens, Lynn M. "Understanding Athletes' Learning Style." *Coaches Information Service*. Retrieved from http://coachesinfo.com/article/index.php?id=272 on November 19, 2006.
- Stipek, Deborah. (2001). Motivated Minds. New York: Holt Paperbacks.
- Taft, Lee. Interview via email, 2006.
- Thompson, Jim. (1995). *Positive Coaching*. Portola Valley, CA: Warde Publishers, Inc.
- Waitley, Dr. Denis. (1979). *The Psychology of Winning*. New York: Penguin Group.
- Walters, Pete. "Sleep and Performance." *Strength and Conditioning Journal*, Vol. 24 No 2, pp 17-24.
- Wein, Horst. "Winning vs. Player Development." *Success in Soccer*. January 2007.
- Verstegen, Mark. "Recovery." *Sports Performance Journal*, March 17, 2006.
- Verstegen, Mark. "Ankle Injuries." *Sports Performance Journal*, April 16, 2006.
- Vickers, Joan. Interview on PBS.org: "Science Hotline." Retrieved from www.pbs.org/saf/1206/hotline/hvickers.htm.
- Yessis, Michael. *Build a Better Athlete*. Terre Haute, IN: Equilibrium Books.

About the Author

Brian McCormick is the Founder of **The Cross Over Movement**, a grassroots effort to improve youth basketball development. Cross Over: The New Model of Youth Basketball Development is one of nine books he has published since 2002.

McCormick is the Performance Director for trainforhoops.com and the Founder of 180Shooter.com. He writes a weekly newsletter received by coaches in over 35 countries and trains youth, college and professional players in Southern California.

McCormick received his B.A. in American Literature and Culture from UCLA, where he directed the UCLA Special Olympics program and rowed for the UCLA Crew team, and a Master's in Sports Science from the United States Sports Academy.

He coached professionally in Sweden, where he was selected to coach in the All-Star Game, and Ireland. He has directed camps in Canada, China, Greece, Macedonia, Morocco, South Africa and Trinidad & Tobago and coached at the college, high school, CYO and AAU levels.

McCormick is a Certified Strength and Conditioning Specialist through the National Strength and Conditioning Association; Performance Enhancement Specialist through the National Academy of Sports Medicine; Sports Performance Coach through USA Weightlifting; and Level I Coach through USA Track and Field.

McCormick consults with youth basketball organizations and basketball facilities in the United States and abroad. For more information, visit **The Cross Over Movement** web site: thecrossovermovement.com. To subscribe to the free Hard2Guard Player Development Newsletter, email hard2guardinc@yahoo.com.

Made in the USA
Las Vegas, NV
28 October 2022

58291400R00116